Multisystemic Treatment of Antisocial Behavior in Children and Adolescents

TREATMENT MANUALS FOR PRACTITIONERS
David H. Barlow, *Editor*

Recent Volumes

Multisystemic Treatment of Antisocial Behavior in Children and Adolescents

SCOTT W. HENGGELER, PhD
SONJA K. SCHOENWALD, PhD
CHARLES M. BORDUIN, PhD
MELISA D. ROWLAND, MD
PHILLIPPE B. CUNNINGHAM, PhD

Series Editor's Note by David H. Barlow

THE GUILFORD PRESS
New York   London

© 1998 The Guilford Press
A Division of Guilford Publications, Inc.
72 Spring Street, New York, NY 10012
http://www.guilford.com

Printed in the United States of America

This book is printed on acid-free paper.

Last digit is print number: 9   8   7   6   5   4   3   2   1

Library of Congress Cataloging-in-Publication Data

Multisystemic treatment of antisocial behavior in children and
    adolescents / Scott W. Henggeler . . . [et al.].
        p.   cm.—(Treatment manuals for practitioners)
    Includes bibliographical references and index.
    ISBN 1-57230-106-6
      1. Conduct disorders in children—Treatment. 2. Conduct disorders
in adolescence—Treatment. 3. Antisocial personality disorders—
Treatment. 4. Combined modality therapy. 5. Family psychotherapy.
I. Henggeler, Scott W., 1950-   . II. Series.
      [DNLM: 1. Social Behavior Disorders—in infancy & childhood.
2. Social Behavior Disorders—in adolescence.   3. Social Behavior
Disorders—therapy.   4. Combined Modality Therapy—methods.
5. Family Therapy—methods.   6. Community Mental Health Services.
WS 350.8.S6 M961 1998]
RJ506.C65M84 1998
618.92′858—dc21
DNLM/DLC
for Library of Congress   98-10618
                                                                CIP

Dedicated to the children we love the most

Jay
Lauren
Lee
Noelle
Phillippe
Russell
Santos
Waylon

and to the many children, adolescents, and families
who have invited us into their homes

Series Editor's Note

Confronting antisocial behavior in children and adolescents is a compelling societal imperative. Yet the cost to mental health professionals attempting to work with these individuals and their families is high. Few are drawn to this extraordinarily important endeavor. One reason is that, until now, there has been little evidence that the extraordinary and sometimes heroic effort necessary to work with this population *has* any meaningful impact on antisocial youth or their social systems. The development of multisystemic treatment, as detailed in this manual, gives mental health professionals a new and powerful tool for this population. Although many children and adolescents occasionally flirt with transient or mild antisocial behaviors, it is children at the extreme end of the continuum, those at risk for out-of-home placement, who can benefit from this program. And the benefits are enormous to both the individual and to society at large in preventing later antisocial and criminal behavior. Drawing on careful analysis of the social-ecological context of antisocial youths, this program does not restrict itself to one theoretical approach, but draws on a full range of knowledge concerning the social systems in which the child is imbedded (e.g., family, neighborhood, school, community). As such, the program represents a cutting edge application of the principles of behavioral and social science to real world problems. As with all recently developed interventions with proven effectiveness, applying the treatment protocol described in this book, systematically and with integrity, is important if one is to reap the fullest benefits of this program (Henggeler et al., 1997). Thus, everyone working with this population will want to become fully aware of the details of this exciting new treatment program.

DAVID H. BARLOW

Reference

Henggeler, S. W., Melton, G. B., Brondino, M. J., Scherer, D. G., & Hanley, J. H. (1997). Multisystemic therapy with violent and chronic juvenile offenders and their families: The role of treatment fidelity in successful dissemination. *Journal of Consulting and Clinical Psychology, 65*(5), 821–833.

Preface

We are very pleased to present this volume to the practitioner, academic, and to policy-oriented communities. Since the first extensive description of the clinical features of multisystemic therapy (MST) was published (Henggeler & Borduin, 1990), several controlled evaluations have supported the ability of MST to reduce long-term rates of antisocial behavior and out-of-home placements for children and adolescents presenting serious antisocial behavior. Several additional controlled studies and research projects are currently extending the application of MST to the treatment of drug dependence and serious emotional disturbance and to a broader array of services implemented within managed care contexts. Moreover, in consideration of the clinical effectiveness and cost savings produced by MST projects, private and public provider organizations have initiated MST treatment programs in numerous sites across the United States and Canada.

MST has the potential to significantly influence the disproportionate allocation of resources currently devoted to largely ineffective and costly out-of-home placements for troubled and troubling children across mental health, juvenile justice, and social welfare service systems. Clearly, we believe that family-oriented services that are based on empirical knowledge regarding the multidetermined nature of antisocial behavior, and that assume high accountability for outcome, hold the greatest promise for changing the current zeitgeist which emphasizes punishment and out-of-home placements as responses to serious antisocial behavior. If nothing else, the findings from studies of MST show that antisocial behavior can be reduced if services focus on changing the known determinants of behavior problems in the natural environments in which children and families live—their homes, schools, neighborhoods, and support systems. This volume details the rationale and method used to produce lasting change in the serious antisocial behaviors of children and adolescents.

Contents

Multisystemic Treatment of Antisocial Behavior in Children and Adolescents

I

INTRODUCTION

1

Empirical, Conceptual, and Philosophical Bases of MST

In this chapter
- The correlates, causes, and costs of antisocial behavior in youth and corresponding implications for the development of effective treatment.
- Systems theory and the theory of social ecology as they pertain to conceptualizations of behavior that inform MST.
- The compatibility of MST with major policy initiatives and consumer preferences shaping the future of children's mental health services.

This introductory chapter provides the empirical, conceptual, and philosophical background for the multisystemic treatment (MST) approach to meeting the mental health needs of children and adolescents who present serious antisocial behavior as well as their families. In essence, the chapter shows that the central thrusts of MST clinical procedures are consistent with (1) extant knowledge regarding the determinants of serious antisocial behavior, (2) a theoretical model of human development and behavior that has become widely supported in the fields of child development and child psychopathology (i.e., social ecology; Bronfenbrenner, 1979), and (3) major policy and consumer initiatives.

Antisocial Behavior in Youth: Correlates and Costs

Antisocial behavior refers to a broad range of activities that reflect social rule violations, acts against others, or both. Such activities include behaviors as diverse as lying, disobedience, truancy, running away, drug use, setting fires, vandalism, theft, and violence against persons. Some antisocial behaviors are relatively common over the course of normal development and are not necessarily clinically significant. For example, the majority of 5- and 6-year-old children engage in problem behaviors such as lying or disobedience toward parents (Achenbach, 1991; Kazdin, 1995), and almost all adolescents commit one or more minor delinquents acts at some point (Elliott, Huizinga, & Morse, 1985; Farrington, 1987). Yet, for most children and adolescents, such antisocial behaviors tend to be isolated, transient, and relatively mild (Kazdin, 1995). On the other hand, when children or adolescents show a pattern of relatively severe antisocial behavior, such behavior is likely to be identified by parents or other adults as a significant departure from normal development and may bring the child or adolescent into contact with the mental health or juvenile justice system. At extreme ends, the severity of the antisocial behavior may place the youth at high risk of out-of-home placement—resulting in referral to an MST program.

Several psychiatric and legal terms are used to denote clinically severe antisocial behaviors in children and adolescents. Within the mental health system, youths who engage in a repetitive and persistent pattern of antisocial behavior are often designated with the psychiatric diagnosis of *conduct disorder* or *oppositional defiant disorder* according to the fourth edition of the *Diagnostic and Statistical Manual of Mental Disorders* (DSM-IV; American Psychiatric Association, 1994). Criteria for diagnosis of conduct disorder are met when (1) three or more of the following antisocial behaviors occurred over the previous 12 months, with at least one of these behaviors present in the past 6 months: bullying or threatening others, starting fights, using weapons, physical cruelty to people or animals, stealing with or without confronting the victim, forcing sexual activity on someone, setting fires, destroying property (other than by setting fires), breaking into someone's property (e.g., house, building, car), lying, staying out late at night, or truancy; and (2) the antisocial behaviors led to significant impairment in the youth's social or academic/occupational functioning. Oppositional defiant disorder is a pattern of negativistic, hostile, and defiant behavior that (1) persists for a period of at least 6 months and includes at least four of the following behaviors: losing temper, arguing with adults, defying adult requests or rules, deliberately annoying people, blaming others, being touchy or easily annoyed by others, being angry and resentful, or being spiteful or vindictive; (2) leads to significant impairment in the youth's social or academic/occupational functioning; (3) does not occur exclusively during the course of a psychotic or mood disorder; and (4) does not meet the criteria for conduct disorder. Evidence suggests that conduct disorder is associated with the same types of family problems (e.g., low maternal monitoring and parental deviance) as is oppositional disorder but to different degrees, which suggests that these diagnoses may represent more or less severe forms of the same spectrum of behavioral problems (see, e.g., Frick et al., 1992; Schachar & Wachsmuth, 1990).

In the juvenile justice system, youths who are arrested for engaging in illegal antisocial activities are designated *delinquent*. Milder or less serious forms of delinquent behavior include those activities referred to as status offenses (e.g., alcohol use, not attending school, staying out late, running away, and incorrigibility); such activities are illegal for youths only and would not be considered offenses if the youths were adults. In contrast to status offenses, index offenses reflect a less common and more serious form of delinquent behavior among youths. Index offenses include murder/nonnegligent manslaughter, forcible rape, robbery, aggravated assault, burglary, larceny–theft, motor vehicle theft, and arson. Other delinquent activities (e.g., damaging property, petty larceny, buying stolen goods, breaking and entering, and joyriding) fall somewhere between status offenses and index offenses in terms of their seriousness and effects on others.

Youths who are arrested for delinquent behavior may or may not meet diagnostic criteria for conduct disorder or oppositional defiant disorder, which require a pattern of multiple antisocial behaviors over an extended period of time. Conversely, youths diagnosed with conduct or oppositional disorder may or may not have any contact with the juvenile justice system or be designated as delinquents. Nevertheless, there is often considerable overlap in the antisocial behaviors of delinquent youths and conduct-disordered youths such that the treatment needs of youths in the juvenile justice system (i.e., delinquent youths) are largely the same as those of youths in the mental health system (i.e., conduct-disordered youths) (Melton & Pagliocca, 1992).

For the purposes of MST treatment planning and delivery and as described extensively in Chapter 2, the practitioner should recognize that diagnostic labeling, whether psychiatric (e.g., conduct disorder and oppositional disorder) or referencing juvenile justice involvement (e.g., violent offender and status offender), usually has little bearing on clinical decision making. As discussed throughout this volume, MST is an individualized treatment model in which families set treatment goals and collaborate with practitioners in designing and implementing interventions to meet these goals. Because treatment goals and strategies to meet these goals are well defined, whether or not the constellation of identified problems meets diagnostic criteria is largely irrelevant. What matters is that a specific behavior is identified as problematic (e.g., stealing from neighbors and staying out all night) because of its consequences for others or the youth, and that this and other possible behaviors resulted in a significant response from the mental health or juvenile justice system. The therapist's task, then, is to collaborate with the family to determine the factors in the youth's social ecology that are contributing to the identified problems as well as those factors that reflect

systemic strengths that might be used to attenuate these problems. In conducting such an analysis, the therapist must possess a great deal of knowledge
about the parameters of complex social relations within the family and
between the family and extrafamilial systems. Citing formal diagnostic criteria, however, is rarely necessary (exceptions discussed in later chapters
include an understanding of mental health difficulties with a significant
biological component such as bipolar disorder and attention-deficit/hyperac-
tivity disorder).

Precursors, Correlates, and Causes of Serious Antisocial Behavior

More than one developmental path leads to clinically severe antisocial behavior in youths. In an excellent review of risk factors that influence the course
of antisocial and delinquent behavior, Loeber (1990) noted at least three
distinct paths leading to antisocial outcomes in youths:

- An "aggressive–versatile path" beginning in the preschool years and
  involving a great variety of aggressive and nonaggressive conduct
  problems, as well as hyperactivity (other labels for this pathway
  include "early starter" [Patterson, Capaldi, & Bank, 1991], "life-
  course-persistent" [Moffitt, 1993], and "childhood onset" [Hinshaw,
  Lahey, & Hart, 1993]).
- A "nonaggressive path" beginning in late childhood or early adolescence and primarily involving nonaggressive conduct problems (e.g.,
  theft, lying, truancy, substance abuse) that are often committed in the
  company of deviant peers.
- An "exclusive substance abuse path" beginning in early to middle
  adolescence and involving no appreciable antecedent conduct problems.

Although evidence for the existence of these different developmental paths is
far from complete, it seems clear that some youths progress more rapidly in
the development of antisocial behavior patterns than do others.

CORRELATES OF ANTISOCIAL BEHAVIOR

Research findings provide strong and consistent evidence that many factors
are linked with and predict development of serious antisocial behavior in
youths (Henggeler, 1996). Empirical research shows that serious antisocial
behavior is multidetermined by the reciprocal interplay of characteristics of
the individual youth and the key social systems in which youths are embedded

(i.e., family, peer, school, neighborhood, and community). In general, the factors linked with antisocial behavior are relatively constant, whether the examined antisocial behavior is conduct disorder (Kazdin, 1995; McMahon & Wells, 1989), delinquency (Elliott, 1994; Henggeler, 1989; Thornberry, Huizinga, & Loeber, 1995; Tolan & Guerra, 1994), or substance abuse (Hawkins, Catalano, & Miller, 1992; Kumpfer, 1989; Office of Technology Assessment, 1991).

1. Individual youth characteristics
   - Low verbal skills
   - Favorable attitudes toward antisocial behavior
   - Psychiatric symptomatology
   - Cognitive bias to attribute hostile intentions to others
2. Family characteristics
   - Lack of monitoring
   - Lax and ineffective discipline
   - Low warmth
   - High conflict
   - Parental difficulties such as drug abuse, psychiatric conditions, and criminality
3. Peer relations
   - Association with deviant peers
   - Poor relationship skills
   - Low association with prosocial peers
4. School factors
   - Low achievement
   - Dropout
   - Low commitment to education
   - Aspects of the schools, such as weak structure and chaotic environment
5. Neighborhood and community characteristics
   - High mobility
   - Low support available from neighbors, church, and so forth
   - High disorganization
   - Criminal subculture

CAUSAL MODELING STUDIES

In light of the multiple known correlates of antisocial behavior, at least 20 research groups have conducted sophisticated causal modeling studies in an attempt to describe the interrelations among these factors. Findings from the fields of delinquency (Henggeler, 1991) and substance abuse (Henggeler, 1997) are relatively clear and consistent:

1. Association with deviant peers is virtually always a powerful direct predictor of antisocial behavior.
2. Family relations predict antisocial behavior either directly (contributing unique variance) or indirectly by predicting association with deviant peers.
3. School difficulties predict association with deviant peers.
4. Neighborhood and community support characteristics add small portions of unique variance or indirectly predict antisocial behavior by, for example, affecting family, peer, or school behavior.

Thus, across studies and in spite of considerable variation in research methods and measurement, investigators have shown that youth antisocial behavior is linked directly or indirectly with key characteristics of youths and of the systems in which they interact. A schematic representation of these characteristics is presented in Figure 1.1.

CLINICAL IMPLICATIONS OF FINDINGS

The clinical implications of the research findings seem relatively straightforward. If the primary goal of treatment is to optimize the probability of decreasing rates of antisocial behavior, then treatment approaches must have the flexibility to address the multiple known determinants of antisocial behavior. That is, effective treatment must have the capacity to intervene comprehensively at individual, family, peer, school, and possibly even neighborhood levels. Indeed, at least in the area of delinquency, several reviewers have so concluded (Henggeler, 1989; Melton & Pagliocca, 1992; Mulvey, Arthur, & Reppucci, 1993; Tolan & Guerra, 1994). As discussed throughout this volume, a crucial feature of MST is its capacity to address the multiple determinants of serious clinical problems in a comprehensive, intense, and individualized fashion. This capacity is one of the key components of the success of MST (Henggeler, Schoenwald, & Pickrel, 1995).

Long-Term Social and Economic Costs of Antisocial Behavior

Longitudinal studies show that aggression and other conduct problems in early adolescence foreshadow criminal behavior in adulthood. For example, Stattin and Magnusson (1989) found a strong association between teacher

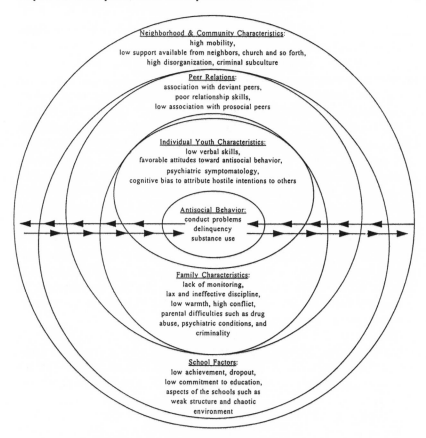

FIGURE 1.1. Correlates of antisocial behavior in youth.

ratings of boys' and girls' aggressiveness at age 13 and their involvement in criminal activities at age 26. Similarly, Huesmann, Lefkowitz, Eron, and Walder (1984) found that for both boys and girls, early aggressiveness as rated by peers at 8 years of age significantly predicted serious antisocial behavior during adulthood (including criminal convictions, spouse abuse, and self-reported physical aggression). Likewise, Farrington, Loeber, and Van Kammen (1990) found that childhood conduct problems at school or in the community were significant predictors of criminal convictions at age 25, and Kratzer and Hodgins (1997) found that conduct problems during early adolescence predicted both criminality and mental disorders (mainly substance abuse) at age 30. Thus, reviewers (e.g., Loeber, 1990; Moffitt, 1993) agree that individuals who display high rates of serious antisocial behavior during adolescence (especially violence) are more likely to continue their antisocial behavior during adulthood than are nonviolent offenders or youth without behavioral problems.

Although the economic costs of adult antisocial behavior to society are not fully delineated, available data suggest that such costs are substantial. For example, in 1992, the average annual cost of housing an adult prison inmate was approximately $18,000, and it was estimated that almost 13,000 new cells (at a cost of $108,000 per cell) would be needed by 1996 to house a projected increase in federal detainees (U.S. General Accounting Office, 1992). Moreover, in 1994, almost $5 billion was spent to construct new prisons in the United States (Mendel, 1995). Recent federal legislation, such as the $30.2 billion Violent Crime Control and Law Enforcement Act of 1994, provided additional funding for prison construction as well as for increased law enforcement and incarceration time. The economic costs related to victimization from serious antisocial behavior are also considerable. Indeed, using several national data sets, Miller, Cohen, and Rossman (1993) estimated that in 1987, physical injury to victims of violent crime resulted in about $10 billion in health-related costs (e.g., medical, psychological, emergency response, and insurance administration), more than $23 billion in lost productivity (e.g., wages, fringe benefits, and housekeeping), and almost $145 billion in reduced quality-of-life costs (e.g., pain and suffering). Although these costs pertain to victims of both adolescent and adult violent offenders, adult offenders in their 20s and 30s accounted for 33% and 25%, respectively, of all persons arrested for violent offenses in 1995 (Federal Bureau of Investigation, 1996).

In addition to increased crime and economic costs, youths who engage in antisocial and delinquent behaviors are at increased risk for several deleterious outcomes during adulthood, including the following:

- Substance abuse and dependence (Farrington, 1991; Pulkkinen & Pitkanen, 1993).
- Physical health problems—higher rates of hospitalization for physical problems (Robins, 1966).
- School dropout and decreased educational ambitions (Laub & Sampson, 1994; Sampson & Laub, 1990, 1993).
- Unemployment, job instability, and lower-status jobs (Farrington, 1991).
- Difficulties in close interpersonal relations, including increased divorce/separation, increased spouse/partner abuse, increased childrearing problems, and decreased relationship satisfaction (Farrington, 1991; Huesmann et al., 1984; Serbin, Schwartzman, Moskowitz, & Ledingham, 1991).

Taken together, these findings suggest that serious and repeated antisocial behavior during childhood and adolescence can have significant negative, long-term ramifications for the individual, for those connected with the individual, and for society. Such outcomes have extremely important implications for the development and utility of MST programs. Extensive discussion of the favorable individual and interpersonal outcomes associated with MST are provided in Chapter 9. In addition, Chapter 9 documents the capacity of MST to produce considerable immediate cost savings when provided to youths at high risk of out-of-home placement and their families. Such favorable outcomes and cost savings serve as significant incentives for policymakers to fund the development and dissemination of MST programs (Office of Juvenile Justice and Delinquency Prevention, 1997). Pertaining to the long-term sequelae of serious antisocial behavior, however, the short-term effects of MST (i.e., 2–4 years posttreatment) may well portend enormous social and economic savings through adulthood. For example, diverting a small proportion of violent juvenile offenders in an MST program from violent adult careers could pay for the program costs many times over.

Theoretical Basis of MST

As discussed previously, an overwhelming body of evidence demonstrates that serious antisocial behavior in youths and their families is multidetermined. To develop an effective treatment for these problems, treatment providers need a theory of human behavior compatible with this evidence. General systems theory (von Bertalanffy, 1968) and the theory of social ecology (Bronfenbrenner, 1979) fit closely with research findings on the causes and correlates of severe emotional and behavioral problems in youth and serve as a foundation for the MST treatment principles discussed in Chapter 2.

Systems Theory

Systems theory reflects a shift in the paradigms the scientific community has been making over the last century—from a mechanistic, linear focus, in which attention is centered on a what-causes-what perspective, to perspectives that understand causality in terms of simultaneously occurring, mutually influential, and interrelated phenomena. With this systemic view, the whole is considered to represent more than the sum of its parts, and the larger picture is taken into consideration (Plas, 1992). A comparison of key features of traditional and systemic paradigms as they pertain to understanding human behavior—and to psychotherapeutic approaches to alter human behavior—follows.

  The traditional scientific paradigm is characterized by binary and mechanistic conceptions of causality (Pepper, 1942; Schwartz, 1982). When behavior is conceptualized from a binary perspective, it is presumed to fit into one category and not another (e.g., a disorder is present or absent). When behavior is conceptualized from a mechanistic perspective, a single cause, or chain of causes, is presumed to have a single effect. Moreover, that journey from cause to effect is presumed to be both linear and direct. That is, *A* causes *B*, which causes *C*, and *C* has no influence whatsoever on *B* or *A*. A systemic paradigm, on the other hand, views behavior as a function of dynamic interactions of elements of the whole system and the system's transactions with the surrounding ecology. From a systemic perspective, *A*, *B*, and *C* mutually influence one another in dynamic ways. In addition, any particular behavior is seen as having multiple causes.

Drawing on the systemic thinking that was evolving in multiple areas of science (e.g., physics and biology) over the past century, Gregory Bateson and his colleagues (Bateson, 1972; Bateson, Jackson, Haley, & Weakland, 1956) developed a psychotherapeutic approach in the 1950s that focused on the family system rather than the individual. This work influenced the development of many models of family therapy, all of which emphasize systemic thinking. Although each of the schools of family therapy may differ somewhat in their interpretation of systems theory, most share a tendency to focus on the family system rather than on understanding the pathological dynamics of the individual client (Plas, 1992). Thus, for example, most family therapists attempt to understand how emotional and behavioral problems "fit" within the context of the individual's close interpersonal relations—emphasizing the reciprocal and circular nature of these relationships. Thus, a therapist working from a systemic conceptual framework would consider not only how parental discipline strategies affect child behavior but also how the behavior of the child shapes and guides the behavior of the parents, and what function any misbehavior might serve in the environment. The systemic clinician might also ask how behavior within the parent–child dyad is associated with the parent's spousal relations, the child's peer and school interactions, and with the extrafamilial relations of individual family members. In addition, the perspectives and feelings of family members regarding identified problems are viewed as important in understanding the fit of identified problems.

Although a discussion of the principles of systems theory is beyond the scope of this text, an excellent overview of systems theory is provided by P. P. Minuchin (1985). In addition, descriptions of the fundamental tenets of traditional (linear and mechanistic) and systems paradigms—and of therapeutic orientations emanating from these different traditions—can be found in most introductory texts on family therapy and in handbooks of psychotherapy (e.g., Bergin & Garfield, 1994).

Social Ecology

The theory of social ecology (Bronfenbrenner, 1979) also played an important role in the development of MST. Although this theory shares some of the basic tenets of systems theory, social ecology is somewhat broader in scope. Bronfenbrenner (1979) likens the individual's ecological environment to "a set of nested structures, each inside the next, like a set of Russian dolls. At the inner-most level is the immediate setting containing the developing person" (p. 3). Each concentric layer is then seen as representing a system or subsystem that plays an integral role in the person's life (see Figure 1.2). As with systems theory, the theory of social ecology views individuals as growing entities that actively restructure their environments while being influenced by those environments. That is, the mutual accommodation of individuals and ecologies occurs as a result of the reciprocity of influence between the two. Like systems theory, social ecology also takes into consideration the individual's subjective definition and interpretation of his or her circumstances.

The theory of social ecology differs from systems theory in its focus on the influence of broader and more numerous contextual influences within a person's life. Whereas the interactions between the individual and family or school are seen as important, the connections between the systems or concentric circles (see Figure 1.2) are viewed as equally important. Hence, a child's achievement in school may be seen to depend as much on the existence and nature of ties between the school and home as on what is taught. A social ecologist would also propose that behavior is influenced by settings and persons who do not come in direct contact with the individual. For example, the conditions of a parent's place of employment may have far-reaching effects on a child's development (Bronfenbrenner, 1979). Likewise, economic difficulties, the portrayal of violence in the media, and prejudice are just a few examples of distal influences that may affect a child's behavior. Importantly, social ecological theory emphasizes the significance of "ecological validity" in understanding development and behavior, that is, the basic assumption that behavior can be fully understood only when viewed within its naturally occurring context (Henggeler et al., 1994).

How Different Perspectives View the Same Problem: A Case Example

To highlight the differences between mechanistic, systemic, and social ecological thinking and the various theories that fall within these domains, we use a case example to outline the ways therapists from some common therapeutic disciplines might approach the same problem.

> Johnny, a 14-year-old male, comes to the clinician's office with his mother who describes him as being impulsive, inattentive and oppositional. He is repeating the seventh grade and in danger of being expelled from school for continued oppositional behavior and class disruptions. He lives with his mother and 12-year-old sister.

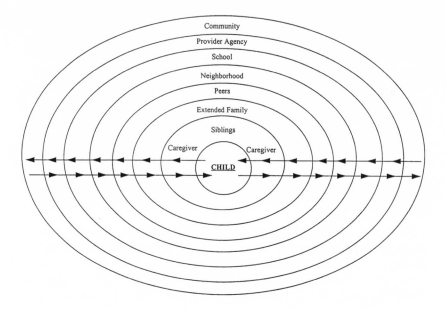

FIGURE 1.2. Ecological environment. Note the reciprocal interactions, represented by arrows, that may occur between any combination of the systems in which the youth and family are embedded. The social ecologist (and MST therapist) will strive to take all interactions into account when attempting to understand factors linked with problem behaviors.

PSYCHOANALYTICAL

The psychoanalytical clinician might view Johnny's oppositional behavior as a function of the interplay between intrapsychic structures (e.g., id, ego and superego) and basic psychosexual conflicts. Upon hearing that mother's new boyfriend arrived on the scene about the time Johnny's oppositional behavior increased, the psychoanalyst may hypothesize that the unconscious conflict between Johnny's id and superego concerning his feelings for his mother and her new boyfriend caused the behavioral problem. This therapist might work with Johnny in individual therapy to try to resolve the unconscious conflict by discussing Johnny's love for his mother and jealousy about her boyfriend ("Oedipal issues" in analytical terms).

PSYCHODYNAMIC

The psychodynamic clinician would emphasize gaining insight into the origins of the conflict fueling Johnny's behavior. This clinician might hypothesize that

Johnny's oppositional behavior is a direct result of the anger he harbors toward his mother for leaving his father when Johnny was 9 years old. The therapist would focus on helping Johnny gain insight into these feelings and the effect they are having on his behavior.

BEHAVIORAL

The behavior therapist may view Johnny's oppositional behavior as a predictable outcome of previous learning experiences that include exposure to certain reinforcement contingencies and behavioral models. That is, the therapist would be looking for ways in which Johnny's mother, mother's boyfriend, and teachers reinforce Johnny's oppositional behavior by, for example, ignoring him unless he becomes aggressive and giving in when he becomes oppositional. Behavioral interventions might involve restructuring contingencies at home and school so that desired behavior was positively reinforced and oppositional behavior was ignored or punished.

COGNITIVE

A clinician trained in cognitive techniques would understand Johnny's oppositional behavior as emanating from the way he perceives his interpersonal environment, organizes information about it, and conceptualizes what is happening in it. The therapist would determine whether Johnny has any cognitive distortions or deficiencies that contribute to the oppositional behavior, and, if so, would help Johnny to develop more realistic views of his circumstances and the capacity to engage proactively in problem solving.

PSYCHOPHARMACOLOGICAL

Given the mother's report of impulsive and inattentive behavior, a physician might search further and uncover a history of behaviors consistent with the diagnosis of attention-deficit/hyperactivity disorder (ADHD). The physician, assuming that the problems were the direct result of ADHD, would most likely prescribe a stimulant medication.

FAMILY THERAPY

In contrast to the preceding examples of mechanistic conceptualizations, the family therapist would base his or her interventions on the premise that Johnny's behavioral problems are closely associated with transactions among family members and the interrelations of family subsystems. Thus, family sessions would be held with various combinations of the Johnny's mother, her boyfriend, Johnny's sister, and Johnny, targeting the reciprocal patterns of interactions between them that might be sustaining Johnny's behavioral problems. In addition, depending on the family therapist's particular theoretical orientation (e.g., strategic, structural, or Bowenian), sessions might emphasize the development of family boundaries, communication skills, or understanding of the intergenerational context of the problems. At any rate, treatment would attempt to alter the family system as a way to improve child behavior.

MULTISYSTEMIC THERAPY

From a social-ecological perspective, assessments would be conducted in the natural ecology of the youth and family (e.g., school, home, and community) and would involve gathering information from multiple sources (parent, youth, siblings, peers, teachers, coaches, etc.) to maximize ecological validity. When the therapist and family have agreed on treatment goals that target their hypothesis of the "fit" of the problem within the broader systemic context, interventions would begin. Again, to maximize ecological validity, these interventions would be implemented primarily by the youth's caregivers in the natural ecology (i.e., home, school, and community). Specific intervention techniques used might include the more empirically based approaches noted previously (i.e., behavior therapy, cognitive therapy, and the pragmatic family therapies), the difference, however, is that design of the interventions would be informed by the strengths and needs of the family's larger social-ecological context and would target key factors within and between the multiple systems in which the youth is embedded. For example, the therapist and family might have developed a hypothesis that several factors contribute directly to Johnny's acting-out behavior in school, including ADHD, poor social skills resulting in more association with deviant peers, a teacher's authoritarian teaching style, seating proximity to other youth with behavioral problems in the classroom, and insufficient parental support of the school's disciplinary efforts. In examining these proximal causes of the youth's antisocial behavior, however, the therapist may find that each is influenced by factors that are more distal to the youth's actual transgressions. For example, failure of the mother to support the school's disciplinary efforts may be associated with conflict between the mother and her boyfriend concerning discipline strategies, a history of conflict between the mother and school personnel, and mother's depressive symptoms. As described throughout this volume, the MST practitioner's task will be to help the family identify and prioritize changes in those aspects of the ecology that have the highest probability of leading to desired outcomes.

The "Fit" of MST with Values Guiding Policy and Service System Change

To fully understand MST, the context within which MST programs began to proliferate should be appreciated. Two notable movements, system of care (SOC) reforms promoted by the federal government and private foundations (Henggeler, 1994) and consumer and family advocacy efforts (e.g., Federation of Families for Children's Mental Health, 1995; Lefley, 1996), parallel the development of MST and helped to generate service system and community environments in which MST can thrive. In return, MST serves as an example of a clinically effective and cost-effective treatment that shares the values espoused by federal, state, foundation, and consumer advocates of children's mental health services reform.

A System of Care

In response to increasing national concern that services for youth with severe emotional disturbances were largely nonexistent, inaccessible, and, when available, inappropriate to the needs of such youth and their families (e.g., narrowly focused and overly restrictive), Congress funded an initiative in 1984 that spawned numerous federal-, state-, and foundation-sponsored efforts to reform children's mental health services. This initiative, the Child and Adolescent Service System Program, was developed with a branch of the National Institute of Mental Health to support states in the development of interagency efforts to improve the systems of care for youth who need mental health services (see Day & Roberts, 1991). The essential blueprint for this extremely influential effort to enhance and reform children's mental health services was written by Stroul and Friedman (1986) in a monograph titled *A System of Care for Severely Emotionally Disturbed Children and Youth*. In this text, the authors described two core values and 10 principles to guide the development of child-centered and community-based systems of care (Table 1.1). These values and principles describe a service system that emphasizes the provision of family- and community-based services that address a wide array of child and family needs (i.e., address the social ecology) and that are individualized to fit the particular strengths and cultural contexts of families.

Readers will see much convergence with the guiding principles of the system-of-care philosophy as they examine this volume, especially the MST treatment principles described in Chapter 2. As MST is designed to be delivered in the natural ecology and to collaborate with the family in setting goals that are family driven, MST is compatible with the core values of the SOC. Thus, as described in subsequent chapters, MST interventions are designed to directly facilitate and coordinate access to needed services (SOC

TABLE 1.1. System of Care Values and Principles

Core values of the system of care

1. The system of care should be child-centered, with the needs of the child and family dictating the types and mix of services provided.
2. The system of care should be community-based, with the locus of services as well as management and decision-making responsibility resting at the community level.

Guiding principles for the system of care

1. Emotionally disturbed children should have access to a comprehensive array of services that address the child's physical, emotional, social and educational needs.
2. Emotionally disturbed children should receive individualized services in accordance with the unique needs and potentials of each child and guided by an individualized service plan.
3. Emotionally disturbed children should receive services within the least restrictive, most normative environment that is clinically appropriate.
4. The families and surrogate families of emotionally disturbed children should be full participants in all aspects of the planning and delivery of services.
5. Emotionally disturbed children should receive services that are integrated, with linkages between child-care agencies and the programs and mechanisms for planning, developing, and coordinating services.
6. Emotionally disturbed children should be provided with case management or similar mechanisms to ensure that multiple services are delivered in a coordinated and therapeutic manner and that they can move through the system of services in accordance with their changing needs.
7. Early identification and intervention for children with emotional problems should be promoted by the system of care to enhance the likelihood of positive outcomes.
8. Emotionally disturbed children should be ensured smooth transitions to the adult service system as they reach maturity.
9. The rights of emotionally disturbed children should be protected, and effective advocacy efforts for emotionally disturbed children and youth should be promoted.
10. Emotionally disturbed children should receive services without regard to race, religion, national origin, sex, physical disability or other characteristic, and services should be sensitive and responsive to cultural differences and special needs.

Note. Adapted by permission from Stroul and Friedman (1986).

Principle 1), utilize individual strengths (SOC Principle 2), provide services in the least restrictive setting available (SOC Principle 3), empower families through a collaborative relationship (SOC Principle 4), and assist parents in coordinating and ensuring quality control for agency services provided (SOC Principle 5), while serving as a therapeutic case manager when indicated (SOC Principle 6). Also, MST interventions are designed to focus on all family members including siblings (SOC Principle 7), emphasize the attainment and generalization of favorable long-term outcomes (SOC Principle 8), advocate for just and fair treatments of clients (SOC Principle 9), and respect human dignity (SOC Principle 10). While a system of care may or may not be in place in the community in which youth receiving MST are embedded, the MST therapist, nevertheless, endeavors to support and exemplify the values embodied in the SOC philosophy.

Consumer Advocacy: The Federation of Families for Children's Mental Health as an Example

The Federation of Families was founded in 1989 and is a national organization run by, and composed of, parents of children and adolescents with emotional, behavioral, or mental disorders and their families. This important advocacy group serves parent organizations in all 50 states by providing information, consulting services, and technical assistance. The Federation of Families also promotes research, prevention, and family support services (Tully, 1995). In Table 1.2, a review of the Federation's principles and policy statements reveals their fundamental compatibility with the SOC philosophy and, as evidenced throughout this volume, with the clinical services provided by MST. That is,

TABLE 1.2. Federation of Families for Children's Mental Health: Principles and Policies

Principles of the Federation of Families for Children's Mental Health

The Federation maintains that children and youth with emotional, behavioral, and mental disorders:

- Have unique needs that require individual services.
- Must be respected for their rights, preferences, values, strengths, cultural, and racial backgrounds.
- Must receive what is necessary to achieve their full potential.
- Belong with families and need enduring relationships with adults.
- Must receive supports necessary to remain with their families: out-of-home placements must be considered as a last resort.

Statement on policies of the Federation of Families for Children's Mental Health

Policies, legislation, funding mechanisms and service systems must utilize the strengths of families by:

- Ensuring that they are equal partners in the planning, implementation and evaluation of services.
- Viewing the child as a whole person and the family as a whole unit, rather than emphasizing the disability.
- Empowering families and children to make decisions about their own lives.
- Encouraging innovative programming which increases the options and promotes the integration of services.

Note. From the Federation of Families for Children's Mental Health (1995). Copyright 1995 by the Federation of Families for Children's Mental Health. Reprinted by permission.

the philosophy and values that characterize SOC reforms, consumer advocacy groups such as the Federation of Families, and MST programs are similar in their emphasis on providing services that are comprehensive and individualized, strength focused, family and community based, inclusive of families in all aspects of treatment planning and delivery, and directed toward maintaining youth in the least restrictive setting possible while empowering families to maintain treatment gains.

2

Clinical Foundations of MST: Nine Treatment Principles, Home-Based Model of Service Delivery, and Guidelines for Clinical Supervision

---

In this chapter
- The importance of treatment specificity and treatment fidelity in obtaining favorable outcomes for families.
- How MST is specified via nine treatment principles.
- The advantages of providing MST via a home-based service delivery model.
- An overview of the MST supervisory processes aimed at promoting therapist adherence to the MST treatment principles.

This chapter provides an overview of the clinical foundations of MST, describing how MST is operationalized (i.e., specified), delivered to children and families (using a home-based model of service delivery), and supported in the supervisory process.

MST Treatment Principles

Treatment specification is a critical task in the development, validation, and dissemination of a therapeutic approach. Some intervention models are relatively easy to specify. For example, behavioral parent training typically occurs through 10 sessions, with well-defined tasks targeted during each session— learning to define and track behavior in session one, learning about positive reinforcement in session two, and so on. Complex, multifaceted, comprehensive, and individualized treatments, on the other hand, can be very difficult to operationalize and specify (Kazdin, 1988).

The same characteristics that contribute to the favorable outcomes achieved by MST (i.e., its flexibility, comprehensiveness, and focus on the social ecology) also make this treatment model difficult to describe in detail. MST does not follow a rigid protocol where therapists conduct sets of prearranged tasks in an invariant sequence. Indeed, when working with challenging cases that present serious and diverse crises and problems, MST therapists must be prepared to shift gears at a moment's notice. Moreover, because MST focuses on a wide variety of possible strengths and weaknesses across the social ecologies of youths and families, fully detailing treatment parameters for each possible combination of situations would be an impossible task. Nevertheless, in the absence of strong specification, the value of MST would be greatly diminished.

To address the conundrum faced in the specification of MST, we used the work of Dr. Fred Piercy (Piercy, 1986), who conducts research on brief family therapy, as a model. Rather than providing session by session breakdowns of recommended clinical procedures, as done in many behavioral approaches, or providing vague conceptual frameworks within which to organize clinical procedures as done in many family therapy models, Piercy developed a treatment manual that used "treatment principles" to guide therapist behavior. These principles organized therapists' case conceptualizations, prioritization of interventions, and the types of interventions delivered.

For the purposes of MST, the use of treatment principles has several advantages over the types of treatment specification that appear in more traditional treatment manuals. First, many therapists who are trained in MST are seasoned professionals who have a wealth of valuable experiences as well as personal strengths and weaknesses. Providing a flexible treatment protocol, within the limits of adhering to the treatment principles, allows therapists the freedom to use their strengths to the family's advantage. Second, the treatment principles can be readily and conveniently used to assist in the ongoing conceptualization and design of MST interventions. Many MST therapists, supervisors, and consultants, for example, keep laminated copies of the principles in their wallet and refer to the principles while planning interventions and during supervision. Third, treatment integrity can be evaluated by measuring therapist adherence to the principles. Indeed, as discussed in more detail in Chapter 9, parent and therapist ratings of adherence to the MST treatment principles have predicted long-term outcomes regarding the criminal activity and incarceration of violent and chronic juvenile offenders (Henggeler, Melton, Brondino, Scherer, & Hanley, 1997).

A primary purpose of this chapter, therefore, is to orient readers to the nine MST treatment principles (see Table 2.1). To facilitate orientation to the principles, we integrate the case of Maggie into the descriptions of each principle.

> Maggie is a 13-year-old white seventh grader who lives with her unemployed, crack-addicted mother, mother's live-in boyfriend, two sisters (age 10 and 8 years), and a daughter of one of mother's crack-addicted friends. Maggie was referred for MST treatment because she perpetrated physical violence at home (e.g., she was arrested several times for assaulting family members), at school (e.g., she beat a classmate with a stick and threatened to kill a teacher), and in the neighborhood (e.g., she was arrested twice for assaulting residents of her housing development). Many of Maggie's aggressive acts occurred following all-night drug binges by her mother. Maggie primarily associates with delinquent peers, was recently transferred to a classroom for behaviorally disordered students, and was recommended for expulsion from school at the time of the referral. The family resides in a neighborhood with high rates of crime and violence, and their only source of income is from welfare benefits.

TABLE 2.1. MST Treatment Principles

Principle 1: The primary purpose of assessment is to understand the fit between the identified problems and their broader systemic context.

Principle 2: Therapeutic contacts emphasize the positive and use systemic strengths as levers for change.

Principle 3: Interventions are designed to promote responsible behavior and decrease irresponsible behavior among family members.

Principle 4: Interventions are present focused and action oriented, targeting specific and well-defined problems.

Principle 5: Interventions target sequences of behavior within and between multiple systems that maintain the identified problems.

Principle 6: Interventions are developmentally appropriate and fit the developmental needs of the youth.

Principle 7: Interventions are designed to require daily or weekly effort by family members.

Principle 8: Intervention effectiveness is evaluated continuously from multiple perspectives with providers assuming accountability for overcoming barriers to successful outcomes.

Principle 9: Interventions are designed to promote treatment generalization and long-term maintenance of therapeutic change by empowering caregivers to address family members' needs across multiple systemic contexts.

Principle 1: The Primary Purpose of Assessment Is to Understand the Fit between the Identified Problems and Their Broader Systemic Context

The goal of MST assessment is to "make sense" of behavioral problems in light of their systemic context. Consistent with social-ecological models of behavior (Bronfenbrenner, 1979) and research on the known determinants of antisocial behavior, MST assessment focuses on understanding the factors that contribute directly or indirectly to behavioral problems. In general, these features pertain to transactions between the child and the multiple systems in which he or she is embedded (e.g., family, peer, school, and neighborhood) as well as transactions between these systems (e.g., family–school interface, family–peer interface). Thus, the MST therapist attempts to determine how each factor, singularly or in combination, increases or decreases the probability of youth problem behaviors. Several steps are required to develop a comprehensive understanding of fit.

METHOD

The assessment of fit proceeds in an inductive manner, systematically examining the strengths and needs of each system and their relationship to identified problems. In light of the complexity of such a broad-based assessment, an Initial Contact Sheet (Table 2.1) was developed to help therapists and supervisors organize assessment information. The Initial Contact Sheet provides space to identify the strengths and needs of each system. Using nonpejorative language, the therapist delineates how the transactions within or between any one or combination of systems exacerbates or attenuates the identified problems.

In Maggie's case, the therapist discovered several factors associated with her violent behavior across multiple settings. As Figure 2.1 illustrates, exacerbating factors included conflicts with adults; threats, insults, and provocation from others; maternal drug binges, poor parenting skills, and family isolation; and modeling of aggressive peers and encouragement from peers to fight. On the other hand, several strengths were identified that might attenuate Maggie's physical aggression, including intelligence, athletic skill, likability (when desired), concern of extended family and mother, an involved counselor at school, and possible supports in the neighborhood.

As suggested by the strengths and needs identified for Maggie and consistent with a multimethod, multirespondent approach to assessment, MST assessment focuses on obtaining information from the key informants in the youth's social ecology. The therapist, therefore, examines perceived strengths and needs from the perspectives of family members, including siblings and extended family when appropriate, school personnel, possibly neighbors and

FAMILY NAME: Maggie   DATE OF ADMISSION:_____

STRENGTHS   NEEDS

Individual

Athletic, enjoys sports.   History of school and
Attractive and likeable.   community aggression.
Average intelligence.   Physically fights mother.
Takes care of siblings.   Victim of child sexual
Antisocial behavior   abuse.
limited to aggression.
Cares deeply for her
mother and wants things
to be better at home and
school. She responds well
to praise.

Family

Extended family lives   Maternal crack cocaine dependence,
close by and are concerned   Poor monitoring. High
about M's behavior and   conflict, crowded living
home life. Grandmother and   conditions. Low financial
aunts willing to do   resources. Mother feels
"whatever it takes."   hopeless about changing her
Mother is seriously   and M's behavior. Mother has
concerned about her drug   minimal parenting skills.
use and M's school and   Family is socially isolated.
home behavior.   Grandmother has cancer.
Childrens basic needs are
met by the mother—she
is a survivor. Strong
family bond.

Peers

Prosocial peers in   Aggressive and antisocial.
grandmother's   peers. Peers have little
neighborhood.   commitment to school.

School

Athletic programs. A   Limited resources. Policy of
counselor has a close   zero tolerance for
relationship with Maggie   threatening teachers. View
and wants her to do well.   behavior problems as moral
                                flaw. Quick to expel
                                students. Poor relationship
                                to surrounding community.
                                History of conflict with the
                                family.

Neighborhood/Community

Several churches located.   Drug infested. Criminal
in the neighborhood.   subculture. Minimal prosocial
                                outlets.

FIGURE 2.1. Initial contact sheet.

family friends, probation officers, peers, and so forth. As the goal of assessment is to obtain a comprehensive understanding of fit, the therapist's task is to integrate data obtained from these multiple perspectives.

Consistent with the emphasis of MST on ecological validity, MST therapists rarely rely on formal psychological testing. The goal of MST assessment is to understand specific problems in real-world contexts, not to delineate vague personality constructs as reported by the youth on paper-and-pencil tests. On the other hand, and as noted in several sections of this volume, formal diagnostic testing can be useful in confirming the presence of psychiatric and academic conditions that have an underlying biological basis and are influencing behavior (e.g., bipolar disorder and attention-deficit disorder). Biological factors are certainly important potential contributors to behavior from a social-ecological perspective.

The integration of information obtained from multiple sources, each containing unique forms of bias, is not a simple task. Therapists must be able to resolve inconsistencies between the views of different respondents and know when the information obtained "does not make sense" of the problems. In resolving inconsistencies, the therapist may need to revisit informants, asking that they help the therapist make sense of divergent perspectives on a particular situation and provide additional information. Moreover, the therapist may need to weigh the preponderance of the evidence when developing and testing hypotheses concerning fit—emphasizing evidence from the more credible respondents (e.g., a drug-free parent or a concerned teacher).

When the therapist conducts a comprehensive assessment but the behavior problems still do not "make sense" (e.g., a youth presenting problems such as Maggie's but living in a stable home and having primarily prosocial peers), the lack of understanding of fit is usually a result of circumstances that are not yet revealed or uncovered (e.g., marital problems, drug abuse, or incest). In such situations, the therapist should engage family members and key informants in developing a more comprehensive conceptualization of the fit by asking specific questions designed to tap possible explanations that were not addressed (e.g., How often do you and your husband disagree about Jim's discipline? How often does [a family member] use alcohol or other recreational drugs? Has anyone in the family touched [the child] in a sexual way?).

HYPOTHESIS DEVELOPMENT

After obtaining the information needed to understand fit, the therapist in collaboration with the treatment team and clinical supervisor develops "testable" hypotheses based on the strengths and needs of the pertinent systems. Generally, hypothesis development takes the form of one element A, contributes to a second element B, for a person, C, under X conditions. In Maggie's case, one hypothesis is that conflict with adults (A) contributes to physical aggression toward peers (B) by Maggie (C) in the absence of adult supervision (X).

Note that all the variables in the hypothesis can be measured. An important prerequisite of testing a hypothesis is that the underlying constructs or relevant factors are concrete and measurable. For example, Maggie's level of aggression (i.e., frequency, intensity, and duration) in the presence or absence of adults is an observable event. On the other hand, a hypothesis that attributed Maggie's aggression to low self-esteem is not amenable to direct observation. As the level of abstraction of hypotheses increases (e.g., aggression due to unresolved psychosexual conflicts with father), the ability to accurately measure and evaluate hypotheses decreases.

In developing hypotheses, MST therapists initially give priority to hypotheses that are based on proximal causes of behavior prior to hypothesizing more distal causes. Nevertheless, proximal effects may mask more distal and indirect effects, and these distal effects often become initial targets of intervention. For example, a boy's aggression toward his siblings may be linked proximally with ineffective parental discipline strategies. Factors contributing to the ineffective discipline strategies (i.e., proximal determinants) may include high family stress, low parent–child bonding, parental drug abuse or psychiatric condition, lack of knowledge regarding effective parenting, a weak social support network, and marital distress; these proximal determinants of ineffective discipline are the more distal determinants of the boy's aggression.

As described next, the targets of intervention are derived from the hypotheses formulated from the assessment data. These hypotheses are then tested through the implementation of interventions, and hypotheses are either confirmed or refuted based on outcomes of interventions. As information supporting or refuting hypotheses is gathered over the course of treatment, understanding of the fit of behavioral problems should remain or change accordingly. That is, the therapist and treatment team develop a process of ruling in or ruling out the various hypotheses thought to influence the child's and family's behavior. *Thus, MST assessment is a reiterative process from the beginning to end of treatment.*

HYPOTHESIS TESTING

Generally, MST therapists test hypotheses by evaluating the effects of interventions derived from the hypotheses. As suggested above, for example, if the hypothesis is that mother–adolescent conflicts precipitate Maggie's aggression at home and school, the therapist would help the family to develop strategies to decrease the frequency of mother–daughter conflicts and then determine whether such changes led to decreased aggression. To evaluate the success of the intervention, the therapist obtains a valid baseline rate of arguments and aggression, as judging "change" requires knowledge of preexisting rates of the targeted behaviors. Next, the therapist must collaborate with the family in selecting a strategy that fits the strengths and needs of the context. Strategies that rely on maternal competence (e.g., teaching mother negotiation and conflict resolution skills) are not likely to be effective as long as Maggie's mother is using cocaine. On the other hand, strategies that take advantage of Maggie's strengths and those of extended family members may be more useful. For example, perhaps Maggie could be engaged in after-school athletics to decrease her contact with her mother, and the extended family could plan for Maggie to spend the evening at their home during times of heightened stress between Maggie and her mother. If Maggie's aggression had not decreased following consistent implementation of this plan, additional hypotheses about factors contributing to the fit would be generated, information would be gathered to support or refute these hypotheses, and interventions would be implemented to test them. Thus, the concept of fit is used in the development of hypotheses and the design of interventions in an ongoing fashion.

Principle 2: Therapeutic Contacts Emphasize the Positive and Use Systemic Strengths as Levers for Change

The successful treatment of serious behavioral problems in children is contingent on engaging the family in treatment collaboration and developing a supportive therapeutic alliance. Unfortunately, working with multiproblem families that may include parental drug abuse, child maltreatment, and other serious problems can engender a host of negative emotions (e.g., frustration, hopelessness, and anger) that can impede the therapist's capacity to engage the family in a strong therapeutic alliance. Such impediments can be exacerbated when attention during supervision sessions and interagency meetings focuses on the youth's and family's deficits, often evidenced by the exchange of anecdotes that exemplify family deficiencies. As the therapist comes to view the family in a negative light, the family senses the therapist's attitude, and the development of a therapist–family partnership becomes very difficult. Hence, a consistent and ongoing emphasis on fostering strength-focused attitudes and communications among MST therapists, supervisors, administrators and professionals from other agencies is critical to the reinforcement of strength-focused therapist–family interactions. Therapists should not be expected to maintain positive and optimistic perspectives when working with difficult and challenging cases if their colleagues and supervisors do not also evidence such perspectives.

Thus, an organizational emphasis on strength-focused attitudes and interactions enhances staff morale and, most likely, improves family-level outcomes for several reasons. Focusing on family strengths:

- Sets the stage for cooperation and collaboration by decreasing the untoward effects of negative affect and builds feelings of hope and positive expectations, which are linked with favorable outcomes (Greenberg & Pinsof, 1986).
- Helps to identify protective factors (e.g., family resources and social supports) that lead to the development of better informed interventions and to solutions that have increased ecological validity and can be sustained by the family over time.
- Decreases therapist and family frustration by emphasizing problem solving (e.g., focusing on how desired changes can happen as opposed to why problems are so bad).
- Bolsters the caregiver's confidence, which is a prerequisite for empowerment.

DEVELOPING AND MAINTAINING A STRENGTH FOCUS

The MST therapist and treatment team can take several straightforward steps to develop and maintain a strength focus.

1. Mandate that MST therapists, supervisors, and administrators use nonpejorative language in verbal (e.g., informal discussions, and group supervision) and written (e.g., Initial Contact Sheet and case summaries) communications. For example, clients are not viewed as "resistant" but as presenting a "challenge." When therapists have difficulty identifying positive aspects of the family, the treatment team should assist.

2. Teach and use techniques of reframing. For example, when Maggie's mother felt hopeless and overwhelmed and blamed herself for Maggie's difficulties, the therapist responded that the mother may or may not have caused Maggie's problems but she is certainly a critical part of the solution.

3. Use positive reinforcement liberally. The therapist should strive to find "evidence" of client effort and improvement and positively reinforce such, regardless of how small. For example, a client should be reinforced for attending sessions, giving his or her best, and so on. During the initial phase of treatment, Maggie's mother felt considerable apprehension, frustration, and hopelessness. The therapist reminded the mother that she was making important progress in helping her daughter by meeting with the therapist and helping to plan for changes.

4. Incorporate and maintain a problem-solving stance. A problem-solving stance emphasizes the examination of factors that can increase the

probability of success as opposed to detailing what failed. For example, when barriers to success arise in treatment, the therapist, family, and MST treatment team should focus their attention on understanding the fit of the barrier, developing hypotheses, and testing the hypotheses by designing interventions to overcome the barrier. In Maggie's case, the mother's drug use was a constant barrier to treatment, and she refused to enter an intensive specialized treatment program for cocaine abuse. Instead of continuing to focus on the barrier presented by this refusal, the therapist took a different tack—enlisting the support of extended family to help serve as parental surrogates and attempting to identify and understand the events and situations leading up to and following the mother's cocaine use (i.e., closely examining the fit of the cocaine use).

5. Provide hope. Many families referred for MST are told repeatedly by family, friends, and social service professionals "how bad things are" for the child and family. To counter this pessimistic stance, the therapist should, through optimism and a "can do" attitude, engender hope among family members and attempt to energize the family and key members of their social ecology to effect change.

6. Find and emphasize what the family does well. The therapist should focus on identifying and encouraging what the family does well. To facilitate this process, breaking large, seemingly insurmountable tasks into small steps is often useful. With Maggie and her mother, for example, the therapist helped to set small, "achievable" daily homework assignments and goals (e.g., saying hello to one another when Maggie got home from school and getting Maggie's homework to grandmother to be checked). These goals were designed to provide incremental progress toward the larger goals of treatment.

Focusing on family strengths does not mean that therapists should take a "Pollyanna" approach that is not grounded in reality. Creating a false sense of hope and unrealistic expectations for success is counterproductive when families are ill prepared to succeed. Rather, staying strength focused means that therapists should realistically appraise family members' ability to use their strengths to accomplish tasks while working to develop additional strengths needed to attain treatment goals.

WHERE TO LOOK FOR STRENGTHS

Identifying strengths begins during the assessment and focuses on the broad ecology of the child and family. Even in families presenting serious clinical problems, the following strengths are often identified and used to facilitate clinical progress.

- *Child*: individual competencies and abilities (e.g., social skills and academic skills), attractiveness, intelligence, hobbies and interests, hygiene, motivation, and temperament.
- *Parent*: social skills, concern, problem-solving ability, attractiveness, frustration tolerance, patience, altruism, and motivation.
- *Family*: financial resources (e.g., money, property, welfare benefits and employment income), basic needs are met (e.g., housing and food), child care is provided, transportation is available, strong affective and instrumental relations between spouses, parents and children, number and variety of social supports (e.g., extended family, friends, neighbors, coworkers, and church members), characteristics of the extended family, and recreational and leisure activities.
- *Peer*: individual competencies and abilities of peers; prosocial activities, hobbies, and interests; family monitoring and involvement in peer activities.
- *School*: appropriate and effective classroom management practices and schoolwide discipline procedures, concerned school personnel, teacher involvement in the community, prosocial after-school activities (e.g., drama, art, athletics, and interest clubs), cultural and community activities held at school, and efforts to engage families in their children's education.
- *Neighborhood and community*: recreational and leisure activities, voluntary associations (e.g., churches, neighborhood associations, sororities and fraternities, and the NAACP), law enforcement, business and industry, human services (e.g., economic assistance programs, housing and transportation support, child care, health care, and legal aid), and concerned and involved neighbors.

As suggested earlier, despite their substantive problems, Maggie and her mother had many important strengths. At the child level, Maggie cares deeply for her mother; is likable, attractive, athletic, and of average intelligence; and wants a better life for herself and her family. At the parent and family level, the mother cares deeply for her children and their welfare, is resourceful, and has provided for the family's basic needs in spite of her drug dependence. In addition, a major strength was the presence of a strong natural support system in the extended family (e.g., grandmother and aunts) who were willing to "do whatever it takes" to help Maggie and her mother. At the peer level, the major strength was the availability of prosocial peers in the grandmother's neighborhood. School-related strengths included the availability of athletic programs and the presence of a counselor who cared about Maggie and was invested in her welfare. At the community level, the major strength included excellent athletic programs at the local community center.

Principle 3: Interventions Are Designed to Promote Responsible Behavior and Decrease Irresponsible Behavior among Family Members

In essence, to achieve the positive outcomes associated with MST (reductions in antisocial behavior, out-of-home placements, and arrests; improvements in family functioning), therapists assist parents and youths to behave responsibly across a variety of domains. Conceptualizing the purpose of MST as enhancing responsible behavior is a point of view that can be readily communicated and understood by diverse groups of individuals, including family members, school personnel, agency colleagues, judges, and legislators. For all parties involved, increasing the responsible behavior of children and parents is a less daunting and more achievable task than treating "psychopathology," which, as reflected in diagnostic labels such as conduct disorder, borderline personality disorder, and so forth, implies a fixed, disease-like, and potentially intractable entity (the "disorder") as the target of treatment.

PARENTAL RESPONSIBLE AND IRRESPONSIBLE BEHAVIOR

Parents have several interrelated responsibilities that are linked with the favorable development, socialization, and well-being of their children. These responsibilities include providing for basic needs, nurturance, protection, advocacy, support, guidance, and discipline (Small, 1990). From an MST perspective, responsible parents engage in behaviors that prepare their children to become competent members of society. Responsible parents constructively and proactively address factors that pose barriers to fulfilling parental responsibilities (e.g., substance abuse, stress, social isolation, and marital discord). Thus, for example, the drug use of Maggie's mother is conceptualized as irresponsible behavior because drug use directly affects the mother's ability to parent. In addition, however, most parents juggle multiple responsibilities (as parent to several children, employee, spouse, daughter of an ailing parent, etc.). In some families, apparent lapses in the execution of parental responsibilities (e.g., failure to monitor a youth's whereabouts consistently and engaging in irritable interchanges) occur because the parent cannot meet his or her responsibilities equally well across multiple domains (e.g., a divorced mother of several young children is employed full time, engaged only in work or child-care activities and therefore relatively socially isolated and mildly depressed). In such instances, enhancing responsible behavior requires engaging others in sharing some of the parent's many responsibilities.

YOUTH RESPONSIBLE AND IRRESPONSIBLE BEHAVIOR

Responsible children engage in behaviors and activities that help them become competent members of their family, community, and society. Youths' primary responsibilities include complying with family and societal rules, attending school and putting forth reasonable efforts, helping around the house, and not harming others. Overall, these responsibilities do not seem too much to ask of children and adolescents. Youth who engage in activities such as drug use, skipping school, and breaking the law are viewed as irresponsible.

PROMOTING RESPONSIBLE BEHAVIOR AND DECREASING IRRESPONSIBLE BEHAVIOR

For children and adolescents, the systematic application of positive reinforcement and discipline is usually used to promote responsible behavior and decrease irresponsible behavior. Social learning theorists have delineated excellent guidelines for the development and application of reinforcement contingencies (see, e.g., Munger, 1993). For example:

- Contingencies should be spelled out clearly on the front end and should fit the nature of the behavior (e.g., missing curfew might result in being grounded the next weekend evening and stealing might require the youth to provide restitution at several times the value of theft).
- Youth should always understand the rationale behind the rules of behavior and should have some input into the rules.
- Using social (e.g., praise) and tangible (e.g., allowance, privilege) reinforcers to promote responsible behavior should be emphasized. Parents should not take "good" behavior for granted but should clearly target such behavior for positive consequences.
- Discipline should be aversive. Constructive disciplines are favored, such as cleaning bathrooms and washing floors. Deprivation of naturally occurring positive reinforcers (e.g., use of phone, Nintendo, and television) can serve as effective discipline.
- For minor transgressions, the sanctions should be minor; for major transgressions, the sanctions should be significant.
- Physical discipline should be discouraged, as they model aggression for youths who already have problems with aggression. In addition, physical discipline can disrupt parent–child affective relations, which are often a focus of MST.
- Punishments should never last so long that the youth has little to lose by continued transgressions (e.g., "You're grounded until you're 18").

Contingencies should always be arranged so that the youth can gain some payoff for behaving responsibly the next day.

Parents often need to be encouraged to increase their levels of responsibility as well. In some cases, parental abdication of parenting responsibilities (e.g., through drug use and personal problems) directly led to the youth's antisocial behavior. As discussed in Chapter 3, the therapist must determine the causes of parental abdication (e.g., lack of necessary skills, mental health difficulties, and family transitions such as divorce and remarriage) and design interventions accordingly. In other cases, a combination of factors (authoritarian parenting style, long work hours at two jobs) reflect sincere but ineffective efforts to be a responsible parent. In either situation, the therapist must always be prepared to reinforce responsible parenting behavior through praise and support for efforts. Critically, the therapist must also help to build natural reinforcements for responsible parenting in the parent's natural ecology (e.g., having grandmother praise her son for helping his son with schoolwork). Improvement in parental responsibility is almost always linked with improved child behavior; thus, as discussed throughout this volume, MST therapists devote a great deal of time to developing and maintaining parental responsibility.

Principle 4: Interventions Are Present Focused and Action Oriented, Targeting Specific and Well-Defined Problems

The overall purpose of this treatment principle is to encourage family transactions that are facilitating clinical progress toward unambiguous outcomes.

PRESENT FOCUSED

MST interventions emphasize changing the family's present circumstances as a step toward changing future functioning. Such an approach contrasts with treatment models that devote a great deal of attention to examining the client's or family's past (e.g., psychoanalysis and Bowenian family therapy). As noted earlier, the MST therapist begins by formulating hypotheses associated with proximal causes of behavior prior to developing more distal (spatial and temporal) analyses of fit. For example, Maggie's history of sexual victimization could have been the primary focus of treatment if distal explanations of aggression were emphasized. Instead, treatment focused on the clear and specific contingencies that were influencing her current aggressive behavior. If changing proximal influences had not proven successful, however, more distal explanations might have been considered.

ACTION ORIENTED

In light of the serious nature of the problems presented by youth and families referred for MST, interventions aim to activate the family and their social ecology to make multiple, positive, observable changes. Making and sustaining such changes requires a high-energy and action-oriented focus. When used within the family preservation model of service delivery, the brevity of MST requires that family members work intensely to solve often long-standing problems. Thus, swift and consistent action is required to enable the family and key players in the social ecology to meet their treatment goals. If (1) the therapist's analysis of fit is correct, (2) the therapist and family agree on appropriate goals and methods to achieve those goals, and (3) the family is working hard on reaching the goals, outcomes should emerge. Moreover, when therapists and family members are action oriented, incremental successes are experienced often; such successes, in turn, can bolster the motivation of family members (and therapists) to sustain their efforts and make additional changes.

TARGETING SPECIFIC AND WELL-DEFINED PROBLEMS

Two types of well-specified treatment goals are used within MST—overarching goals and intermediate goals. *Overarching goals* refer to the family's ultimate aims by the end of treatment (e.g., have the youth pass to the 10th grade). *Intermediate goals* refer to the daily nuts and bolts of reaching the overarching goals (e.g., completing homework assignments each evening, studying for exams, parental reward for academic efforts, and linking parents and school to support educational efforts), and development of the intermediate goals is usually led by the therapist. An ultimate goal in Maggie's case, for example, was for her mother to provide consistent structure and discipline at home. Many intermediate steps, however, were necessary for the mother to achieve this goal: therapist and mother developing a collaborative relationship, assessment of mother's parenting strengths and skill deficits, determination of other barriers to mother's implementation of parenting skills (e.g., drug abuse), implementation of interventions to overcome barriers, problem solving and redesigning interventions when barriers are not overcome, developing a natural support system to reinforce mother's favorable parenting behaviors, and so forth.

Targeting well-defined problems (i.e., objective, measurable, and jargon free) and, correspondingly, setting well-defined treatment goals have several advantages.

- Family members, therapists, and other participants are fully aware of the direction of treatment and the criteria that will be used to measure success.

- Intervention effectiveness can be monitored closely and accurately.
- Unambiguous positive outcomes can motivate subsequent efforts toward change.
- Clear treatment termination points are set (i.e., when goals are met).

Principle 5: Interventions Target Sequences of Behavior within and between Multiple Systems that Maintain the Identified Problems

This principle orients the practitioner toward modifying those aspects of family relations and of the social ecology that are linked with identified problems. Thus, interventions are based on the therapist's assessment of the sequences of behavior within the family (i.e., family interactions) that attenuate or contribute to the behavioral problems. Such an approach contrasts, for example, with treatment models that emphasize the development of individual insight among family members or with treatments that, a priori, assume that families with problem children require a specific type of standardized treatment such as parent training, communication training, or improved problem-solving skills. With MST, the types of family interactions targeted for change are highly individualized and, hence, interventions vary from family to family. Similarly, because youths are embedded in multiple systems, interactions that contribute to or attenuate the youth's difficulties within these systems are addressed (see, e.g., youth's peer group [Chapter 5]; school transactions, [Chapter 6]) specifically, and often intensively, by MST.

One of the defining features of MST, and a characteristic that differentiates MST from the vast majority of treatment models, is the significant attention devoted to transactions between systems that are associated with identified problems. Thus, for example, MST often attempts to empower parents to disengage youths from deviant peer groups while facilitating their involvement with prosocial peers (i.e., the family–peer mesosystem [Chapter 5]). Similarly, significant attention is devoted to the ways that parents can promote their children's educational performance and develop positive working collaborations with school personnel (i.e., the family–school mesosystem [Chapter 6]). Serving as a catalyst to enhance family members' relations with each other and the family's transactions with the community, MST also devotes considerable resources to helping the family develop a prosocial and indigenous support network composed of neighbors, friends, extended family, church members, and so forth. Thus, whether addressing problematic family interactions or helping to build the family's relations with extrafamilial systems, *MST focuses on interpersonal transactions as the mechanism for achieving treatment goals.*

Principle 6: Interventions Are Developmentally Appropriate and Fit the Developmental Needs of the Youth

Children and their caregivers have different needs at different periods of their lives, and interventions should be designed in consideration of such. For example, the nature of family-based interventions will vary with the developmental level of the youth as well as the developmental stage of the caregiver. For children and young adolescents, considerable efforts may be extended to increasing parental control. For older adolescents (e.g., 17-year-olds), interventions might be more viable if they focus on preparing the youth for entry into the adult world. Here, for example, the therapist and parents might use individual interventions with the adolescent to increase his or her social maturity or to develop strategies for overcoming the financial and logistic barriers to independent living.

In designing such individual interventions, however, the practitioner must consider the youth's level of cognitive and social development. A 17-year-old who has a mental age and social maturity of a 14-year-old will be treated very differently than a 17-year-old whose friends are all in their 20s. Therapeutic tasks, therefore, must not exceed clients' developmental or functional capabilities, nor should tasks underestimate abilities. For example, most professionals would agree that a 17-year-old who has been out of school for several years would benefit more from interventions designed to prepare the youth for entry into the job market than from academic remediation. However, the youth in question might be emotionally and intellectually functioning at a much younger age; consequently, preparing the youth for entry into the job market would be premature. Similarly, asking 13-year-old Maggie to self-monitor (i.e., record in an anger journal) her thoughts and feelings would involve several complex skills, including attending to internal stimuli, accurately recording internal events while in a heightened emotional state, and writing. Although some 13-year-olds might have the capacity to engage in such complex cognitive processes, many will not.

The developmental stage of the caregiver is also an important factor when designing interventions. For example, grandparents who are thrust into the role of primary caretaker may have different developmental needs than a traditional parent. Although grandparents may function well as grandparents (i.e., seeing their grandchildren periodically), the role of primary caregiver to a youth presenting serious antisocial behavior requires a great deal of energy and fortitude. Thus, because of age and possible medical factors, some grandparents may not have the physical and emotional strength needed to raise youth engaged in serious antisocial behavior. In Maggie's case, for example, asking her grandmother to assume primary responsibility for structuring and monitoring Maggie's school and community behavior would have overburdened grandmother, in spite of her many strengths. Hence, grandmother was asked to provide nurturance and some physical care while Maggie's aunts provided the structure and monitoring. Thus, the general strategy was to activate a strong social support network to reinforce the grandmother's capacity as a caregiver.

Another example of the importance of considering caregiver developmental needs pertains to situations in which a young mother may have a child in his or her teens. Sometimes, the mother's developmental level is closer to that of the adolescent than to other parents of teenagers (e.g., a 28-year-old mother who is more like a sister or competitor than a parent to her 14-year-old daughter). In such cases, a grandparent has often functioned as the primary caregiver throughout the child's life, but the grandparent is not capable of dealing with the intensive and pervasive difficulties that an adolescent can present. Here, as suggested previously, the therapist must examine the capacity of the full ecology vis-à-vis appropriate parenting. Sometimes the parent can develop the needed parenting capacity if given the requisite resources and support. Other times, the parent has limited cognitive and social maturity, and the therapist needs to pull together a parenting collaboration among a variety of adults who are emotionally connected with the youth.

Finally, designing developmentally appropriate interventions also pertains to the individual's transactions with extrafamilial systems. For example, adolescence is a period when youth are developing increased independence from their family and increased emotional intimacy with peers. As such, adolescents need substantial opportunities for peer involvement. Unfortunately, youths presenting serious antisocial behavior often develop relations with peers who exert negative influences. Keeping the youth at home after school and not allowing him or her to visit friends on the weekend are not developmentally appropriate solutions for the problem of association with deviant peers because they interfere with an important developmental task of adolescence. Rather, interventions should focus on determining ways in which friendships with prosocial peers can be developed and on eliminating barriers (e.g., attitude and availability) to the development of such friendships.

Principle 7: Interventions Are Designed to Require Daily or Weekly Effort by Family Members

A basic assumption of MST is that therapists can help families resolve their problems more quickly if everyone involved (e.g., caregivers, extended family, siblings, friends, neighbors, and social service personnel) works together diligently. This assumption is predicated on the family and therapist agreeing on and collaborating with the goals of treatment. By default, when agreeing on the goals of treatment, the family and therapist are also agreeing to address any barriers that interfere with achieving these goals. Thus, the expectation is that when a therapist and family are working collaboratively on agreed goals, maximum effort should be evident in the daily behavior of all involved.

Designing interventions that require daily and weekly effort provides several advantages.

1. Identified problems can be resolved more quickly if everyone involved is working on them.
2. Backsliding and nonadherence to treatment protocols become readily apparent. Consequently, therapists can respond immediately to identify and address barriers to change.
3. Treatment outcomes can be assessed continually, which provides many opportunities for corrective actions.
4. Because intervention tasks occur daily, family members have frequent opportunity to receive positive feedback in moving toward goals, praise from therapist and others in the ecology, and satisfaction inherent in completing tasks. Such reinforcers promote family motivation and maintenance of change.
5. Family empowerment is supported as families learn that they are primarily responsible for and capable of progressing toward treatment goals.

In Maggie's case, several interventions required daily effort by family members. First, the grandmother assigned Maggie household chores and monitored their completion daily. If Maggie completed them, the grandmother provided rewards and informed the mother. However, if she did not complete them, the grandmother, mother, and aunts would confer on the appropriate consequence based on a menu of alternatives. This intervention helped provide Maggie much needed structure while slowly building the mother's parenting capacity. Second, the aunts monitored Maggie's social behavior at school in collaboration with the school counselor and at home on a daily basis in collaboration with the mother and grandmother and provided previously agreed consequences. Third, the aunts and grandmother took turns contacting the mother each day to support her abstinence from drugs (and monitor drug use), and the therapist conveyed the results of random drug screens to the aunts and grandmother. Social reinforcers from the mother's family were based on the mother's capacity to remain drug free. Thus, key members in Maggie's extended family were engaged in a continuing process of changing her social ecology in a way that would promote responsible behavior in Maggie and her mother.

Principle 8: Intervention Effectiveness Is Evaluated Continuously from Multiple Perspectives with Providers Assuming Accountability for Overcoming Barriers to Successful Outcomes

This principle ensures that the therapist will have a continuous and relatively accurate view of treatment progress and, therefore, receive ongoing and prompt feedback regarding the viability of interventions. Most interventions, when applied appropriately, can be expected to begin to have positive results within a short time (1–2 weeks at the most). If an intervention is not working, prompt feedback allows the therapist and family to consider alternative interventions or alternative conceptualizations of the targeted problem. Problems can usually be resolved in multiple ways, and therapists are encouraged to consider alternative solutions when the present ones are not effective. Likewise, MST therapists are strongly discouraged from providing "more of the same" when interventions are not working (assuming that the interventions are being implemented as intended).

Multiple informants and multiple methods should be used to evaluate the ongoing effectiveness of interventions. Informants can include parents, the youth, siblings, teachers, peers, classmates, neighbors, and other professionals working with the family. Three important points should be kept in mind when choosing informants. First, the informant should be reliable and accurate and have access to the behaviors of interest (i.e., teachers are better informants of classroom behavior than are caregivers). Second, the therapist must remain aware of any biases that the informant might have regarding the validity of reports. For example, the reports of the teacher who Maggie threatened to kill might be biased toward negative reporting even if interventions are successful. Third, the therapist must follow confidentiality protocols while asking informants for relevant client information. Thus, the therapist must obtain a "release of information" from the client family prior to contacting informants for specific information. In addition, if possible, multiple methods should be used to tap the behavior of interest. For example, three methods of assessing drug use by Maggie's mother were used: random urine screens, self-reports, and other-reports from extended family. Finally, by examining outcomes from multiple perspectives and using multiple methods, the ecological validity of MST assessment and treatment are further emphasized.

Principle 9: Interventions Are Designed to Promote Treatment Generalization and Long-Term Maintenance of Therapeutic Change by Empowering Caregivers to Address Family Members' Needs across Multiple Systemic Contexts

Ensuring that treatment gains will generalize and be maintained when treatment ends is a critical and continuous thrust of MST interventions. Stokes and

Baer (1977) defined generalization as the occurrence of relevant behavior under different, nontraining conditions—across subjects, settings, people, behaviors, and time. If Maggie, for example, learned to be respectful toward her mother and, although not taught, she started being respectful to her teacher or other adults, Maggie's respectful behavior would have generalized. Maintenance, subsumed under generalization, refers to the tendency of new behaviors to persist over time.

Designing interventions that promote treatment generalization and maintenance is a very active process that has several important implications for the MST practitioner. Therapeutic interventions should do the following:

1. Emphasize the development of skills that family members will use to navigate their social ecology.
2. Develop the capacity of family members to negotiate current and future problems.
3. Be delivered primarily by caregivers, with therapists playing primarily supportive and consultative roles.
4. Accentuate and build family strengths and competencies.
5. Make abundant use of protective and resiliency factors available in the natural environment.

EMPOWERMENT

Each of the preceding implications can be subsumed under the rubric of empowerment. Empowerment from an MST perspective refers to families having the capacity to deal effectively and independently with the inevitable challenges of raising children (Henggeler, Cunningham, Pickrel, Schoenwald, & Brondino, 1996), and empowerment is the vehicle through which treatment generalization and maintenance occur.

Empowering clients requires MST therapists to possess at least three attitudes or characteristics. First, therapists must restrain themselves from entering the family system and affecting change through the force of their own personalities and skills. Instead, MST therapists must maximize the capacity of family members to affect changes in their own lives. Practitioners, therefore, should demonstrate "benevolent demanding" (Linehan, 1993), which recognizes the client's existing capacities, reinforces adaptive behavior and self-control, and refuses to take care of clients when they can care for themselves. Second, MST therapists must recognize that families are composed of autonomous individuals with the right to decide what they do and what happens to them. Families have a right to choose the goals of treatment and clinicians must respect their choices. A corollary of this second point is that MST therapists must assume families have competencies when given appropriate opportunities and resources. Third, MST therapists must be creative in finding indigenous resources for families to use in gaining control over their lives. As suggested next and discussed in Chapter 8, priority is clearly given to the development of natural resources (i.e., friends, neighbors, and extended family) versus agency resources (i.e., case managers). These resources must be in place by the time MST treatment is terminated.

DESIGNING INTERVENTIONS FOR GENERALIZATION AND MAINTENANCE

Therapists can increase the probability of treatment generalization and maintenance by taking several straightforward steps.

1. Teach relevant behaviors or skills in the environments and under the conditions in which clients will eventually behave. For example, the therapist taught Maggie's mother behavior management techniques at home and had her use the skills as she was consequating Maggie's behavior after school.
2. Encourage and reinforce the development of problem-solving skills. Reinforce families for (or their efforts toward) identifying problems (i.e., well-defined and specified), generating alternative solutions, evaluating solutions, analyzing possible barriers to solutions, choosing an alternative, and preparing for possible consequences of the solution.
3. Find individuals in the ecology who can and will reinforce family members' new behaviors and skills across settings (e.g., home, school, and community).
4. Alert significant others (e.g., teachers, probation officers, and case managers) to the new behaviors of the family members.
5. Provide positive reinforcement when generalization occurs. For example, the therapist taught the mother to reinforce Maggie when she exhibited "respectful behavior" to siblings and peers, not just to adults.
6. Allow clients to do as much of the development and implementation of interventions as they can.

Throughout the treatment process, the MST practitioner must determine and help to develop the support and resources necessary to maintain clinical gains after the therapist leaves. If, for example, the caregiver is an effective disciplinarian, except under conditions of high stress, indigenous supports must be developed and readied to assist the family during times of high stress. Similarly, if a parent needs a small loan on occasion to make ends meet, an appropriate resource should be identified. As discussed in Chapter 8, considerable attention to reciprocity between the family and the supports (i.e., quid pro quo) must be given if natural support networks are to be maintained over time.

Providing MST via the Home-Based Model of Service Delivery

As described throughout the presentation of the MST principles, a core feature of MST is its emphasis on altering the social ecology of youth and families in ways that promote positive adjustment and attenuate emotional and behavioral difficulties. By definition, therefore, MST interventions must be highly involved in the natural environments of youths and families. When addressing the needs of families in which one or more children are at imminent risk of out-of-home placement (i.e., incarceration or placement in a residential treatment center, group home, or psychiatric hospital), the intensity of clinical need requires an equally intensive clinical response. Thus, in the vast majority of MST research projects and programs, MST was provided via the home-based (or family preservation) model of service delivery. Key characteristics of this model include the following:

- Low caseloads, typically three to six families per full-time therapist.
- Provision of services in the family's natural environment—home, school, and neighborhood settings.
- Time-limited duration of treatment, 3–5 months per family depending on the seriousness of the problems and success of interventions.
- Therapist functioning within a team of three to four practitioners, though each has an individual caseload.
- 24-hour-per-day and 7-day-per-week availability of therapists, or at least one practitioner on the MST team.
- Scheduling appointments at the family's convenience, such as evening hours and weekends.
- Daily contact, face to face or by phone, with families.

Thus, the intent of the home-based model is to provide very intensive clinical services, services that prevent an out-of-home placement. Although, at first glance, many professionals and administrators think that the intensity of a home-based model is prohibitively expensive, this could not be further from the truth. For example, assuming that a team of three MST therapists and the requisite organizational infrastructure can treat 50 families per year at the cost of $5,000 per family (an assumption based on program costs at several existing MST program sites), the annual cost of the entire MST program (i.e., $250,000) would be offset and savings realized by preventing four 12-month placements in a residential treatment center at $80,000 per placement or seven such placements at $40,000 per placement. As described in Chapter 9, the potential cost savings associated with successful MST programs are substantial, and such documentation is becoming increasingly available. The key, however, is for the MST program to focus on those youths who are truly at high risk for out-of-home placement and their families.

In addition to having the capacity to provide intensive services, the home-based model has several other advantages over more traditional models of service delivery (e.g., outpatient treatment and hospitalization).

1. Assessment data, which form the basis of treatment planning, have much greater validity when gathered in locations where the problems occur (i.e., home, school and neighborhood) and from multiple members of the youth's real-world ecology. The validity of the assessment data greatly increases the probability that planned interventions will fit the needs and strengths of the youth and family, and, therefore, be implemented and achieve results.

2. Providing home-based services greatly decreases barriers to service access in a population (i.e., families of youths presenting serious antisocial behavior) that has very high "no show" and dropout rates from traditional institution-based services. Indeed, in a recent study of MST with substance-abusing and dependent juvenile offenders and their families, fully 98% completed a full course of MST treatment (Henggeler, Pickrel, Brondino, & Crouch, 1996).

3. Going to families and communicating on their turf sends a message of therapist commitment and respect that can greatly facilitate family engagement and the development of a therapeutic alliance—prerequisites for achieving desired outcomes.

4. Treatment progress can be monitored more validly, and, thus, midcourse corrections in treatment plans can be implemented quickly and reliably. For example, when the therapist spends considerable time each week discussing progress in the family's living room, the reality of such progress is much more likely to become clear (whether dad has stopped drinking, whether parental discipline and child compliance have improved).

Thus, although providing home-based services is a major shift from the historic reliance of mental health on institution-based services (Santos, Henggeler, Burns, Arana, & Meisler, 1995), such a shift is fully compatible with and responsive to (1) extant knowledge regarding the determinants of serious antisocial behavior, (2) social-ecological models of behavior, (3) SOC principles (Stroul & Friedman, 1986), and (4) the high therapy dropout rates for populations presenting serious antisocial behavior (e.g., Stark, 1992). Moreover, the home-based model can be cost-effective when used with populations at imminent risk of out-of-home placement, or even with populations not an imminent risk but presenting serious antisocial behavior (e.g., Schoenwald, Ward, Henggeler, Pickrel, & Patel, 1996).

MST Clinical Supervision

Recent research in the field of child and adolescent psychotherapy underscores the importance of clinical supervision in facilitating treatment effectiveness. Meta-analyses examining treatment as conducted in university- versus community-based settings indicates that provision of *structure* (e.g., through treatment manuals) and *monitoring* (e.g., through review of therapy tapes) to foster adherence to treatment plans were among the factors associated with the apparent superior effectiveness of child psychotherapies provided in research settings (Weisz, Donenberg, Han, & Kauneckis, 1995; Weisz, Donenberg, Han, & Weiss, 1995). Earlier in this chapter, the nine MST treatment principles were discussed, along with the role that these principles play in structuring MST interventions. Here, we describe the characteristics of MST supervision that provide the monitoring and consultation required to support treatment fidelity. Importantly, high adherence to MST treatment principles is linked with reductions in the recidivism, psychiatric symptomatology, and incarceration of violent and chronic juvenile offenders (Henggeler, Melton, et al., 1997). Hence, supporting MST treatment integrity is a priority at all levels of program implementation—supervisory, administrative, fiscal, and interorganizational.

In clinical trials of MST, on-site supervision for teams of MST clinicians was provided by the initial developers of MST; by doctoral-level psychologists and psychiatrists who were members of the research team developing, refining, and evaluating MST; and by master's-level mental health professionals who were not involved in the development of MST but were hired to provide clinical supervision (e.g., Henggeler, Melton, & Smith, 1992; Scherer, Brondino, Henggeler, Melton, & Hanley, 1994). When investigators were remote to the treatment site, weekly telephone consultation to on-site supervisors occurred. This model of clinical supervision, in which on-site clinical supervision is supported by remote consultation from MST experts, is a central feature of the training and consultation protocol that emerged in response to requests for training made by public and private agencies remote from the Family Services Research Center. The guidelines for clinical supervision described in this chapter were developed on the basis of our experiences with clinical trials and with organizations implementing home-based services using MST through contractual arrangements in which training and consultation are provided by MST experts remote to the site.

Objectives of MST Clinical Supervision

The overarching objective of clinical supervision is to facilitate clinicians' acquisition and implementation of the conceptual and behavioral skills required in MST. These skills are critical to attenuating or eliminating identified problems and achieving positive, sustainable outcomes. Thus, the primary functions of MST supervision are to ensure that clinicians are able, on a consistent basis to do the following:

1. Develop and refine a multisystemic conceptualization of the causes of identified problems presented by each client family.
2. Design and effectively implement intervention strategies that embody the nine treatment principles.
3. Identify barriers to the successful engagement of key participants (family members, school personnel, sources of parental social support) and implement strategies to overcome these barriers.
4. Logically and clearly connect intermediary goals to ultimate goals and intervention strategies to both intermediary and ultimate goals.
5. Identify barriers to the successful implementation of interventions and implement strategies to overcome them.

To assist clinicians in carrying out these frequently complex functions, supervisors reinforce critical thinking throughout the treatment process. That is, supervisors encourage clinicians to engage in hypothesis testing when they have hunches, beliefs, or theories about the causes and correlates of particular problems in a family, the reasons that improvements have occurred, and the barriers to change. Figure 2.2 depicts these functions, the relationships among them, and the analytical process used to identify and execute them.

Assumptions Underlying MST Clinical Supervision

Key assumptions underlying the MST approach to clinical supervision are as follows:

1. Each clinician implementing MST is a hard-working, competent professional who brings unique personal strengths and professional experiences to the treatment process.
2. Ongoing clinical supervision is necessary to monitor adherence to MST and to achieve positive, sustainable outcomes with youth presenting serious clinical problems and their families.
3. The purpose of clinical supervision is to enable clinicians to adhere to the nine principles of MST in all aspects of treatment—engagement

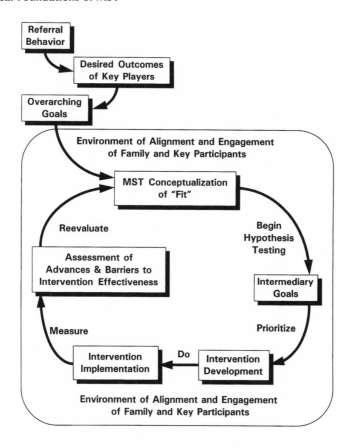

FIGURE 2.2. MST analytical process.

of client families, case conceptualization, intervention design and implementation, and evaluation of outcomes.

4. The process of clinical supervision should mirror the process of MST. That is, supervision is present focused and action oriented and targets specific and well-defined problems that the clinician appears to be having in (a) conceptualizing the "fit" of referral problems with the family's ecological context, (b) identifying and using strengths as levers for change, (c) designing interventions, (d) implementing interventions adequately, and (e) overcoming barriers to intervention implementation or success. Supervision should also enable clinicians to sustain MST-like conceptualization and intervention skills across cases (generalization).

5. Clinicians and clinical supervisors (and the provider organization that houses the MST program) are accountable for outcomes.

Structure of Supervision

MST supervision occurs in a small group format. A team of three to four clinicians and the clinical supervisor meet for 1½ –2 hours and address 12–15 cases addressed within that time frame. As with MST treatment contacts, the amount of time and effort directed toward a particular case in supervision varies in accordance with the needs of the clinician and family during a given week. When a referral is new to the team, relatively more supervision time is spent discussing the clinician's initial assessment of the strengths and needs in each system, examining the fit of identified problems with the family and its ecology, articulating the family's goals, and identifying initial targets of treatment. When evidence clearly indicates that interventions are successful and families are making observable progress toward ultimate goals (Principle 8), very little time is spent discussing the case. When progress is slow or setbacks occur, the team devotes relatively more time to the case.

The group supervision format helps team members to become familiar with developments in all cases and with supervisory feedback regarding those developments. This familiarity, in turn, enables clinicians to reinforce the multisystemic nature of therapeutic efforts throughout the week, to generalize as appropriate from supervisory discussion of colleagues' cases, and to sustain continuity of care while covering for one another during vacation, weekend, and personal time. In addition, individualized supervision is immediately available when developments arise that pose serious threats to the safety of a family member (e.g., suicidal, homicidal, or psychotic behavior; evidence of physical or sexual abuse or serious neglect; and incidents of domestic violence) or to the youth's continued placement in the home (e.g., court or agency recommends out-of-home placement).

Figure 2.3 reflects the general structure of the inquiry and problem-solving processes embodied in MST supervision and the nature of the information required to efficiently engage in that process. This structure was originally developed to assist clinicians and clinical supervisors in remote sites to prepare for clinical consultation with an MST expert. Anecdotal reports from supervisors indicate that the information requested on this form facilitates their acquisition of the skills needed to conduct supervision in an MST-like fashion, and clinicians report that completing the forms for client families each week assists them in retaining the multisystemic focus of case conceptualization and intervention.

CLINICIAN RESPONSIBILITIES

Responsibility for clinical supervision is shared by the team and the clinical supervisor, though the supervisor carries more of the responsibility for ensuring the productivity of the supervisory session. To maximize the value of

Family: _____ Therapist: _____ Date: _____

<u>Weekly Review</u>

I. Overarching/Primary MST Goals

II. Previous Intermediary Goals   Met   Partially   Not

III. Barriers to Intermediary Goals

IV. Advances in Treatement

V. How has your assessment of the fit changed with new information/interventions?

VI. New Intermediary Goals for Next Week

FIGURE 2.3. Case summary for MST supervision and consultation.

clinical supervision for team members and their client families, supervisors discourage clinicians from using supervision to narrate extensively regarding case details, as fascinating, challenging, and dramatic as these details often are. Instead, clinicians are strongly encouraged to prepare for the group supervision session by thinking about these details in terms of what they suggest about the multisystemic fit of referral problems, strengths to be used as levers for change, barriers to change, and strategies to overcome those barriers.

SUPERVISOR RESPONSIBILITIES

Whereas the primary focus of the clinician is on the interactions within the family and between family members and school personnel, peers, neighbors, and so on, the primary focus of the clinical supervisor is on the clinician's thinking, behavior, and interactions with the family and with the systems in which the family is embedded. Supervisors must understand enough of the "nuts and bolts" about a client family and its ecology to assist clinicians in all aspects of treatment (i.e., engagement and alignment, conceptualization, intervention design and implementation, designing strategies to overcome barriers to change, and assessment of outcomes). In addition, the supervisor should be able to assess and facilitate the development of the clinician's MST skills across all cases. When clinicians new to MST for example, conceptualize fit too narrowly, overlook the importance of getting parents on board, and/or implement interventions prematurely across several cases, the supervisor would target these skills for improvement. When it appears that a clinician lacks the training or experience to identify, design, or execute needed intervention strategies (marital treatment, cognitive behavioral interventions for a mildly depressed mother, etc.), the supervisor provides guidance, instruction, and references of materials relevant to those intervention strategies. If instruction is obtained elsewhere (e.g., the clinician attends a workshop on cognitive-behavioral therapy with depressed adults or reads a treatment manual pertaining to enhancement of marital communication), the supervisor monitors the clinician's acquisition of the needed skills and application of those skills in interventions designed in accordance with the MST principles.

Supervision Process Guidelines

Consistent with the MST approach to treatment contacts with families, clinical supervision is collaborative and goal oriented. Liberal doses of humor are used and verbal praise is freely given as clinicians make progress toward and achieve positive outcomes with families. To be effective, supervision should be viewed by the participants as an enjoyable and useful activity.

SUPERVISORY QUESTIONS THAT REINFORCE AN MST FOCUS

In guiding interactions with team members during supervision, supervisors often ask some version of the following questions.

• How does the child's behavior *make sense* in the context of all the systems in the child's and family's life? In asking this and similar questions, the clinical supervisor is seeking a response that indicates that the clinician conceptualizes the bases of identified problems in terms of some *combination* of identifiable everyday interactions in the family, at school, between school and family, with peers, and in the neighborhood (Principle 1). If the clinician's responses to such questions suggest that he or she is conceptualizing problems in accordance with other theoretical orientations (e.g., psychodynamic or Bowenian family therapy) or personal beliefs (e.g., "I think any parent who really loved his or her child would . . . "), assumptions about causality that are not testable (e.g., the child experienced rejection by the dad when he was a toddler), diagnostic labels (e.g., he's oppositional defiant), or historic events as a primary determinant of current problem behavior (e.g., the fact that the child was molested by a distant relative 6 years ago), additional prompts are often provided to assist clinicians in conceptualizing the fit of referral problems in multisystemic terms.

• What repeated, predictable patterns of family interactions have you observed that might explain the problem behavior?

• How are the parents interacting with the school, community (church, employers, neighbors), and peers? Which interactions suggest strengths in the relations between systems (e.g., family–school and family–peers), and which interactions seem to contribute to the problems?

• What is the *evidence* supporting your idea that [any clinician's hypothesis about why things do or do not happen in a family, at school, etc.] is contributing to the problems? How can you test the hypotheses you have about what contributes to what?

• What are the *strengths* of the parent(s)/caregivers, child, and naturally occurring supports (relatives, neighbors, friends of parents, etc.). How can we reinforce those strengths? How can we use those strengths to help change aspects of the family's life that contribute to the identified problem?

• What are the family's goals for treatment?

• Are the parents "on board" with the goals and intervention plans?

• If not, what are the barriers to getting a parent on board? What have you done to cultivate an alliance or working partnership with the parent to get him or her on board? What is the evidence that you have cultivated such a relationship? What are you doing to maintain the alliance when addressing barriers to change?

• If the parent is not on board, what will you, the clinician, need to understand about the parent and his or her social network to increase the probability of successful engagement. What will you have to do to get the parent on board?

• What has the family done this week to achieve intermediary goals?

• What has the clinician done this week to assist the family in achieving intermediary goals? Is there any evidence that achieving these goals is leading toward the attainment of ultimate goals?

• When interventions are either partly implemented, not implemented at all, or not successful, what are the barriers to success? What is the evidence supporting your assessment that these barriers are the ones that interfered with the intervention's implementation or success? How can you test which are the greatest barriers to change?

MANAGEMENT OF TEAM INTERACTION DURING SUPERVISION

Although supervision should be lively and enjoyable, the overarching objective is to facilitate therapists' implementation of MST and the attainment of favorable client family outcomes. Because 12–15 cases must be covered in a 1–2 hour supervisory session, such sessions must be relatively task oriented and goal directed to achieve their objectives (note the similar goal-oriented purpose of MST sessions conducted with families). In our experience, task oriented clinical supervision is a rarity in the field of mental health, where supervision usually focuses on administrative issues, storytelling, and providing emotional support. When working with therapists who are inexperienced in MST, therefore, supervisors may need to learn methods to effectively redirect the flow of case discussion when MST supervisory objectives are not being pursued.

Early in their implementation of MST, clinicians often provide extensive narrative about details, events, conversations, or treatment sessions that were particularly interesting, amusing, or disturbing to them. The following questions may help supervisors to evaluate the utility of the narrative in terms of MST case conceptualization and intervention design: (1) Does the narrative convey new information that changes the team's overall case conceptualization or understanding of the fit of the identified problems with the family's ecology; and (2) Does the narrative provide new information about potential strengths that can be used as levers for change, or about barriers to change previously unknown to the family and therapist? If the clinician's accounts of details confirm previously identified patterns of interaction, the supervisor should inquire as to the purpose of the narrative. What is the clinician hoping to accomplish in telling the story? If the narration reiterates what is already known, the supervisor points this out and moves on.

Take, for example, an interaction in which a clinician is describing the details of a heated argument she observed between Jake and his stepfather (see Chapter 3). The clinician may be describing the details of the interaction because she did not know what to make of it in MST terms but suspected that the argument might alter her conceptualization of the interactions patterns that contribute to Jake's runaway behavior. Under these circumstances, supervision would focus on (1) the extent to which this interaction is consistent with, or differs from, the team's understanding of the fit of the identified problem with family interaction patterns (i.e., conflict between stepfather and Jake is a nearly inevitable sequelae of school–family contact and ineffective maternal efforts to punish Jake for inappropriate behavior at school); and (2) the implications of any changes in conceptualization for intermediary goals and intervention strategies currently being implemented. The incident would not become a focus of supervision if the clinician is describing the father–son altercation because she was uncomfortable witnessing it, but the incident simply confirmed what is already known about the fit of the problem with relations within the family and between the family and school. Instead, the supervisor and team would acknowledge the clinician's discomfort, assess whether the discomfort is a barrier to engagement or intervention with the father, and move on.

Just as MST interventions should be designed to generalize across time and situations, so too should supervisory feedback. The objective of clinical supervision is to have clinicians think and do MST in the field, on the spot, when no supervision is available. Thus, before giving advice, supervisors may ask clinicians to articulate their evidence for a particular formulation of fit, the intervention strategies they are considering, and the barriers they anticipate. Initially, supervisors may tell clinicians what to think and do without first understanding the clinician's rationale for a particular intervention plan. This pattern sometimes leads to clinician compliance in the absence of understanding, which, in turn, decreases the likelihood that the clinician will generalize from the supervisory session to other cases. Clues that compliance is occurring without understanding include supervisory advice repeatedly given that is not implemented by the clinician, advice implemented in one case but not in another where it would be useful, and advice openly rejected.

Potential Barriers to Clinician Implementation of MST

Group supervision or individual meetings should be used to explore barriers to clinician implementation of supervisory recommendations. Tools that may be useful in assessing the barriers to implementation include review of audiotaped treatment sessions and live supervision in the field. On the other hand, the barriers may relate to the supervisor's behavior. For example, recommendations may "miss the mark" because they were based on inadequate information or recommendations may be communicated poorly. In the context of MST, clinician *and* supervisor behavior are considered possible strengths and barriers to change and thus are open to critical evaluation.

CLINICIAN CHARACTERISTICS

Gaining therapists' engagement in group supervision and adherence to MST treatment principles can present significant challenges to supervisors when the therapists are midcareer professionals who practiced relatively autonomously prior to their involvement with an MST program. The demands associated with developing the conceptual and intervention skills required to implement MST may engender anxiety or even resistance. Clinical training programs often encourage trainees to develop a specific theoretical orientation, which, in turn, becomes the clinician's basis for clinical practice and may become central to the personal and professional identity of the clinician. If the theoretical orientations and therapies associated with them are subsequently shown to be ineffective, clinicians "face a difficult choice: Persist in the preferred orientation and its methods despite a lack of supporting evidence, or learn new ways of construing and intervening with clinical problems" (Weisz, Donenberg, Han, & Weiss, 1995, p. 698). Doing so may require "replacing hard-won, familiar, and conceptually appealing ways of thinking and intervening" (Weisz, Donenberg, Han, & Weiss, 1995, p. 698). Thus, clinical supervisors should be sensitive to the fact that new agency initiatives, such as the development of an MST program, can be perceived as questioning the competencies and contributions of clinicians who view themselves, and are viewed by others, as capable and productive. Consistent with recommendations in the technology transfer literature (Brown, 1995) and with the strengths focus of the MST treatment model, clinical supervision should capitalize on clinicians' existing skills and experiences while helping them to develop proficiency in the implementation of MST.

Anecdotal impressions were also developed regarding other clinician factors that may facilitate readiness to adopt MST principles and practices. Desirable personal characteristics include intelligence, flexibility, creativity, open-mindedness, and a serious work ethic. Professional training and experience consistent with MST in terms of treatment focus (family, ecology), epistemology underlying the treatment model (empirically based), and emphasis on measurement of, and accountability for, clinical outcome appear to enhance clinician adoption of MST practices. Conversely, clinician training and experience that focuses on the individual child, is informed primarily by non-empirically based treatment models, and eschews measurement of and individual accountability for outcomes appear to interfere with clinician adoption of MST principles and practices.

COMMON "STARTER" DILEMMAS

In our experience, common dilemmas for clinicians learning MST appear to be as follows:

- Engagement of the child, rather than the parent figure(s).
- Failure to engage one or more key players (i.e., someone with power to influence treatment).
- Failure to collect evidence to support or refute personal hypotheses about the fit of referral problems.
- Framing of fit in terms of trait-like, steady-state attributes of individuals or unobservable motivations (e.g., he has an anger problem or she is dependent).
- Personal implementation of interventions by the therapist when MST

would dictate facilitating implementation by others (e.g., parent, teacher, or neighbor).

- Avoidance of assessment and intervention activities due to discomfort or lack of experience or skill (e.g., avoids stepfather because he is loud and angry or avoids assessing the role of marital interaction in the fit of referral problems because the clinician has not previously conducted marital therapy).

Clinical supervisors should be alert for signs that clinicians are facing these dilemmas. Common "red flags" that arise in the context of clinical supervision and on clinicians' weekly case summaries include the use of blaming terms in descriptions of family members; clinician avoidance of interactions with certain members of the family, school, peer group, or neighborhood; and descriptions of fit that are not consistent with MST or rely heavily on untested hunches (e.g., "Kim's mother is trying to turn Kim against her ex-husband because she is jealous of the time Kim spends with him").

COMMON BARRIERS OBSERVED DURING SUPERVISION

Given the complexity of the cases referred for MST, challenges often emerge in initiating and maintaining progress. Such challenges arise even when teams and clinical supervisors have extensive experience translating MST treatment principles into concrete intervention strategies. In our experience, when the team struggles consistently in assisting families to make even incremental gains, several sources of the problem should be considered.

1. The MST conceptualization of the fit of identified problems is incomplete or off base. For example, the therapist has not yet learned that the mother is financially dependent on her boyfriend who has not been engaged in the treatment process, parents of deviant peers allow the youths to use drugs in their homes, and marital problems are interfering with parental monitoring.

2. Team members are persisting in conceptualizing the case from theoretical perspectives that are not consistent with the goal-oriented, present-focused, and pragmatic nature of MST. For example, rather than developing and implementing specific solutions to specific problems, the therapist may proselytize regarding the roles of prejudice and social injustice in contributing to the problems of disadvantaged youths and families. Even though such conceptualizations may be true, they do little to help a particular family engage their son in a particular school or prevent him from associating with fellow gang members.

3. The conceptualization is sufficiently multisystemic and comprehen-

sive, but interventions do not follow logically from the conceptualization. For example, the clinician working with Jake and his family noticed a pattern of interaction that often precipitates Jake's staying away from home overnight or longer. The pattern (described in further detail in Chapter 3) is that news from school about Jake's misdeeds prompts Jake's mother to reprimand her son, which she does ineffectively. The reprimands are met with angry responses from Jake, mother and son begin to argue, the stepfather coaches his wife to use harsh discipline, and he and Jake sometimes come to blows. In spite of this multisystemic conceptualization, the clinician listed "increase anger management skills for Jake" as an intermediary goal for this week.

4. Interventions are inadequately specified. An example of weak specification is as follow: "Recommend parents provide more structure." Increased structure may be a reasonable intermediary goal (though a better operational definition of structure is needed), but interventions need to describe the how and wherefore of achieving such goals. Thus, interventions should indicate specifically what is needed for the parent to provide structure, what should be said and done differently by the parent and child, and how the clinician plans to facilitate these events.

5. The interventions were incompletely implemented. For example, the clinician helps a family to develop a set of rules but does not list rewards and consequences. The clinician helps a parent set a curfew but does not examine the possible strategies that the youth might use to circumvent the curfew and develop a set of counterresponses for the parent.

6. The implementation of interventions is not monitored adequately by family or clinician. As a common example, the clinician reports that the parent implemented rules and consequences for several days, but contingencies are having no effect on child behavior. However, no system was put in place to track whether adolescent behavior is being consequated consistently, and other family members cannot verify whether the rules are being enforced.

7. The conceptualization and interventions are accurate, and interventions were applied properly, but previously unknown barriers were encountered in trying to apply the interventions. Now, clinical conceptualizations must be altered accordingly and new interventions must be designed to better fit the new information.

Conclusion

Through the use of treatment principles, MST was specified in a relatively user-friendly format. Importantly, the treatment principles are validated in research that showed that therapist adherence to these principles predicted favorable long-term outcomes for violent and chronic juvenile offenders and their families. In addition, providing MST via a home-based model of service delivery facilitates family engagement and greatly enhances the ecological validity of assessment and treatment. An important research goal in the forthcoming years is to test anecdotal impressions regarding the role of supervision in facilitating therapist adherence to MST—and subsequent child and family outcomes. To facilitate the validation of the MST supervisory protocol, a supervisory manual is being written and subsequent studies will empirically link supervisory adherence with therapist adherence and, in turn, with youth outcomes.

II

CLINICAL PROCEDURES

3

Assessment of Family Functioning

In this chapter
- The framework of effective family functioning that informs MST.
- The theoretical and empirical rationale underlying this framework.
- The ongoing process for assessing family ecology and the family's strengths.

Families come in many forms. They may be headed by two biological or adoptive parents, one biological and one stepparent, a single parent who is divorced or who was never married, one or more grandparents, or relative(s) acting as parents. The diversity of family forms has broadened in recent years, and increased numbers of children are raised by divorced, remarried, and/or never-married parents (Emery, 1994; Pecora, Fraser, Nelson, McCroskey, & Meezan, 1995). Similarly, increasing numbers of youth coming into the care of state agencies (child welfare, juvenile justice, mental health) were born to never-married parents and to teenage parents (Pecora et al., 1995). Regardless of the particular form a family takes, all families must carry out several essential functions to raise reasonably well-adjusted children.

Multisystemic conceptualizations of effective family functioning are guided by social-ecological and family systems theories and by research on child development, developmental psychopathology, parenting practices, marital relations, and individual parent and child characteristics associated with positive and negative outcomes for youth. Across these literatures, five broad categories of family phenomena are implicated in the etiology of serious antisocial behavior. These categories are (1) interactions throughout the family system; (2) parenting styles and the knowledge, beliefs, and skills that support them; (3) marital interactions; (4) characteristics of the individual parent figure and his or her social ecology that impact parenting tasks; and (5) concrete and practical aspects of the family's ecology (e.g., housing and transportation). The ongoing MST assessment of family functioning, strengths, and needs is directed toward identifying, for each client family which particular combination of these factors contributes to the referral problem and/or can be used as levers for change.

The first section of this chapter describes effective family functioning in terms of systemic concepts and parenting typologies, and presents the theoretical and empirical rationale for this conceptualization. Effective functioning is discussed in terms of the instrumental and affective aspects of systemwide, parent–child, and marital relationships associated with positive and negative developmental outcomes for youth. Also, this section describes the adjustments required to maintain effective functioning in families experiencing transitions due to divorce, remarriage, and single parenthood. The second section describes the ongoing assessment process MST practitioners use to identify the specific combination of systemic, parent–child, and marital factors that compromise effective functioning and contribute to referral problems in a particular family. We introduce two case examples to illustrate the MST assessment of family functioning, and these cases are discussed throughout this chapter and in Chapter 4, which describes interventions used to improve family functioning.

Effective Family Functioning

The Family as a System

The MST perspective on effective family functioning embodies systems theories and the assumptions of multicausality and reciprocity of interactions that characterize these theories. Thus, the behavioral and psychological functioning of all family members is understood in terms of ongoing and repetitive patterns of family transactions rather than in terms of unidirectional and linear interpersonal or intrapsychic processes. Family problems are seen as both affecting and being affected by how the family interacts as a whole. Consistent with pragmatic (i.e., focused on changing behavior in the present) as versus esthetic models of the family and family therapy (see Alexander, Holtzworth-Munroe, & Jameson, 1994; Henggeler, Borduin, & Mann, 1993), MST family interventions aim to change the everyday patterns of interaction thought to sustain the identified problems. The present-focused and solution-oriented nature of MST is particularly consonant with structural (S. Minuchin, 1974) and strategic (Haley, 1976) models of family therapy.

STRUCTURAL FAMILY THERAPY

The structural model conceptualizes the family in terms of marital, parental, and sibling subsystems that are constructed along generational and role lines.

Each subsystem has boundaries such that all family members do not have equal access to the subsystem. Boundaries should be flexible, however, to facilitate the capacity of the family system to respond to the needs of individual family members or to environmental demands. The structural model views child emotional and behavioral problems as signs that subsystem boundaries are too weak or too strong. Terms such as enmeshment and disengagement describe family interaction patterns in which boundaries are excessively porous or rigid. Porous boundaries, for example, can fail to promote the emancipation and independent achievements of children; rigid boundaries can limit the family's capacity to respond to environmental stress and meet the affective needs of family members. Constructs such as triangulation and parent–child coalition describe transactional patterns that confuse parent–child and spousal boundaries, often in ways that involve the child in the negotiation of adult subsystem conflict. Treatment-related changes in these patterns are associated with improvements in the antisocial behavior of adolescents (Mann, Borduin, Henggeler, & Blaske, 1990).

STRATEGIC FAMILY THERAPY

Strategic formulations also inform the MST clinician's assessment of family functioning. To design interventions that effectively address interactions within and between systems (Principle 5), the MST practitioner undertakes assessment of the "recursive sequences of behavior" (Haley, 1976) associated with an identified problem. The strategic family therapy tenet that emotional and behavioral problems are intimately linked with recurrent sequences of family interactions is consistent with research on the etiology of childhood aggression and conduct disorder. This research identifies predictable and repetitive cycles of aversive interaction between parents and children and among siblings as contributing factors in the development of antisocial behavior (Patterson, 1982; Patterson & Reid, 1984).

The Parent–Child Subsystem

Family systems constructs can render the complexity of interactions among multiple family members understandable and predictable, and, therefore, alterable. Systems principles do not, however, address the central issues and topics around which family interactions occur, namely power/control and affection/intimacy (Emery, 1994; Seaburn, Landau-Stanton, & Horwitz, 1996). Systems constructs are also of limited utility in predicting which types of problems (externalizing vs. internalizing problems, eating disorders vs. delinquency) are associated with which types of family structures (enmeshed, disengaged) and interaction patterns. Research on child development and parent–child socialization practices explicitly addresses these issues and informs the MST perspective regarding the components of effective functioning in the parent–child subsystem. This research provides consistent evidence that parental control and warmth are the major dimensions along which parenting practices vary, and, importantly, these dimensions are associated with numerous child outcomes.

WARMTH

The warmth dimension of parent–child relations reflects verbal and nonverbal behaviors that are emotional in tone, ranging from warmth to rejection. Warm parents are relatively accepting and nurturing and use frequent positive reinforcement when they interact with their children. Such affection provides an emotional bond between parent and child that is satisfying to both and establishes and maintains a positive mood during interactions. On the other hand, neglecting parents are low in nurturance, and rejecting parents are both low in nurturance and relatively hostile, tending to use criticism and even aggression when interacting with their children. When children do not have positive experiences of parent–child interaction, they have difficulty having positive experiences in interactions with others. Thus, children who experience low levels of positive affection (emotional neglect) and high levels of negative affection (emotional rejection) are at risk for the development of interpersonal and behavioral difficulties and often have difficulty trusting, responding positively, and developing empathy for others.

CONTROL

Parental control strategies have several important functions in child development. They teach the child frustration tolerance, which is essential to the development of successful interpersonal relations. Control strategies also teach the child socially acceptable norms of behavior, including the avoidance of aggression, cooperation with others, and respect for authority. When parents allow their child to behave aggressively toward family members or consistently give in to the child's demands, they are teaching the child social norms that promote aggression and noncooperation in the child's relations with peers. Similarly, when parents do not teach the child to respect their authority, the child is likely to have considerable difficulty interacting with adults outside of the home. The child's lack of respect for authority or belief that he or she has the same rights and privileges as do adults may lead to problems in the child's interactions with teachers, with adult leaders of youth groups (coaches, band directors, Scout leaders), with neighborhood residents, and, eventually, with the legal system. Hence, parental control teaches the child to manage emotions and behavior through the internalization of a socially sanctioned set of norms. This learning process prepares the child for interactions with peers and other adults throughout the life span. Thus, a primary responsibility of parenthood is to implement reasonable controls over child behavior. Indeed, research indicates that many child and adolescent behavioral disturbances are direct reflections of ineffective parental control strategies (Olweus, 1980; Patterson & Stouthamer-Loeber, 1984). And, as noted in Chapter 1, harsh control strategies, inconsistent application of discipline, and lack of monitoring are identified as aspects of the control function that predict delinquency and drug use in adolescents.

PARENTING STYLE

Research consistently demonstrates that parental warmth, inductive discipline (i.e., involving sanctions based on means–ends reasoning), and consistency in childrearing are each associated with positive developmental outcomes in children (Maccoby & Martin, 1983) and adolescents (Steinberg, Lamborn, Darling, Mounts, & Dornbusch, 1994) and that discipline is most effective when provided in the context of generally positive interactions between parents and their children (Wierson & Forehand, 1994). *The use of inductive discipline within the context of a warm parent–child relationship describes the authoritative parenting style, the development of which is a critical goal in many MST cases.* Authoritative parenting is one of four styles in a parenting typology developed in the early 1970s and validated in numerous studies of child development. Formulated on the basis of longitudinal studies of the impact of socialization practices (i.e., childrearing) on child outcomes (Baumrind, 1967, 1971, 1978, 1983), the four parenting styles are authoritative, authoritarian, permissive, and neglectful. These styles represent different areas on the intersecting dimensions of warmth and control (high warmth could be combined with low control, low warmth with low or high control, etc.).

Authoritative parents are responsive to the reasonable needs and desires of the child but also make maturity demands appropriate to the child's stage of development. Parents have clear and well-defined expectations and rules regarding the child's school performance, participation in household chores, and interpersonal behavior with family members, peers, and adults and authority figures outside the home (teachers, other relatives, neighbors, coaches, etc.). Authoritative parenting is associated with a range of positive outcomes, such as positive academic achievement, social responsibility, and positive peer relationships.

Authoritarian (high control, low warmth) parents are directive and overcontrolling, and require that children have an unquestioning obedience to parental authority. When a child deviates from parental rules, punishment tends to be severe and is often physical. When teaching the child new skills, behaviors, or tasks, the authoritarian parent is directive, giving direct verbal orders and often physically taking over the activity being taught. Thus, the parent's responsiveness to the child's needs is often overridden by his or her efforts to direct or control those situations. Authoritarian parents also fail to make appropriate maturity demands. By rigidly prescribing child behavior, the child rarely participates in making choices and decisions and therefore has little opportunity to grapple with the consequences of his or her own choices and decisions (Baumrind, 1989). Authoritarian parenting is linked to child aggression, social withdrawal from peers, poor self-confidence, and internalized distress (Baumrind, 1989; Steinberg et al., 1994) as well as continuity of such patterns into adolescence (Baumrind, 1991; Lamborn, Mounts, Steinberg, & Dornbusch, 1991; Steinberg et al., 1994).

Permissive (high warmth, low control) parents provide their children with little structure and discipline, make few demands for mature behavior, and tolerate even those impulses in children that meet with societal disapproval. Permissive parents are typically warm and responsive but not demanding. Permissive parenting is associated with aggression (Olweus, 1980), impulsivity, and a lack of social responsibility and independence in children (Baumrind, 1989, 1991) and with school misconduct, drug and alcohol use, and heightened orientation toward and value of peer activities and norms in adolescents (Baumrind, 1991; Steinberg et al., 1994).

Neglectful (low warmth, low control) parents offer little affection or discipline to their children and appear to have little concern for or interest in parenting. That is, neglectful parents are neither responsive to the reasonable needs and desires of the youth nor demanding of responsible, age-appropriate behavior with respect to tasks or interpersonal relationships. Of the four parenting types, neglectful parenting is most strongly related to children's distress. Children from neglectful homes are characterized by poorer adjustment on many indices of functioning than children from permissive or authoritarian homes, and this negative trajectory continues through adolescence, when neglectful parenting is associated with sizable increases in adolescent delinquency and drug use (Steinberg et al., 1994).

In general, findings of recent studies continue to highlight the benefits of authoritative parenting and the deleterious effects of neglectful and authoritarian parenting for children and adolescents across various ethnicities and cultural contexts (Baumrind, 1991; Lamborn et al., 1991; Steinberg et al., 1994). These studies also suggest, however, that several effects of parenting style may be moderated by the adolescent's ethnicity such that authoritative parenting has the most beneficial effects on youth of European American and middle-class families while the negative consequences of authoritarian parenting may not be as severe among minority youth as among their European American counterparts. Perhaps minority youth, if living in economically disadvantaged circumstances, may benefit from a relatively more authoritarian parenting style (Steinberg et al., 1994) in which parents are more strict, vigilant, and controlling.

The Marital Subsystem

In families headed by two married adults, the marital relationship is the foundation of the family system. Generally speaking, successful marriages require that partners be able to love and feel loved, to honor their commitment to monogamy, and to experience the marital relationship as one in which they receive at least as much as they give. Throughout the course of a marriage, couples must deal with transitions associated with the development of each of their children, with work, with financial circumstances, community changes, and so forth. Major crises occur on occasion. To weather these changes, families need to be adaptable but not so adaptable that they are disorganized and unstable. Thus, marital partners must balance the need for stability and structure with the need for flexibility.

INTIMACY AND POWER

Just as the major dimensions of parent–child interactions are warmth and control, so the major dimensions of marital interactions reflect intimacy and power (Emery, 1992, 1994). Intimacy refers to the strength of the emotional bond between adults, and a positive emotional bond is important to the longevity of intimate relationships. Power refers to the relative influence of each member of the couple on the affective and instrumental aspects of the relationship. On the instrumental level, couples need to make decisions about financial concerns (earning, budgeting, spending), household tasks, parenting tasks, and obligations to families of origin and civic institutions. When marital roles are not clearly defined or couples lack the skills or motivation needed to successfully resolve conflicts about affective and instrumental aspects of the relationship, the marriage suffers. Similarly, when the emotional bond of marriage is strained by conflict, distance, or chronic imbalances in power, all family members can sustain deleterious outcomes. On the other hand, when couples are emotionally bonded and have the ability to resolve conflicts, family members are more likely to have secure emotional attachments, and stressors and crises are not likely to threaten the integrity of the family system.

CONFLICT

Research indicates that conflict between parents is associated with a host of problems in children and families, including externalizing problems, childhood aggression (particularly in boys), depression in mothers, inconsistent parenting practices, and increased parent–child conflict (for reviews, see Cummings & Davies, 1994; Grych & Fincham, 1992). The frequency and intensity of conflict and the presence of both verbal and physical conflict (Fantuzzo et al., 1991; Vissing, Strauss, Gelles, & Harrop, 1991) are associated with higher levels of conduct problems in youth. Several mechanisms may account for the association between marital conflict and child behavioral problems. Marital problems may be linked with behavioral problems because the resulting emotional distress interferes with parental responsiveness to children's needs, marital conflicts interfere with parents' abilities to deliver consistent discipline, parents in conflict may be modeling poor conflict-resolution skills, and the emotionally charged environment may be stressful to children.

Family System Transitions: Divorced, Remarried, and Single-Parent Families

The fact that divorce is often followed by remarriage and/or living in a single-parent family means that many children experience more than one set of the multiple and sometimes difficult transitions (Cherlin, 1992) described next.

DIVORCED FAMILIES

Longitudinal research indicates that divorce is a developmental process during which a series of "partially predictable events" often occurs (Emery, 1994, p. 17). This developmental perspective and the family systems framework of divorce articulated by Emery (1994) are consistent with the principles of MST. Within this framework, the central tasks facing all family members are the renegotiation of boundaries around intimacy and power. Relations between ex-spouses and between the children and each parent are renegotiated. Behaviorally, family members must often assume the tasks and responsibilities of the absent parent. Cognitively, ex-spouses and their children must understand the new roles in the family.

Recent reviews of the psychological and behavioral impact of divorce on children and adolescents indicate that whereas most children function competently following divorce and do not experience psychological disorder (Emery, 1994; Hetherington & Clingempeel, 1992), they often undergo distress, longing, disappointment, confusion about divided loyalties, and periods of relationship strain with one or both parents. In addition, reviewers (e.g., Amato & Keith, 1991; Emery, 1988) have concluded that divorce can be linked with difficulties in children's school achievement and psychosocial adjustment. Data from some longitudinal studies suggest, however, that problems attributed to the effects of divorce may have predated the divorce by many years (Block, Block, & Gjerde, 1986; Doherty & Needle, 1991). Thus, when behavioral problems resulting in referral for MST occur in the context of a divorced family, the practitioner cannot assume that the divorce is the cause of the problems. Nonetheless, for some children the fit of the identified problems can be explained, in part, by the practical, relational, instrumental, and affective changes that occur in many divorcing and remarried families.

REMARRIED FAMILIES

As with divorce, research on the reconstitution of families through marriage supports a developmental, family systems perspective (Hetherington & Clingempeel, 1992). Remarriage requires renegotiation of relationships, roles, and boundaries among all members of the two families coming together to form a new family group. The new marital partners have primary responsibility for defining the roles of stepfamily members and for enhancing the stability of the new system. Unlike newlyweds without children, couples in remarried families must negotiate marital intimacy and power relations while parenting children, and the "honeymoon" period after remarriage is either short-lived or nonexistent (Hetherington, 1993; Hetherington & Clingempeel, 1992). Practical and concrete issues such as relocation of one or both families to a new home and school, allocation of physical space within the home, and distribution of financial resources in the blended family must be negotiated. Affective bonds between the stepparents and stepchildren must be actively cultivated, and the roles of the step and biological parent regarding discipline must be clearly delineated and commensurate with the differential strength of the affective bonds between biological and step relations. Similarly, if the reconstituted family includes children from two marriages, the affective bonds between stepsiblings may need to be cultivated, as stepsiblings may compete for affection and resources; instrumental responsibilities such as chores must be defined for all children. In sum and as concluded in recent reviews (Dunn, 1994; Hetherington & Clingempeel, 1992), children's adjustment to remarriage is associated with several family processes, including the quality of the relationship with the custodial parent, the quality of the relationship with the stepparent, the clarity of parent and stepparent roles in parenting, renewal of the children's loyalty dilemmas with respect to the noncustodial parent, practical challenges such as relocation and financial stresses, resumption of custody battles between ex-spouses, and contact by ex-spouses.

SINGLE-PARENT FAMILIES

Many families headed by a single parent function effectively to meet the instrumental and affective needs of the children and the parent. In some families, the responsibilities of childrearing are supported by, or shared with, another family member such as a grandparent or another relative. Just as adult relationship and parent–child boundaries must be renegotiated in divorced and remarried families, the adult relationship between the parent and family member and between each caregiver and the children must be renegotiated in single-parent families. Some single parents never or rarely become involved in adult intimate relationships, others develop long-lasting relationships that may or may not result in remarriage, and still others experience frequent and relatively brief relationships. Sometimes these adult relationships do not compromise the parent's ability to be responsive to the affective and instrumental needs of his or her children. In other cases, the significant other moves into the household and/or the relationship alters the nature of family interactions in ways that appear to contribute to the fit of a child's behavioral problems.

KIN AS PARENT FIGURES

In a significant percentage of families with a youth presenting serious antisocial behavior, grandparents or other relatives are the surrogate parents, often assuming guardianship, if not legal custody, of the youth. In some of these cases, surrogate parents had substantial involvement with the youth prior to assuming primary parenting responsibility. In other cases, parenting responsibilities previously were shared by several kin, simultaneously or in succession. As with all families, the MST practitioner assesses the family ecologies of kin acting as parents for the child. When the child and his or her kin have not lived together for extended periods of time, careful attention should be paid to assessing the affective connections between the caregivers and the youth and to adult relationships within the kin network that can be used to support the caregiver and child, or that may present barriers to the development of a stable kin-and-child family group.

Assessing Family Functioning

Assessment of family functioning is an ongoing process initiated when the practitioner first meets the family and refined throughout treatment as interventions are implemented and their effects are observed. Together, the practitioner and family members observe and try to tease out the specific family interactions that are the most powerful, proximal predictors of the identified problems. Throughout this process, practitioners do the following:

1. *Develop hypotheses* (e.g., explanations, hunches, or beliefs a practitioner or family member develops regarding the possible causes of the referral problem) regarding the relative contributions of familial factors to problem behaviors. Consistent with MST Principles 4 and 5 (present focused, targeting specific, well-defined problems; targeting sequences of behavior within or between multiple systems), hypotheses focus primarily on observable interactions and behaviors.

2. *Gather evidence* (i.e., information that was observed, self-reported, or concretely monitored, such as checklists, charts, check-in phone calls by the parent, other family members, school personnel, neighbors, etc., and the practitioner) to support or refute those hypotheses.

3. *Implement interventions* that target the hypothesized contributing factors.
4. *Observe* whether the interventions result in *changes* in problem behaviors.
5. *Identify* barriers to intervention success.
6. *Design interventions* to overcome these barriers.

These steps are part of the iterative process of MST case conceptualization and intervention implementation depicted in Figure 2.2 of Chapter 2.

Case Examples

In this chapter, the cases of Jake Jackson and Kim Taylor are introduced to illustrate the MST approach to assessment of family functioning. Figures 3.1 and 3.2 are the genograms and initial assessment forms completed by the MST practitioner for Jake, and Figures 3.3 and 3.4 are the genograms and initial assessment forms for Kim. The initial assessment form identifies the strengths and weaknesses/needs that characterize each system in the youth's ecology. This form is used as a tool to organize information the practitioner obtains through direct observation in multiple settings (home, school, neighborhood) and from multiple sources, including family members, teachers, peers, and archival records. The form is updated as needed to reflect additional information obtained throughout the treatment process.

> Jake Jackson is a 15 year-old ninth-grader who lives with his mother and stepfather. He was referred for MST treatment because of delinquent activities, runaway incidents, and school misconduct. Jake has lived with his stepfather and mother, Mr. and Ms. Jackson, for 3 years. His biological father is in prison, as is his 19-year-old brother. Mr. Jackson has a disability that prevents gainful employment, yet he provides financial support for two children from a previous marriage. He also has intermittent problems with alcohol abuse. Ms. Jackson works rotating shifts at a local paper factory. Jake was arrested four times while committing acts of vandalism and car theft, and one of these arrests included an assault charge. Some of the arrests occurred when he stayed out all night after major family altercations.

> Kim Taylor, a 14-year-old eighth-grader, is the eldest of three children living with her mother, Ms. Taylor, who has been divorced from Kim's father for 4 years. Mr. Taylor lives in another state, and Kim and her siblings see him once or twice a year. Kim was referred to MST by her probation officer for possession of marijuana and a misdemeanor charge related to a shoplifting incident. She is failing the eighth grade, and barely passed the seventh grade. When she does attend school, she often

Family: Jake_____ Therapist: _____ Date: _____

Genogram

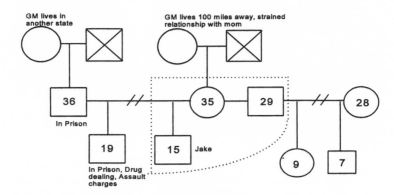

Reasons for Referral

1. School suspensions
2. Runaway incidents
3. Arrest for car theft
4. Arrest for vandalism

Initial Goals/Desired Outcome

Participant	Goal
1. Mother	No more school suspensions for Jake No more runaway incidents No more Juvenile Justice involvement Reduce physical and verbal conflict between Jake and stepfather
2. Stepfather	No Juvenile Justice involvement for Jake Get Jake to "mind" stepdad
3. Jake	Get off probation Stepdad to "stay out of things" related to school, friends, etc.
4. School	Reduce aggressive behavior to be allowed to stay in class; otherwise, permanent expulsion
5. DJJ	Meet probation terms

FIGURE 3.1. Case summary for supervision and consultation: Genogram for Jake. GM = grandmother; DJJ = Department of Juvenile Justice.

Family: Jake_____ Therapist: _____ Date: _____

Systemic Strengths   Systemic Weaknesses/Needs

Individual

History of average grades   Stays out late, especially when
until middle school; likes   mother works nights; leaves
MTV and tries to play music   school when suspended and does
"by ear" as he watches;   not notify parents; threatens
likes video games; average   physical violence when he and
athletic skills; likes to   stepdad argue; some question
tinker with cars, and helps   regarding drug use.
mother with hers.

Family

Mother works; mom obtained   Biological father and older
GED after Keith was born   brother in prison; mother leans
when she was 16; mother   toward permissive parenting,
left physically abusive   stepfather toward authoritarian;
marriage; mother and Jake   significant conflict between
love each other; some   Jake and stepfather; some
positive relationship   marital conflict; stepfather's
between mother and   alcohol abuse is associated with
stepfather; stepfather   increased conflict between
wants Jake to "make   stepfather and Jake, stepfather
something of his life."   and mother; stepfather's
                                 disability checks go to his
                                 former wife and children.

School

One teacher "goes to bat"   Principal has threatened
for Jake; school has some   permanent expulsion; history of
music and athletic organ-   negative interactions between
izations; school is close   teachers and Jake, mother.
to family home.

Peers

Some peers are not involved   Several friends are involved in
with Department of Juvenile   vandalism, car-theft activities;
Justice (DJJ); some friends   some drug use is suspected by
go to video arcade, one   DJJ but no solid evidence is
friend is on football team;   available; one friend in jail
one friend has a part-time   for selling drugs; Jake runs to
job.   that friend's home during some
                                 runaway incidents.

Community

DJJ and police neighborhood   Several antisocial kids and
watch staff have good work-   families nearby; drug-dealing
ing relationship; city gym   corner nearby; some transience;
has free activities for   some neighborhood violence,
teens; Veterans Hospital 30   burglaries.
miles away has some drug
and alcohol programs for
vets.

FIGURE 3.2. Case summary for supervision and consultation: Intial assessment
form for Jake.

Family: Kim _____ Therapist: _____ Date: _____

Genogram

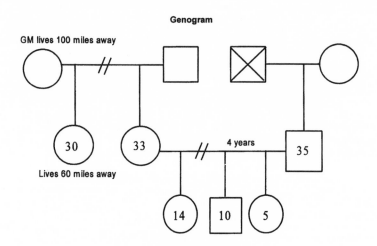

Reasons for Referral
1. Truancy, misbehavior at school
2. Misdemeanor charge for shoplifting
3. Failing eighth grade
4. Suspected drug use

Initial Goals/Desired Outcome

Participant	Goal
1. Mother	Kim to get to school, stay in school, get average grades Kim to "mind" mother
2. Kim	Mother to "get off my back" Get DJJ out of her life More time to hang out with friends, less baby sitting for sibling
3. School	No truancy Passing grades
4. DJJ	Meet terms of probation

FIGURE 3.3. Case summary for supervision and consultation: Genogram for Kim. GM = Grandmother; DJJ = Department of Juvenile Justice.

Family: Kim   Therapist: _____   Date: _____

Systemic Strengths	Systemic Weaknesses/Needs

Individual

Above-average grades until seventh grade; attractive; likes "doing" her friends' hair; baby-sits for her siblings while mother works.	"Follower" of older, somewhat antisocial peers; failing four of six classes due to lack of performance; truancy; sexually active with 16-year-old boyfriend.

Family

Mother works; some intimate mother-daughter moments when mother talks about divorce; siblings have minimal behavior problems so far; Kim likes grandmother, aunt (mother's sister); mother has some parenting success, skills, with younger children.	Conflictual relationship with own mother and sister, who could be source of support; frequent verbal conflict between Kim and mother; blurred boundaries between mother and daughter; some increased sibling conflict when Kim baby-sits; mother has limited range of discipline strategies, uses those exercised by Kim's father; mother fairly socially isolated.

School

Kim was involved in extra-curricular activities until seventh grade; Kim likes two classes and usually attends those; Principal willing to talk with mother if she will come in.	Teachers see Kim's mother as unresponsive to school feedback; truancy officer "fed up" with Kim.

Peers

Some prosocial peers in some classes; boyfriend (16) still in school.	Shoplifting incident occurred with girls arrested for shoplifting previously; some peers at school are known drug users; 16-year-old boyfriend may not finish high school.

Community

Church family used to attend has a youth group.	Few community activities for girls.

FIGURE 3.4. Case summary for supervision and consultation: Initial assessment form for Kim.

falls asleep, "talks back" to teachers, and "cuts" classes. Kim's mother, Ms. Taylor, works as a waitress in a local restaurant. Teachers report that Ms. Taylor does not respond to school communications regarding Kim's behavior. When initially contacted by the MST practitioner, Ms. Taylor announced that she planned to "send Kim off if she doesn't straighten up." Ms. Taylor also stated that the so-called help provided by counselors, probation officers, and school personnel was "useless."

Assessing Systemic Structure and Interaction Patterns

KIM

The initial assessment of family strengths and needs in Kim's case illustrates the influence of structural principles in MST case conceptualization. As seen in Figure 3.4, the clinician listed "blurred boundaries" in the "weaknesses/needs" category of the family assessment. To support the hypothesis that parent–child boundaries were blurred in this family, the clinician noted that, on the rare occasions when Kim and Ms. Taylor were on speaking terms, conversations often revolved around Ms. Taylor's frustrations with her ex-spouse. Next, the clinician identified the possible impact of the boundary transgression on all family members (Kim, her mother, her younger siblings, her father) and on the relationships between them. One apparent benefit was a momentary increase in intimacy between mother and daughter, whose interactions were generally highly conflictual. On the other hand, the mother's credibility as an authority figure and her capacity to execute effective discipline strategies for Kim was low. Given Kim's problems in school (truancy, failing grades, problems with authority figures) and with antisocial peers (suspected drug and alcohol use, shoplifting), the benefits of increased mother–daughter intimacy obtained by transgressing generational boundaries did not appear to outweigh the costs.

The MST clinician recognized that other factors within and outside the family system might maintain Kim's behavioral problems and gathered evidence regarding the relative impact of these factors in compromising Ms. Taylor's parental effectiveness. These factors were lack of knowledge of parenting strategies for a 14-year-old (mother's eldest), lack of skill enforcing discipline because the father had been the disciplinarian prior to the divorce, lack of energy due to the demands of working while raising three children ages 5 to 14 years, and relative social isolation since the divorce. The practitioner's observations of family interactions, examination of Ms. Taylor's work schedule, and conversations with Ms. Taylor confirmed her hypotheses about the importance of these factors in maintaining Kim's behavioral problems.

Thus, in contrast with traditional structural and strategic conceptualizations of the family, the MST practitioner concluded that a combination of the mother's inexperience as the disciplinarian, work schedule and reliance on Kim to baby-sit for her siblings were as important as the boundary transgression in compromising Ms. Taylor's parental effectiveness. In trying to make sense of the fit for Ms. Taylor of the mother–daughter discussions of her marital problems, the clinician observed that Ms. Taylor experienced both emotional distress and increased social isolation after the divorce, and that these factors contributed to her initiation of conversations about her ex-spouse with Kim. Thus, the clinician's original systemic hypothesis regarding the primacy of inappropriate boundaries in maintaining Kim's behavioral problems was refined to incorporate practical (work schedule), parenting, and social support factors.

JAKE

The case of Jake illustrates the incorporation and expansion of strategic concepts in MST. From an MST perspective, the recursive sequences of family interaction that sustain a particular problem are often viewed as part of a longer, more complex chain of interactions among participants within and outside the family that sustain problem behaviors. During the clinician's first family visit, Ms. Jackson reported that Jake's runaway incidents were precipitated by intense stepfather–stepson conflicts punctuated by mutual threats of physical violence. Neither Jake nor his stepfather volunteered his perspectives on the problem. Ms. Jackson also reported that Jake's delinquent activity occurred primarily while Jake was on runaway status, though Mr. Jackson disagreed with this assessment. The MST practitioner had not yet obtained independent verification of this information (from police records, school teachers, neighborhood sources, family homework assignments tracking conflicts and behavioral problems, etc.).

As she continued her assessment, the practitioner noted that variations of the following sequence of interactions within and between systems were critical to understanding the fit of Jake's runaway and delinquent behavior. In recent months, the sanctions usually issued were in-school or out-of-school suspensions. When issued an out-of-school suspension, Jake did not go home, nor did he inform his mother or stepfather of the suspension. Thus, the school's perception was that Jake's parents were unresponsive to school efforts to sanction Jake's behavior. When the school and Ms. Jackson did connect, she became angry and frustrated with Jake and with the school. Seeking support from her husband, she complained to him about Jake's behavior and about the school's apparent inability to control Jake and to contact her. Mr. Jackson responded by blaming Jake's behavioral problems on his wife's lenient parenting practices. Marital arguments ensued. If Jake was at home or returning home as these events were occurring, he would interrupt the marital disagreement and defend his mother verbally, which angered his stepfather and brought mixed responses from his mother, who was now angry with Jake and with her husband. The conflict between Jake and his stepfather escalated until the two threatened one another with physical harm. At that point, Jake often stormed out of the house and did not return until the next day or evening.

Assessing Parenting Style

The assessment of parenting style (i.e., affect and control dimensions) begins almost at the moment the MST practitioner meets the family at the home. At that time, the therapist taps information in three distinct ways:

1. *Directly questioning family members* about their own behavior and their perceptions of other family members' behavior. Here, each family member is asked to give his or her view of the presenting problems and about the "good" qualities of each family member. In making this request, the practitioner obtains important information about areas of agreement and conflict in the family.
2. *Observing family interactions.* The therapist arranges to observe the parent and child interact long enough to obtain a sample of (a) the parent's discipline strategies and the child's response to them and (b) expressions of positive emotion among family members.
3. *Asking family members to monitor and record particular behaviors daily.* For example, the therapist may ask parents to monitor all discipline attempts and responses to them or to track the children's good behaviors. Such monitoring should be done daily to provide an adequate picture of the control strategies employed by parents and the responses of the children and adolescents as well as a sense of the emotionally positive interactions between the parents and children.

CONTROL

To assess parental control strategies, practitioners observe and ask parents to document sequences of parent–child interactions that involve discipline efforts. Specifically, the therapist can request that the parents keep a daily record of (1) child misbehaviors, (2) each parent's discipline in response to these misbehaviors, (3) the child's compliance or noncompliance with each disciplinary attempt, and (4) each parent's response to the child's compliance and noncompliance. The practitioner examines the parents' records to assess their disciplinary strategies, perceived effectiveness of these strategies, and parenting style—authoritarian, permissive, neglectful, or authoritative—reflected in these strategies.

Over a 2-day period in the Jackson family, for example, four out of five interactions about chores that occurred between Mr. Jackson and Jake involved Mr. Jackson issuing a command and shouting the command and physically grabbing Jake to redirect him if the command was unheeded. The frequency and consistency of similar interactions and the complete absence of efforts to explain the rationale for the commands or to negotiate the activities on the chore list led the therapist to note "authoritarian parenting style" under the "needs/weaknesses" column of the initial MST assessment form. Other evidence of authoritarian parenting included the following: punishment is often harsh or physical, punishment is not calibrated to the seriousness of the infraction (i.e., the punishment is excessive relative to the "crime"), and discussion or negotiation regarding rules is absent or rare, even when such discussion would be developmentally appropriate, as is the case in families with adolescents.

In contrast, therapist observations and a checklist completed by Ms. Taylor regarding her efforts to discipline Kim indicated that outside clearly established expectations regarding Kim's baby-sitting for her sister when Ms. Taylor was at work, no other rules regarding curfew, homework, or chores existed. Moreover, Kim was left to make decisions for herself that, at her age, typically require adult guidance (e.g., when to come in on weeknights and whether to get into cars with older boys). This and other evidence prompted the therapist to identify "permissive parenting" as a factor potentially contributing to Kim's behavior problems.

AFFECT

At times, an overall lack of positive interactions between parents and their children seem to contribute to problematic interactions pertaining to discipline. The affective tone of parent–child interactions can range from warm and nurturing to neglectful (i.e., low in nurturance but relatively neutral in affective tone when engaged in interactions) and rejecting (i.e., low in nurturance and relatively hostile when engaged in interaction). To assess affective relations, the therapist obtains information about (1) verbal and nonverbal messages exchanged between parents and their children in everyday interactions about instrumental issues (taking out the trash, completing homework on time); (2) parental expressions of interest in the youth's experiences at school, with peers, with other family members, and regarding hobbies or extracurricular activities; (3) parental praise in response to the youth's successes or positive behaviors; and (4) expressions of concern regarding things that are not going well for the youth.

In some families with generally positive affective parent–child bonds, strong negative affect arises in the context of parent–adolescent conflict, as occurred frequently in the Taylor family. Although Ms. Taylor initially voiced anger and frustration about Kim, the therapist obtained ample evidence (frustration gave way to concern once a therapeutic alliance was established; mother–daughter heart-to-heart talks occurred occasionally) of a positive parent–child bond. At the same time, however, arguments often escalated into shouting matches in which insults were hurled by both mother and daughter. Although the reduction of such conflicts was an intermediary goal for treatment, such conflicts were not construed as a sign of a neglectful, rejecting, or poor parent–child bond.

Such expression of negative parental affect may be evidence of a poor parent–child bond if the negative affect occurs in the context of ongoing parent–child interactions that should be neutral or positive in affective tone. When this is the case, the practitioner should assess whether emotional neglect or rejection is occurring, as evidenced by minimal parental responses to the youth's positive behaviors, rejection of youth efforts to engage in verbal interactions or parent–child activities, minimal awareness of the youth's concrete and emotional needs, and, in the case of rejecting parenting style, consistently critical, belittling, or hostile responses to the youth even when he or she is engaged in neutral or positive behaviors.

PARENTING STYLE

Although ineffective parenting style (permissive, authoritarian, neglectful) is often identified as part of the fit of the referral problem, the factors that sustain a particular parent's style can vary from family to family. For some parents, a combination of work schedule, caring for younger siblings, and marital problems contributes to permissive parenting practices; for others, lack of knowledge

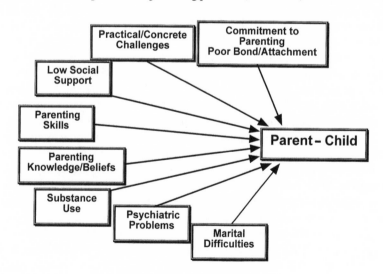

FIGURE 3.5. Barriers to effective parenting.

about effective discipline practices for adolescents and concern that warm parent–child relations will be damaged if the parents set limits sustains permissive practices. An authoritarian parent may implement harsh and arbitrary punishment because he or she believes such punishment to be effective and necessary, while another authoritarian parent verbalizes that he or she has tried to reason with the child to no avail and thus resorts to physical punishment.

One schematic tool often used by clinicians to clarify the factors that influence a particular parent–child dyad, is illustrated in Figure 3.5. Common factors include concrete needs (housing, heat, transportation, etc.); knowledge, beliefs, and skills specific to childrearing; commitment to childrearing; parental depression or anxiety, mental illness, or substance abuse; child characteristics; and problems in the marital (divorced, remarried) subsystem. Intervention strategies to alter parenting style are tailored to the particular constellation of factors that support ineffective practices, and these factors and guidelines and strategies for altering them are described in Chapter 4.

Assessing Marital Functioning

In contrast with couples who actively seek marital therapy in traditional outpatient settings, couples treated in the context of MST may not immediately identify marital difficulties as primary concerns because the serious behavioral problems of their children were the cause for referral for treatment. Whereas some couples may acknowledge marital difficulties openly, others may only allude to them in the context of conversations about other topics, such as discipline. When describing a child's behavioral problems, for example, a husband may report that he punishes the child for "backtalk" while his wife does not. Or, a teenager may report that when her mother says she cannot go out on Friday night, she asks her father, who gives her permission. Both of these examples signal interparental inconsistencies in discipline strategies, which, in turn, are often part of the fit of referral problems. In many instances, disagreements about parenting practices occur in the context of a troubled marriage; in some instances, other aspects of marital functioning are adequate and the couple does not consider disagreement about parenting practices important until they are able to see that such disagreement contributes to the child's behavioral problems. Finally, complaints about the way a spouse spends time and money or comments that suggest that too much or too little time is spent with children, at work, or in leisure activities away from the home may signal marital difficulties.

MARITAL INTIMACY

If the practitioner suspects that marital difficulties are contributing to the referral problem, he or she should arrange to interview the couple about their marriage when the children are not present. The initial interview with the couple should be used to assess the level of intimacy and extent to which affective relations are positive or negative. A modicum of a positive bond is needed to motivate the couple to work toward the resolution of what often turn out to be long-standing problems and conflicts. Information about affect can be obtained from both verbal and nonverbal cues (how closely partners sit, whether they make eye contact, the tone of voice used, whether a question is sincere or rhetorical, when a request is really meant as a command, etc.). Information about marital affect can also be obtained by asking the spouses to describe each other's positive characteristics. Practitioners must be aware that sociocultural differences sometimes influence the types of qualities listed by partners during this exercise. Whereas highly educated and relatively affluent individuals may respond that a spouse's humor or caring are positive qualities, less advantaged spouses may value the fact that the husband is a good provider and the wife is a good cook. Because MST interventions are tailored to the unique strengths and needs in a marriage, the practitioner must understand the marriage from the perspective of the couple's sociocultural context.

If either spouse has extreme difficulty describing positive qualities of the other, that spouse may truly feel that the other has little redeeming value. On the other hand, the prolonged conflict in the marriage may have temporarily biased the spouse's view of the relationship. Couples who have experienced prolonged conflict usually devote considerable attention to the negative aspects of their relationship and little or no attention to the positive aspects. Parents whose children have a chronic history of behavioral problems may also view the relationship negatively because the majority of their marital interactions and interactions between the couple and the institutions (i.e., schools), agencies (i.e., juvenile justice, mental health, social services) and individuals (neighbors, parents of their child's peers) involved with the family are negative.

When spouses have difficulty describing the positive aspects of their mates, the therapist might ask the couple to describe what the relationship was like when they first dated, what attracted them to one another, what they used to do for fun, and so forth. The practitioner's goal is to determine whether feelings of optimism can be generated about the relationship. The quality of a couple's sex life is also an indicator of the affective relationship in a marriage. Quality can be assessed by direct questioning about frequency of, and each spouse's satisfaction with, lovemaking. Couples who rarely make love tend to be distant and those who have an active love life tend to be more intimate, but there are many exceptions to this rule of thumb. An active sex life can occur within the context of a marriage characterized by serious disagreements. Again, sociocultural sensitivity should be used in assessing sexual aspects of the marital relationship. Men and women who subscribe to traditional roles, for example, may construe frequent lovemaking as a wifely duty; in such cases, frequent lovemaking may not be an indicator of intimacy or mutual satisfaction.

MIXED MESSAGES

Often couples who have experienced months or years of hostile interactions have grave doubts about whether their marriage will improve. Because practitioners of MST are apt to be assessing the marital relationship in a family context characterized by multiple stressors and serious child behavioral problems, serious doubts about the marital relationship may not surface in the initial family interviews. Should such doubts become apparent, the practitioner may decide to investigate the issue with the doubting spouse before meeting with the couple, as that spouse is more likely to tell the practitioner how he or she really feels when the other spouse is not in the same room. During the interview, the practitioner should state directly that he or she senses such doubt. The practitioner should ask about the spouse's investment in marital therapy and in the marriage itself. During such an interview, the practitioner can help clarify mixed messages in a way that opens the spouse up to considering marital therapy.

PREDOMINANTLY NEGATIVE MESSAGES

Sometimes when practitioners probe apparent ambivalence, they find that the spouse no longer wants the marriage. This is usually an implicit decision that was made over the course of one or more years. Typically, the spouse has not acted overtly on these feelings for a number of reasons (fear of losing custody of the children, economic support, the social support of in-laws or relatives, etc.).

Adjustment to Family Transitions: Divorce, Remarriage, Single Parenthood

MARITAL SUBSYSTEM CHANGES

For divorcing spouses, the overarching tasks are to redraw boundaries around intimacy (e.g., which areas of a former spouse's life the other spouse is allowed to access, under which circumstances, and for how long) and power (influence over the events that occur in one another's lives with respect to children, finances, etc.) and to separate their marital roles from their parental roles. The inherent difficulty here is that although their marital roles end, their parental roles are retained after divorce, and these roles are often confused following divorce. The practitioner should be attentive to communications signaling role confusion, for example, disagreements regarding such issues as the apparel a child is wearing on returning from one parent's home, leisure activities provided by one parent but not the other, and visitation schedules. Such disagreements may signal a parent's reluctance to relinquish control over the parent–child relationship between the ex-spouse and the child, or over the spouse him- or herself. Frequent unplanned phone calls to a former spouse, ostensibly regarding child-related matters, may also signal reluctance to accept the reduction in marital intimacy between spouses that occurs as a function of divorce.

PARENT–CHILD SUBSYSTEM CHANGES

When it appears that parenting practices contribute to referral problems in a family affected by divorce, the MST practitioner should assess whether current practices predated the divorce or emerged after the divorce occurred, as interventions may vary accordingly. In Kim's case, for example, several aspects of parent–child relations contributed to the referral problem: Ms. Taylor had a permissive parenting style, was unable to monitor Kim's whereabouts consistently, and relied periodically on Kim for emotional support. The permissive style predated the divorce, while the monitoring and emotional support issues emerged as a result of the divorce.

CONCRETE AND PRACTICAL CHALLENGES

Concrete and practical issues raised by divorce may also contribute to behavioral problems, and the practitioner should assess the concrete and practical impact of the divorce on family members. Divorce may give rise to challenges such as working longer hours to compensate for financial losses associated with the divorce, moving to a different dwelling following divorce, accommodating parent visitation schedules, and interacting with the legal system regarding divorce and custody issues. When divorce significantly reduces family income, the residential parent, typically the mother, may return to full-time employment outside the home or, if already employed, obtain a second job. Increased work hours may reduce adult monitoring of the children and negatively influence the mother's own adjustment. The mother may also become isolated from her social support network when all her time is spent at work or engaging in child-care responsibilities, as was the case for Ms. Taylor.

PARENTAL DISTRESS

A parent's coping strategies may also contribute to the development of child behavioral problems. Some ways of coping, such as depression or chronic hostility and anger, are particularly likely to interfere with the parent's capacity to engage in appropriate parenting practices. Interventions to address parental depression, anxiety, and social isolation are described in Chapters 4 and 7.

REMARRIED FAMILIES

Because the adults and children in most remarried families have experienced divorce, the divorce-related issues identified previously may also need to be assessed and addressed when working with remarried families. In addition, the formation of a new family group presents additional challenges, and the practitioner should understand the extent to which remarriage enhances or compromises effective family functioning. For some families, the addition of a stepparent without children relieves financial stresses incurred as a result of the divorce, bolsters the effectiveness of the custodial parent, increases the availability of adult supervision and monitoring, and is accompanied by minimal, but predictable, conflicts about how things are to be done in the new family group. For other families, such as Jake's, the potential benefits of the stepparent's presence are mediated by the stresses of that parent's previous financial obligations (to an ex-spouse and children from a previous marriage), by mental health or substance abuse problems, and by persistent conflict that arises out of unclear expectations and role relationships.

Again, as with families in which divorce has occurred, it is important to assess the extent to which the problems in question predated the remarriage, were exacerbated after the remarriage, or first emerged after remarriage, as interventions may vary accordingly. If, for example, a child's aggressive behavior and the permissive parenting style that appeared to maintain such aggression predated the current marriage, a hypothesis suggesting that the new stepfather's authoritarian parenting is the primary contributing factor to the child's problems would miss the mark. On the other hand, the child's preexisting problems and parent–child interactions that maintained them may be currently exacerbated by the stepfather's attempt to become the chief disciplinarian in the absence of an adequate affective bond with the child, as occurred in the case of Jake.

SINGLE-PARENT FAMILIES

When single-parent status occurs as the result of a divorce, the practitioner should be sensitive to the potential contribution of divorce-related factors described earlier to the referral problem. In addition, the role that significant others play in the life of the family when a single parent begins to date may need to be assessed. In many cases, the impact of parental dating is minimal, as the parent draws appropriate boundaries around the intimate relationship and parenting responsibilities. The extent to which the children experience the relationship as beneficial or detrimental is likely to vary in accordance with the factors that come into play in families reconstituted through marriage, namely, quality of the relationship with custodial parent and with the significant other, clarity of parenting roles, and so on. If positive bonds exist between the child and significant other and family functioning is enhanced or at least not compromised by virtue of the adult relationship, the end of the relationship may be experienced as a loss at instrumental and emotional levels for the child. If, on the other hand, the end of the relationship returns family functioning to a more positive pattern for the child, the end of the relationship may be welcomed with relief. In any case, when the pattern of relationships established by an adult caregiver regularly alters the experiences of children in the family, the children are likely to experience multiple transitions. As with children in remarried families, such experiences may result in diminished willingness to accommodate each successive transition.

In some cases, a parent's intimate relationships negatively affect family functioning, either because the boundaries between the adult and parent–child relationships are too porous (e.g., mother's boyfriend is allowed to discipline the children) or because the parent focuses on the adult relationship at the expense of the parent–child relationship. Sometimes, the parent becomes involved in successive relationships and the nature of parent–child and family interactions change each time a relationship starts or ends. When the MST practitioner suspects that a parent's intimate relationships with others contributes to the fit of the referral problem, he or she should identify the constellation of individual, familial, and ecological factors that contribute to the pattern in which the parent becomes involved with successive partners and allows that involvement to compromise effective family functioning. Is the parent's struggle to make ends meet eased when a partner is found? Does a single mother obtain relief from the stresses of monitoring and disciplining her children when the boyfriend steps in? What are the parent's sources of social and emotional support? Does he or she have the requisite social skills to develop a support system? Is this a parent who first became a mother while still a teenager and whose social development in the realm of adult relationships was therefore compromised?

4

Family Interventions

In this chapter
- Treatment modalities commonly used in MST family interventions.
- Guidelines for applying parent–child, marital, and systemwide interventions.
- Strategies for overcoming barriers to intervention success.

This chapter describes interventions used to improve family functioning. First, the chapter describes general strategies for altering ineffective parenting styles and family structures. Within the context of MST, however, these strategies are individualized to address the particular combination of individual, intrafamilial, and extrafamilial factors that contribute to the ineffective style. Because one or more of these factors often emerge as a barrier to changing parenting style, the next section of the chapter describes interventions used to address these barriers. The final section of the chapter focuses on marital interventions and describes interventions to enhance effective functioning in divorced, remarried, and single-parent families. Discussion of family interventions does not readily lend itself to a step-by-step or "cookbook" approach because MST interventions are individualized to address the specific constellation of intrafamilial and extrafamilial factors that sustain a particular adolescent's behavioral problems. Thus, this chapter describes intervention strategies often used in MST and provides guidelines for assessing which combination of strategies may be necessary to effect change in a particular client family. In actuality, decisions regarding which interventions are implemented for which problems, and in what order, vary in accordance with the needs and strengths of the particular youth and family. In all cases, however, these decisions are informed by the continuous MST assessment process, through which evidence regarding multiple possible explanatory factors are "ruled in," "ruled out," and judged to be more or less proximal (as opposed to distal) contributors to behavior problems on the basis of ongoing observation, implementation of interventions, and assessment of intervention outcomes (see Figure 2.2, Chapter 2). Throughout this chapter, the examples of Jake Jackson and Kim Taylor, introduced in Chapter 3, illustrate family interventions used in MST.

MST family intervention is not a single therapeutic modality but includes several different types of interventions integrated from structural and strategic family therapies, behavioral family systems approaches (Robin & Foster, 1989), behavioral parent training (Forehand & Long, 1988; Patterson, 1979; Wierson & Forehand, 1994), behavioral family intervention (Sanders, 1996), and cognitive-behavioral therapy (Kendall & Braswell, 1985, 1993). Interventions to change parenting styles may range from simple, focused behavioral interventions that some parents can implement with little assistance from the practitioner, such as establishing behavioral charts, to more complex series of interventions organized by the practitioner to simultaneously address multiple problems such as marital conflict, maternal depression, and parent–child discipline practices. With most families referred for MST, simply giving advice and assigning homework rarely suffices, and interventions addressing parent–child and marital interactions, skill deficits, and social and practical barriers to effective parenting generally require the implementation of several interventions with ongoing monitoring of progress toward desired treatment goals.

The flexibility of MST and the array of interventions available to the MST therapist can lead to confusion in determining the specific foci and sequence of intervening. Several factors influence the practitioner's decision to use a particular family intervention:

- A comprehensive MST assessment of the fit of the particular problem with the ecology (MST Principle 1).
- The other eight principles of MST.
- Empirical literatures regarding the effectiveness of the modality or technique with a particular problem.
- The therapist's good clinical judgment.
- Therapist skill level regarding the treatment technique.
- Therapist creativity.

Consistent with MST Principles 4, 5, and 6 (interventions are present focused, action oriented, targeting specific and well-defined problems; interventions target sequences of behavior within and between multiple systems; interventions should promote treatment generalization), decisions regarding the nature of interventions, and the order in which they are implemented, are most often guided by "first order" factors. First-order factors are immediately observable events in the everyday interactions within families and between families and external systems. An emphasis on such factors contrasts with the emphases of other mental health treatments that focus on past events, personality constructs, and the like. Thus, for example, in a family characterized by practical challenges (e.g., lack of transportation, inadequate and overcrowded living conditions, and parent's evening work schedule), limited parental knowledge and skill, and parental social isolation, interventions targeting the practical and parent knowledge and skill problems would likely be implemented prior to interventions designed to increase social support, though the latter might follow quickly on the heels of the former.

Changing Parenting Practices

When it becomes apparent that a child's behavioral problems are being maintained by ineffective parenting styles (e.g., permissive, authoritarian, or neglectful), the practitioner and parent figure(s) identify factors across the family's social ecology that might be sustaining the ineffective style (see Figure 3.5, Chapter 3), as intervention strategies vary depending on the role each of these factors plays. Then, the practitioner tailors interventions to the particular strengths and needs of the parent, family, and social ecology.

Sustaining Rapport and Building Parental "Buy-In"

Parents are often frustrated with their child's misbehavior and with the challenges of trying to control such behavior. A parent in this situation does not need another outsider (e.g., the therapist) indicating, implicitly or explicitly, that the parent is "at fault" for the child's problems. Thus, practitioners generally should provide emotional support to the parent and highlight any positive aspects of parenting (Principle 2) while assessing family factors that might be linked with identified problems. Some parents are easily able to acknowledge their frustration and openly ask for help, as was the case with Jake's mother. For other parents, like Kim's mother, frustration leads to angry pronouncements that the child is at fault and to rejection of others' suggestions that change is possible and may require effort on the part of the parent.

In light of the variety of ways that parents can respond to the suggestion that parenting practices might need to be altered, therapists should have several strategies in their response repertoire. The goal of each strategy is to avoid unnecessary confrontation with the parent while ensuring that the importance of change is understood. Some parents, for example, respond positively to practitioner explanations of the deleterious effects of continuing current parenting practices. Others do not, and respond more positively when they see for themselves the negative consequences of continuing current practices. Gaining such "insight" can be facilitated through recordkeeping, therapist-designed family interactions, homework assignments, or conversations with others (a trusted grandparent, a teacher, etc.). For some parents, pointing out the negative consequences of current parenting practices for their own lives (frequent absence from work to deal with the child's school and legal problems; aversive interactions with school, neighbors, police, etc.) is more effective initially than pointing out the negative consequences for the adolescent, who, in the parent's eyes, may appear outwardly to suffer little from his or her misdeeds. In any case, the parent must truly believe that change is necessary before alternative parenting practices can be successfully developed.

Changing Discipline Strategies

When it becomes apparent that a child's behavioral problems are being maintained by a parent's discipline strategies, the MST practitioner has three general tasks in providing parent figures with alternative strategies. First, parents must learn to set clearly defined rules for the child's behavior. Second, parents must develop sets of consequences that are inextricably linked to the rules. That is, when a child complies with the rule, positive reinforcement occurs; when a child does not comply, a negative consequence (i.e., punishment) occurs. Third, parents must learn to effectively monitor a child's compliance or noncompliance with rules, even when the child is not in the parent's presence.

Munger (1993) detailed many of the steps involved in accomplishing the three tasks listed previously in a simple (but not simplistic) book for parents. The volume gives concrete examples of parenting practices that typically characterize families in which children appear to have as much or more control as parents and provides step-by-step instructions for parents about how to get control back. Although we rarely provide parents with the book as a part of treatment, MST practitioners have found this book useful when teaching parents more effective methods of handling behavioral problems. Several of the concepts and practices that practitioners should be able to teach are summarized next.

RULES

Consistent with MST Principle 4 (target well-specified problems), the primary purpose of rules is to clearly define desired and undesired behaviors, as all or some portion of these will become goals of treatment. The following guidelines should be followed when helping parents make and enforce rules.

1. The expected behavior should be defined so clearly and specifically that anyone else (a baby-sitter, grandparent, older sibling, etc.) can tell whether the behavior has occurred.
2. Rules should be stated in terms of positive behaviors (e.g., Jim will be inside the house at 9 P.M. on school nights, as opposed to Jim will not be late).
3. The privilege that will be given or withheld when the rule is kept or broken should be listed with the rule.
4. Rules should be posted in a public place in the home (e.g., the refrigerator).
5. Rules should be enforced 100% of the time.
6. Rules should be enforced in an unemotional manner. Munger recommends that the parent bring the child to the posted rule and read the rule and its associated privilege aloud.
7. Privileges should be dispensed or withheld every time a child complies with, or breaks, a rule.
8. Praise should be used in addition to the dispensation of the privilege.
9. When two parents are involved, rules should be mutually agreed on and enforced by both parents. (Factors underlying a couple's apparent inability to collaborate as parents, and potential remedies, are discussed later in this chapter.)

REWARDS AND PUNISHMENTS

To teach their children good behavior, parents have to identify and control belongings and privileges the child wants and enjoys. "Basic privileges" (e.g., shelter, food, clothing, and love), however, should not be manipulated (Munger, 1993). Note that basic food refers to meals; not to snacks, desserts, chips, and so on, which may be used as optional privileges. In addition, activities that contribute to the child's prosocial development (e.g., church groups, athletic teams, and Scouts) are considered "growth" activities, and, generally speaking, should not be withheld. On the other hand, playing video games, going out on Saturday night, and using the phone are not growth activities.

Any reinforcer that is not a "basic" or "growth" privilege is considered an "optional" privilege and can be given as a reward for good behavior and withheld as punishment for problem behavior. To be effective, the punishment must be experienced as aversive by the child, and the reward must be highly desired. Consistent with MST Principle 6, effective rewards and punishments will vary with children's developmental level. For younger children, optional privileges may include such activities as playing with Nintendo, watching television, or having a favorite snack. For adolescents, optional privileges may include going to the mall, nonbasic clothes, telephone time, or watching television. Similarly, younger children generally find activities with a parent, such as going to a park or baseball game as rewarding, whereas adolescents would rather spend time with their peers. Many activities and items fall into the optional category, and parents may need help identifying them.

Several guidelines should be followed for the effective the dispensation and withdrawal of privileges.

1. As noted earlier, the privilege must be highly desirable to the child/adolescent.
2. The younger the child, the more frequently the desired behavior must be rewarded.
3. For youth of all ages to see that good behavior "pays off," the behavior must be rewarded frequently.
4. The privilege must be tied to a specifically stated rule about a behavior that is desired.

The link between the rule and the positive or negative consequence is critical to the success of behavioral interventions. Parents must bear in mind the age of their child when making rules. A child should not be required to perform a task for which he or she is not physically or cognitively equipped. On the other hand, as noted previously, rules that make maturity demands are necessary. The therapist may need to help parents match their expectations and demands to the cognitive, emotional, and physical capacities of their children.

Finally, parents must discuss the nature of the rules and privileges with their children before the structure is implemented. Indeed, many parents include the children in the development of the rules, privileges, and linkages between the two. When a child is being raised by two parents, the parents must develop rules and consequences jointly and enforce them consistently. Children and adolescents should understand what is changing, what will be expected of them, and what to expect from their parents when strategies designed to change their behavior are put in place. Modifying the cognitive expectations of children and adolescents can expedite desired changes in behavior.

INCREASING CHANCES FOR SUCCESS

The therapist should prepare parents for the likelihood that their child or adolescent will react negatively to increases in family structure, and parents should expect that youth will "test" the new rules. In anticipation of such testing, the therapist should be prepared to support the parent in "sticking with" the program and finding support for appropriate parenting from other adults (spouse, relatives, other parents) in the natural environment (see Principle 9). Permissive parents are particularly likely to need support when their children test new rules. Such parents sometimes feel they would rather live with the child's obnoxious behavior than with the negative reaction the child displays in response to new rules. To address this understandable feeling, parents must come to recognize that the consequences of giving in are likely to extend beyond their home and negatively affect their child. Thus, for example, the highly stressed single mother of a juvenile offender may need to be reminded that although she is willing to live with the verbal abuse her son directs toward her, doing so supports his antisocial behavior outside the home (with concomitant risks of injury and incarceration) and sets a poor example for younger siblings. Such a reminder is not intended as a scare tactic (which would violate the principles of MST) but is intended to help parents understand the linkages between the child's behavior in the home and outside of the home.

As noted previously, parents should try to enforce rules in an unemotional way. Parents should avoid badgering the child or adolescent to follow the rules and allow the child to make the decision regarding compliance. If rules are well written, there should be little argument about whether the rules were followed. Thus, the parent should not respond to the child's attempts to argue about this issue. Families are not courts of law, and parents should feel free to run the household as benevolent despots, especially when dealing with youths who are presenting serious behavioral problems. Moreover, parents are more likely to enforce rules if punishments provide some payoff to the parents. With adolescent antisocial behavior, for example, punishments might include washing the parent's car, cleaning the bathroom, and scrubbing windows.

Occasionally, when dealing with adolescents who engage in serious antisocial behavior, the youth's behavior does not change even when the parent learns and consistently exercises appropriate control strategies (use of rules and concomitant provision and withdrawal of privileges, use of punishments aversive to the teen and helpful to the parent, etc.). In such cases, the therapist and parent may consider implementing more drastic consequences for behavior. A teenager may be informed, for example, that failure to meet curfew will result in the parents' solicitation of formal service systems' assistance (calling local police to escort the youth home; calling the probation officer if meeting curfew is a term of probation). Although such a consequence may result in additional consequences from the service system (i.e., curfew violation may result in extended probation), such an extreme approach may be needed to increase the probability that the youth will begin to respond to treatment efforts. Radical strategies should be undertaken only after other approaches fail, after supervision is sought, and after local law enforcement and social service agencies are informed of the parents' plan. Such strategies are occasionally used in MST, are generally successful in changing the teenager's behavior, and do not result in harm to the child or in legal difficulty for the therapist. Again, ethical and legal implications of such strategies must be carefully considered and discussed with the clinical supervisor, provider agency, and community agencies that have legal mandates either to protect or to prosecute youth or their families.

CASE EXAMPLE

Tasha, 15, lived in a residential treatment facility for a year prior to returning to the home of Ms. Cole, her mother. Within weeks after her return, Tasha took up old habits of sneaking out of the house at night, hitchhiking to a nearby town, and meeting up with older boys who bought her alcohol and cigarettes in return for sex. MST interventions initially targeted Ms. Cole's permissive parenting style and lax monitoring, cultivation of adult contacts who would support Ms. Cole's new discipline and monitoring practices, decreasing the apparently reinforcing (in terms of attention) dramatic interactions (yelling, crying, making new promises) that followed Tasha's return, and increasing Tasha's involvement with same-aged peers. Tasha responded positively for 2 weeks before sneaking out and staying away overnight. Upon Tasha's return, Ms. Cole administered previously agreed on consequences, although phone support from the therapist and an acquaintance were needed to prevent her from backing down in the face of Tasha's efforts to normalize her behavior as a natural response to "tasting freedom" after the year in placement and to evoke Ms. Cole's guilt about that placement. After a second such incident, Ms. Cole and the therapist drove to the next town to look for Tasha, enlisted the help of the town's sheriff in finding her, and identified the 18-year-old boys with whom she had been seen. The parents of one boy were contacted; the other boy lived on his own, having been emancipated at age 16. Thus, Ms. Cole, the therapist, and the one parent met with the town's sheriff to devise a plan for return of Tasha should she appear in the town. This plan was enacted twice in the following 4 weeks, at which point Tasha stayed out for two nights. After a reexamination of the fit of Tasha's sneaking out and barriers to intervention success, the therapist and Ms. Cole decided to file a runaway report with local police on the basis of her overnight absence. The sheriff, department of social services (the entity legally mandated to protect children from abuse and neglect), and Tasha's probation officer were alerted to the plan. The police were asked to escort Tasha to the police station, release her to Ms. Cole, and contact her probation officer rather than filing a new "unruly" charge; the filing of such a charge would have resulted in a new family court appearance and court-ordered detention-setting placement. Thus, by engaging the assistance of formal service systems (police, probation officer), Ms. Cole was able to increase the negative consequences of Tasha's staying out all night (being picked up by police and brought to the station;

having probation time extended) without evoking new legal charges and out-of-home placement.

Addressing Factors That Contribute to Ineffective Parenting Styles

The extent to which a particular parent can alter his or her parenting style and adopt the discipline strategies described earlier (i.e., set clearly defined rules for behavior, link consequences to rules, and effectively monitor a child's compliance) is often influenced by one or more of the factors shown in Figure 3.5, Chapter 3. If these factors are not taken into account when interventions to alter parenting practices are initially designed, they may emerge as barriers to intervention success. Thus, in the initial design of parenting interventions, and when trying to understand why an intervention may have failed, the clinician and team should examine the following potential barriers to success-ful outcome.

COGNITIONS ABOUT CHILDREARING (KNOWLEDGE AND BELIEFS)

Numerous studies demonstrate associations between parental knowledge, beliefs, attributions, and parenting behaviors and child outcomes (for reviews, see Baumrind, 1993; Cohen & Siegel, 1991). Knowledge regarding child development (e.g., at what age can children anticipate the future and think abstractly) and beliefs about the motivations of children's behavior are associated with irritable, harsh parenting practices and with conduct disorder and aggression in children. In assessing the role of beliefs and cognitions in maintaining ineffective parenting practices, practitioners should attend to parental language signaling unrealistic expectations about their child's capaci-ties and motivations and should collect evidence regarding the correspondence between these beliefs and parent behavior. A parent may state, for example, that a 10-year-old should "know better" than to loiter near gang territory after school or that a 14-year-old can decide for himself whether attending school is in his best interest. Some parents, often those with authoritarian parenting styles, protest that rewards are "bribes," and that children should comply with parental requests and demands simply on the parent's authority, as the parent did when he or she was a child.

When evidence indicates that parental misconceptions or faulty beliefs are helping to sustain ineffective parenting practices, the practitioner should attempt to understand the bases for the beliefs prior to making attempts to change those beliefs. For example, a parent's continued use of harsh physical punishment may be associated with a belief that "it was good enough for me." That is, the parent points out that he or she was raised similarly and "turned out fine." If the MST practitioner has developed a strength-based approach to treatment, he or she, indeed, is likely to recognize many ways in which the parent has "turned out fine." Thus, we have rarely found it useful to dispute the parent's stance, appeal to changing times, or cite facts and figures about the deleterious effects of harsh physical punishment. Instead, we often point out ways in which this particular adolescent appears to be suffering difficulties (e.g., suspensions, involvement with the law and whatever other reasons resulted in the youth's referral for MST) that may warrant alternative, perhaps even radical-sounding, approaches to discipline. Such an approach may increase parental receptivity to the idea that the parent may need to modify his or her behavior to benefit this unique child. By focusing on the parent's ability to help the child and on the long-term negative consequences of the youth's present behavior, parental cooperation in treatment is more likely to follow.

While assessing parental beliefs, the practitioner may find that both the parent and adolescent possess cognitive distortions that contribute to parent–adolescent conflict. Common distortions in families with high conflict include parental beliefs that their children should respond with absolute obedience (authoritarian parent) or that child misbehavior is motivated by malicious intent aimed at the parent. Adolescents may believe that their parents' behaviors will ruin their lives, are unfair, and threaten their independence (Robin, Bedway, & Gilroy, 1994). To assist families in changing distortions that contribute to the fit of an identified problem targeted for MST treatment, the practitioner helps family members to identify various aspects of unreasonable thinking. Then, interventions are designed that allow family members to disconfirm those beliefs, and tasks are assigned that reinforce more accurate beliefs. A session-by-session description of techniques used to accomplish these goals in the context of weekly, office-based behavioral family systems therapy (Robin & Foster, 1989) appears in a recent collection of treatment manuals (Robin et al., 1994). This description may prove useful to practitioners with limited familiarity with family communications training and problem-solving techniques. The MST practitioner tailors these techniques, and the timing of their delivery, in accordance with MST principles and with the needs, treatment priorities, and goals of a particular family. Thus, in the Jackson case introduced in Chapter 3, sessions in which all family members discussed and tried to problem solve their divergent beliefs about Mr. Jackson's role in parenting and family expectations, rules, and consequences for Jake did not occur until after marital interventions and interventions targeting Ms. Jackson's permissive style began.

Methods used to increase parental knowledge regarding effective childrearing practices are geared according to the practitioner's assessment of the amount of teaching, practice, and practitioner involvement needed to increase the likelihood that a particular parent figure will be able to implement the new strategies. Some parents, such as Mr. Jackson, may need to be explicitly reminded that children and adolescents *learn* to behave correctly, and that such learning occurs when good behavior is rewarded. Such learning requires *both* explanation and parental action. Parents who use reasoning alone (as permissive parents may) to try to change the behavior of a child are not likely to be successful, particularly with a young child (under the age of 12 years), because young children may not have the cognitive capacities to use language to control their behavior. Thus, although a 4-year-old may understand a parent's words (e.g., "If you touch that, it will break"), the child's ability to translate the words into desired behavior (e.g., staying away from the breakable item) requires that he or she both hear the explanation and experience a consequence when engaging in the undesirable behavior (e.g., touching the item). On the other hand, children have considerable difficulty learning what is appropriate and what is inappropriate behavior when consequences are delivered without explanations (as sometimes occurs with authoritarian parents, described earlier).

Just as interventions implemented with parents should be sensitive to the developmental needs of the child or adolescent (Principle 6), so, too, the practitioner should assess the level of cognitive development of parent figures when designing interventions. We work with many families in which the primary caregivers had stroke-related memory problems, were characterized by very concrete thinking, or were borderline or below in intellectual functioning. In these cases, we generally seek expert consultation from professionals in neuropsychology and adult developmental disabilities to assist in translating the objective of an intervention (i.e., increasing parental monitoring) into intervention plans that could be effective given the parent's memory problems or developmental disability. In one case, for example, a system in which colored stickers differentiated calendar days was used to prompt a grandmother to call the school. In another case, an alarm clock was set for 6 P.M. daily and the phone numbers of two neighbors were placed on the alarm to facilitate a mother's ability to retrieve her 11-year-old son at curfew time and seek assistance from neighbors if she could not find him.

PARENTAL SOCIAL SUPPORT

Research consistently points to the negative effects of parental social isolation on parenting practices and child behavior (Dumas & Wahler, 1985) and on the adjustment of parents and children to divorce (see Emery, 1994). Social isolation and lack of social support are consistently associated with maternal depression; irritable, inconsistent, and harsh parenting practices; and negative parent attributions about children's behavior. Conversely, the availability of social support is consistently linked with positive marital adjustment, effective management of parent–child problems, and a host of other positive family outcomes (Pierce, Sarason, & Sarason, 1995).

By virtue of the MST practitioner's frequent contact with multiple aspects of the family and neighborhood and community in which the family is embedded, he or she is in a strong position to assess the quantity and quality of social support available to family members. Circumstances that constitute evidence indicating a lack in social support include parents who engage in few social interactions outside work and childrearing, are unaware of the experiences other parents may be having with their children, or complain that there is no one to talk with.

Some parents report regular contact with a family member outside the home, a colleague, or a friend. In such cases, the practitioner should assess the nature of the interactions that occur when contact is made. When does the parent see or talk to the person? What do they do or say when they get together? Not all social contact can be automatically construed as social support. For example, in one study (Dumas & Wahler, 1985; Wahler & Graves, 1983), social contact consisted mostly of negative interchanges about the mother's poor parenting practices and failure to attend to the needs of the person she was visiting, in many cases, her mother. Alternatively, parents may have positive interchanges with other adults, but those adults may support the very parenting or adult relationship practices that contribute to a child's behavioral problem. Thus, an authoritarian parent may report that his buddy at work advocates the use of harsh punishment, or a potential love interest may persuade a divorced mother that her 13-year-old child should provide baby-sitting each evening so that he and the mother can spend time together.

Although the MST practitioner is often a significant, and sometimes the sole, source of social support to the parents as they attempt to alter parental, marital, and extrafamilial interactions, sources of support within a parent's indigenous environment (in the neighborhood, at work, at church) must be identified and cultivated early in the treatment process. Failure to cultivate such support in the parent's natural environment and to ensure that the parent can sustain the support (e.g., by providing a quid pro quo for any support and assistance received from others) will likely result in attenuation of treatment gains following the termination of treatment (see Principle 9). For effective parenting to be maintained, an indigenous support system must be available to help parents during times of heightened stress and distress. In the case of Kim Taylor, introduced in Chapter 3, an important intermediary goal was to decrease Ms. Taylor's reliance on Kim for emotional support related to the divorce, and the first steps in meeting that goal involved the therapist providing the emotional support. After helping Ms. Taylor distinguish among the aspects of her distress that could be attenuated through "venting," and those that might benefit by taking instrumental action (e.g., filing for additional financial support for her children), the therapist suggested she identify a neighbor or coworker who might become a friend and source of support. Ms. Taylor indicated that she did not want others at work or in her immediate neighborhood knowing her business. Thus, she and the therapist called the local chapter of Parents Without Partners. At the time of termination, Ms. Taylor had been able to attend only one formal meeting because of her work schedule, but she had arranged to meet one member of the group for coffee on several occasions.

PSYCHIATRIC DISORDERS

When the practitioner suspects that a parent is experiencing depression, anxiety, or more serious psychiatric disturbance, he or she should take several steps. First, the practitioner should obtain information regarding the intensity, severity, and duration of the problems from the parent, other family members, and, as appropriate, professionals who may have treated the parent. This information is needed to determine the extent to which (1) the psychiatric problem contributes to the referral problem or presents a barrier to change, (2) the psychiatric disorder can be safely and effectively addressed by the MST practitioner, and (3) periodic or ongoing collaboration with a psychiatrist may be required to ensure safe and effective pharmacological treatment for the parent.

To understand the fit between a parental psychiatric disturbance and identified child problems, and vice versa, the practitioner observes interactions within and between systems (Principle 5). For example, a mother who is somewhat depressed may experience increased hopelessness after receiving a phone call from the school regarding her child's misbehavior. This hopelessness may be accompanied by self-talk suggesting that nothing the mother can do will change the child's behavior. Thus, when the child returns from school, the mother halfheartedly upbraids the child for his aggressive school behavior but administers no consequences. Here, the mother's narrow repertoire of parenting skills comes into play, as her typical discipline strategy is physical punishment. Because the mother lacks the energy to exert such punishment, she does nothing. Moreover, she resolves to avoid answering the phone during school hours for fear that school personnel could be calling to complain about her son. Thus, the school–family linkage, already strained, further deteriorates. In addition, the failure to answer the phone results in increased social isolation. The isolation, in turn, exacerbates the mother's depression, which further compromises her attentiveness to parenting responsibilities and affective relationships with her children, which exacerbates their behavioral problems, which increases her depression, and so on.

When the assessment process indicates that depression interferes with the parent's response to the affective needs of his or her children, to appropriate monitoring and discipline of the children, or to needed social support, the practitioner should introduce the possibility that individually oriented interventions with the parent may be necessary. Again, in contrast with adults who seek office-based treatment for depression, parents in families referred for MST are often focused on the behavioral problems of the child and may find the practitioner's attempt to focus on the individual parent puzzling, frustrating, or irrelevant. Thus, the therapist might need to make explicit linkages for the parent between suspected depression and the child behavioral problems for which the parent wants treatment ("When you can't get out of bed because you feel so sad, Jim is late for school, the teacher calls and complains, you feel even worse," and so on).

Consistent with all aspects of assessment in MST, when a problem such as parental depression is identified, the individual and social-ecological factors that maintain or contribute to the problem should be delineated (e.g., irrational thought processes, marital difficulties, realistic family problems, substance abuse, social isolation, trauma, and recent loss). To address the identified multiple determinants of mild to moderate levels of depression, for example, the MST practitioner might implement cognitive-behavioral techniques for irrational thought processes, engage the parent in increased levels of activity (e.g., cleans the house with the parent, goes for walks with the parent), and help the parent identify and cultivate sources of social support. Practitioners who have limited familiarity with empirically validated cognitive-behavioral techniques for depression should review published texts and manuals, such as *Cognitive Therapy: Basics and Beyond* (J. S. Beck, 1995) and may require additional MST supervision when first implementing these interventions. As discussed in Chapter 7, cognitive-behavioral treatments are highly focused, target specific and well-defined problems, and require that the practitioner engage in frequent, active, and directive teaching. These interventions provide ample opportunities for the parent to practice changing thoughts and behaviors and for the therapist to monitor changes in the parent's cognitions and behaviors.

When social isolation contributes to depression, the practitioner may need to help identify and cultivate sources of social contact and activity. Consistent with the theoretical foundation of MST, the reciprocal nature of behavior must be kept in mind when encouraging a depressed parent to seek social support, as ample research indicates that depressed people often elicit negative responses from others because they deprecate themselves and others during interpersonal interactions. Thus, practitioners may need to augment cognitive-behavioral treatment with attention to social skills (e.g., guiding clients to focus on the positive aspects of life during interactions vs. the negative). Intermittent delivery of such interventions is less likely to be effective, so, as with most MST interventions, the practitioner should convey to the parent that treating depression is likely to require daily effort (Principle

7). Because the prospect of having to expend effort is often daunting to persons suffering from depression, practitioners may find it useful to motivate clients through appeals to desired outcomes, hopes, or dreams the parent may have for her or his life and the lives of the children.

Symptoms of social anxiety or phobia sometimes arise as barriers to the implementation of interventions to garner social support for parents. Practitioners should be sensitive to the possibility that adults with long-standing histories of relative social isolation may, in addition to showing signs of depression, have serious concerns about their ability to interact comfortably with strangers. Thus, prior to recommending that a parent make connections with neighbors, the parents of other children, or formal support groups at church or in the community, the practitioner should attempt to understand the range of experiences, skills, and concerns the parent possesses with respect to engaging in unfamiliar social contact. Such understanding of fit is then considered in the design of interventions.

Sometimes families referred for MST are affected by more serious disturbances such as severe clinical depression, bipolar disorder in a parent, or schizophrenia in a relative. When the disorders are more severe, the practitioner works with the family to identify an ecologically minded psychiatrist who will collaborate closely with the practitioner and family members in the process of providing any needed psychopharmacological treatment. In general, the responsibility for providing psychosocial aspects of treatment remains with the MST practitioner, unless homicidal, suicidal, and floridly psychotic behavior on the part of the parent requires hospitalization or continued assertive community treatment (ACT; see Santos et al., 1995) by a team of psychiatric physicians and nurses. In such cases, however, the practitioner remains responsible for understanding the nature of treatment being provided to the family member, assists the family in obtaining needed information from professionals treating the family member, and designs interventions and engages community resources that will increase the family's capacity to cope with what may turn out to be a chronic and difficult problem. ACT programs are often a great benefit in treating chronic, severe mental illness, and the MST practitioner should assist the family in exploring the availability of such programs in the community.

When the psychiatric problems of a family member who is not a parent figure (a grandmother with Alzheimers' disease, a grown sibling who returns home during manic episodes of bipolar disorder) demand significant attention from family members, the practitioner faces two assessment tasks. The first is to determine whether, when, and how the family member's psychiatric problems are linked to the behavioral problems targeted for treatment. Does caring for the grandmother leave a parent with little energy to monitor the children? Does the adult sibling disrupt household functioning when he returns home after stopping his medication? The second task is to determine whether the primary caregivers and other family members possess the knowledge, skills, resources, and linkages with community and professional resources needed to help that family member function more adaptively. If not, the practitioner assists the family in obtaining needed knowledge, skills, and support. In so doing, the therapist must acquire a level of expertise regarding the chronic condition that is sufficient to help the family make adjustments to managing the chronic illness and to ensure that interventions do not undermine other treatment goals of the family.

PARENTAL SUBSTANCE ABUSE

Parental substance abuse is targeted for intervention when it diminishes parenting capacity in ways that sustain the youth's behavioral problems or present barriers to change. Because substance abuse is often denied by those it most affects, the therapist should gather ample evidence that substance abuse (as vs. use) is occurring and is linked with problems targeted for change before broaching the topic of intervention with the parent and family. Physiological symptoms are one indicator of substance abuse. Alcohol produces specific intoxication and withdrawal symptoms, the latter when consumed regularly in significant quantities. Signs of alcohol intoxication include mood changes (from euphoric to irritable), motor incoordination (from slurred speech to staggering gait), the breath odor of alcohol, and, in some cases, inability to remember what occurred while under the influence of alcohol (so-called blackouts). Cocaine intoxication produces hyperactive behavior, pressured speech, increased affect, racing heart, paranoid thinking, and, at the extreme, frank disconnection from reality with psychotic thinking and perceptions. This stimulant drug is rapidly intoxicating and therefore significantly addicting. As a result, persistent cocaine users often experience peaks of energy and mood followed fairly rapidly by depressed energy and mood. Marijuana intoxication produces increased appetite, giddy euphoric to docile mood, sleepiness, apathy, and a lingering distinct odor if the marijuana was smoked. Withdrawal symptoms are psychological and can include significant irritability and marijuana craving.

Functional indicators of substance abuse include missed days or poor performance at work; heightened marital or parent–child conflict; unexplained changes in the parent's availability at home or work; frequent private visits with previously unknown adults or the appearance of such adults in the home; changes in the parent's social circles; and unexplained changes (i.e., not due to recent unemployment, reductions in support checks, divorce, and unusual medical or housing expenses) in the amount of money available to the family for food, clothing, and school. To determine whether such life problems are linked with substance abuse, the practitioner interviews the parent and family members and observes whether variations in the parent's behavior are associated with episodes of substance use or the after-effects of such episodes. In the Jackson case, for example, interactions between Jake and Mr. Jackson, although ordinarily conflictual, escalated more quickly to physical violence if they occurred while or after Mr. Jackson was drinking. In other cases, parental substance use affects multiple aspects of family functioning even when the parent is not intoxicated. Mr. Smith, for example, was a single parent of two adolescent daughters who were on probation for truancy and runaway behavior. A construction worker, Mr. Smith went to a neighborhood bar with buddies on the way home from work several times a week and usually arranged for his sister to stay with the daughters on these occasions. Although Mr. Smith stated that his social drinking did not interfere with his family life, his sister and daughters reported that he was sometimes loud and irritable and other times overly affectionate and "sloppy" when he returned from the bar. At these times, the younger daughter avoided Mr. Smith, while the older daughter made critical comments that led to arguments both in the moment and whenever he tried to implement curfew, monitoring, and discipline strategies with her. Thus, even when he was not drinking, Mr. Smith's ability to make needed changes in parenting practices (monitoring, increasing control) was compromised by his drinking pattern.

Treatment programs for substance abuse have proliferated in recent years, giving rise to clinical specialization (some states certify practitioners as substance abuse specialists!) in the absence of an adequate knowledge base regarding the effectiveness of various treatment models. The following highlights from the empirical literature on substance abuse treatment should assist the practitioner in deciphering prevalent clinical lore and designing more individualized, empirically informed interventions to address parental substance abuse in the context of MST.

- Controlled research provides no evidence that more restrictive (hospital, residential) settings are safer or more effective in decreasing drug or alcohol use in the short or long term.
- Community-based psychotherapies such as supportive–expressive therapy, family therapy, group therapy, and interpersonal psychotherapy yield poor outcomes, whereas behavioral therapies show more promise.
- Multicomponent behavior treatment (MBT; Higgins & Budney, 1993) integrating contingency management procedures with interventions targeting changes in the client's ecology (family, vocational/educational, and social/recreational systems) had the best outcomes with cocaine dependence.

Chapter 7, on individual interventions, presents guidelines for the development of interventions targeting parental substance, along with case examples.

PRACTICAL CHALLENGES AND BASIC NEEDS

Family members have great difficulty learning, growing, and changing when their primary physical, health, and safety needs are not being met (Wahler & Dumas, 1989). For example, parent–child affect and parental monitoring of child behavior may be difficult to improve when the parent works two jobs for an income that leaves the family at subsistence levels. Indeed, most models of family preservation services were developed on the premise that families at risk for child abuse and neglect were characterized by serious practical problems that interfered with parenting (Hooper-Briar, Broussard, Ronnau, & Sallee, 1995; Nelson & Landsman, 1992).

When practical problems in living interfere with a parent's capacity to meet the child's needs, therapist strategies typically focus on helping the family to connect with people who can provide additional services and support. If, for example, a parent works long hours for subsistence-level wages and is, therefore, both unable to monitor her teenage son's whereabouts and too exhausted to cultivate positive affective interactions with him, several strategies can be indicated. One course of action might be to determine whether neighbors, members of the extended family, or friends are able and willing to assist with monitoring the son after school so that he is not "on the streets" while the mother is at work. Note that consistent with Principle 9, emphasis is placed on developing indigenous family supports versus agency supports. Second, the therapist may assist the mother in finding higher-paying employment or in accessing sources of financial support made available through public service agencies. In such a case, parent–child affective relations may improve when financial stressors are attenuated and monitoring strategies are sufficient to reduce the son's troublemaking in the streets. In either case, the therapist's primary responsibility is to help the family develop and implement strategies to overcome identified barriers to change.

LACK OF COMMITMENT TO PARENTING

In some cases, multisystemic strategies to change parent–child interactions are met consistently with halfhearted attempts, inadequate follow-through with homework, or sheer lack of response from the parent. Usually, such responses are related to the factors described previously (e.g., knowledge, beliefs, concrete needs, and depression) or because the MST clinician is pursuing goals not shared by the parent, has not implemented interventions properly, or has implemented interventions that do not match the nature of the problem.

Periodically, however, assessment of the factors sustaining ineffective parenting and presenting barriers to change indicates that a substantive lack of commitment to parenting is present. As always, assessment and subsequent intervention require that the therapist understand the parent's perspective: Why have the parents decided to raise children but not attend to their affective and instrumental needs adequately? For some parents, career aspirations or economic necessity are the first priority, and the long hours devoted to income-generating activities sap the time and energy needed to attend to their children. Alternatively, the demands associated with caring for other, more apparently needy family members such as a chronically ill child or older parent may render the needs of the child referred for treatment less than pressing in the eyes of the parent.

When evidence clearly suggests that lack of commitment is a primary barrier to meeting a child's emotional and developmental needs, therapist strategies typically focus on helping the parent change his or her attitudes and behaviors. Such change can sometimes be accomplished by helping the parent to understand the child or adolescent's need for affection, focusing on the importance of the love and guidance the parent has to offer the child and examining the long-term costs of ignoring the child. Laying the groundwork for change may require identifying aspects of the parent's life that may be enriched by increasing involvement with the child. For example, Mr. Watson perceived that his business, reputation, and marriage suffered considerably because of his son's criminal behavior and the demands of court appearances, attorney's fees, and restitution. Thus, Mr. Watson did not wish to engage in activities related to his 16-year-old son, stating that if the boy was "old enough to be a criminal," he was "old enough to be on his own." In this case, appeals to salvage the son's future fell on deaf ears. Instead, pointing out that the father's increased involvement with his son might reduce the criminal behavior and, therefore, the need to leave work, pay legal fees, and prop up his own reputation in the community resulted in some willingness on the father's part to engage in treatment. Once he agreed to work with the therapist, initial discussions focused on the ways in which the father's "hands off" approach and angry stance toward his son failed to have an impact on the son's behavior, on alternative strategies that might be effective, and on the many ways in which the boy needed his fathers guidance.

NEGLECTFUL AND ABUSIVE PARENTING STYLES

When the practitioner learns that neglect, psychological maltreatment, physical abuse, or sexual abuse of a minor is occurring or has occurred in the past, he or she immediately faces legal, ethical, and clinical imperatives to ensure the child's safety. Assuming that the practitioner's legal and ethical obligations (e.g., mandated reporting and assisting the family with reporting) are executed promptly and that any potential threats to the therapeutic alliance resulting from such execution are managed, the practitioner assists the family in ensuring the safety of the child and considers how the maltreatment fits with the other identified problems.

The fit of maltreatment with the specific problems targeted for MST treatment is likely to vary across children and families and forms of maltreatment (sexual, physical, psychological, neglect), and as a function of the temporal relationship of the maltreatment to MST treatment. We have worked with cases in which past sexual abuse of a delinquent youth was revealed during the course of MST treatment and clearly identified as contributing to the fit of the problems being targeted for treatment. On the other hand, we have also treated families in which the adolescent had a known history of sexual abuse, but assessment of the factors sustaining current delinquent behavior indicated that the abuse was not contributing to such behavior.

These contrasting experiences, one in which past abuse appeared to be a significant contributor to current behavioral problems and one in which it did not, are consistent with the known heterogeneity of symptoms associated with abuse and neglect and with the moderators of symptom expression and severity. Research indicates that child abuse and neglect can compromise the emotional, social, cognitive, and behavioral functioning of children and adolescents *and* that the severity and variety of the negative effects vary substantially in accordance with multiple moderating factors (for a recent review, see Becker et al., 1995). Reports recently published by the American Psychological Association (APA) Coordinating Committee on Child Abuse and Neglect (APA, 1995) provide an up-to-date review of research on the psychological effects of various forms of maltreatment and on the outcomes of treatment and prevention programs targeting children suffering the effects of abuse and families in which child maltreatment occurred. Readers are referred to these reports, and to the studies reviewed therein, for a more comprehensive understanding of the issues than can be provided in the context of this chapter.

Although the causative factors of maltreatment have not yet been definitively identified, research indicates that abusive behavior is multidetermined, encompassing individual, familial, and ecological variables such as social networks, neighborhoods, and community resources (Ammerman, 1990; Becker et al., 1995; Cohn & Daro, 1987; U.S. Department of Health & Human Services, 1993; Walker, Bonner, & Kaufman, 1988). Because research on treatment for maltreated children and maltreating families is characterized by numerous definitional (e.g., multiple types of maltreatment) and methodological (lack of control groups, etc.) problems, and because evidence regarding the effectiveness of these treatments in reducing symptomatology in the child and attenuating maltreatment is mixed, the practitioner seeking to make informed decisions regarding interventions most likely to be effective faces a daunting task. Studies of individual, group, and family therapy interventions indicate that parents at high risk for abusive behavior may benefit from intensive, comprehensive treatment that addresses both interpersonal and concrete needs of all family members (Cohn & Daro, 1987; U.S. Department of Health & Human Services, 1993). Intensive approaches that are very brief, however, do not appear to be effective.

MST interventions for maltreating parents conform to the treatment recommendations developed by leading researchers (e.g., combination of strategic and structural family therapy techniques and behavioral parent and child training techniques) (U.S. Department of Health & Human Services, 1993; Walker et al., 1988) and were supported in one randomized trial (Brunk, Henggeler, & Whelan, 1987). Briefly, the following interventions are often used by MST therapists treating families in which child maltreatment was identified.

- Parents of youth with antisocial behavior who engage in neglectful or abusive behavior tend to be very insecure about parenting and other personal issues. These insecurities are often long-standing and may have been reinforced by the behavior of other professionals (e.g., teachers, previous therapists, and judges) toward the parent. Thus, in most cases, the therapist must align strongly with the parent from the outset of therapy to alleviate the parent's fears of failure and to establish a cooperative, rather than an adversarial, relationship. Interventions designed to enhance effective parenting skills, decrease parent–child conflict, and enhance or rebuild positive affective ties between family members are unlikely to be successful in the absence of a strong therapeutic alliance.

- When marital discord or marital aggression is associated with child maltreatment, practitioners should design marital interventions, which are described in the next section of this chapter.

- Parents whose arousal and responsivity to aversive behaviors (e.g., crying infants, noncompliant children, and rude adolescents) lead them to act impulsively and harshly may benefit from impulse control and anger management techniques such as self-instruction and social problem solving. Stress management and relaxation techniques may also be useful adjuncts. Relaxation training exercises, such as progressive muscle relaxation, should be demonstrated by the therapist before instructing parents in their use (see Gambrill, 1977; Swenson & Kolko, 1997; Walker et al., 1988, for descriptions of these interventions).

- In light of the well-established association between maltreatment and parenting stress, and the role of social support in attenuating such stress, interventions designed to provide social support for parents are often a primary focus of MST. Although the first line of action would be to link the parents with naturally occurring supports such as neighbors, members of the extended family with whom the parent has a *positive* relationship, and church members, evidence also suggests that parent support groups are a useful adjunct to family-based treatment (Cohn & Daro, 1987; U.S. Department of Health & Human Services, 1993).

• When the antisocial behavior of the youth is associated with abuse-related anxiety, depression, or posttraumatic stress disorder (PTSD), the therapist may need to augment family-based interventions with individual therapy or with manualized group therapies for child abuse victims that are well structured and target specific and well-defined problems (Principle 4). Evidence suggests that programs designed to increase stimulation, enhance language skills, and improve overall functioning produce some positive outcomes for young children; and that the severity of abuse-related anxiety symptoms may be decreased through the inclusion of relaxation techniques in a child treatment program (Walker et al., 1988). Referral to agencies that have expertise in conducting individual and group treatment with child victims of physical and sexual abuse may be warranted in such cases. Prior to making a referral, however, the practitioner should become familiar with the treatment techniques used by the agency or professional in question. Abuse-specific treatment is not recommended when the child has no identifiable symptoms of abuse-related anxiety, fear, intrusions, or avoidance of activities. Similarly, treatment techniques that are vaguely defined and general, as is the case with generic talk therapies and play therapies, are *not* recommended. Indeed, the value of play therapy in attenuating childhood problems of any kind is highly suspect (Lenhart & March, 1996). Thus, the therapist should ensure that the agencies or professionals to which referrals are made do not engage in such ineffective practices. In addition, the therapist should assist the family in monitoring the quality and effectiveness of the treatment by cultivating a collaborative relationship among the therapist, external professional, and family. Such a relationship will facilitate the family's ability to monitor the effectiveness of the treatment being provided by the external professional and to ensure the consistency of the treatment objectives with MST treatment goals and intervention plans.

VICTIMS AND PERPETRATORS OF SEXUAL ABUSE

Although treatment programs for sexually abused children and perpetrators of sexual abuse are widespread, the vast majority of these programs have no demonstrated effectiveness. Perpetrators span all ages and socioeconomic classes and are characterized by a variety of psychological difficulties, which may or may not include sexual deviance. Until the results of rigorous treatment outcome studies with perpetrators and with children are available, MST practitioners should be sensitive to the fact that perpetrators will require additional individual and/or group treatment and that a child whose symptoms are specifically related to the sexual abuse may require the same. Thus, although MST can be effective in helping families cope with the multiple intrafamilial and ecological stressors that may be associated with abuse, in preparing the family for reunification if a child has been removed, and in preventing unnecessary institutionalization or placement of a child, MST should not be construed as a substitute for perpetrator treatment. Generally speaking, the recommended course of action in such cases is to (1) work with family members and extrafamilial systems willing to protect the child from further abuse in ways that strengthen their capacity to do so, (2) work closely with social service and legal professionals on behalf of the victimized child and protective family members, (3) refer a child with trauma-related symptoms to a psychologist or psychiatrist who has expertise in treating such children, and (4) refer the perpetrator (if not incarcerated) to a structured treatment program.

Marital Interventions

When the family assessment indicates that marital (or adult relationship) problems contribute to the youth's antisocial behavior, the MST practitioner must prepare to design and implement marital interventions. Although discussion of the research on marital therapies and their outcomes is beyond the scope of this chapter, practitioners may find recent reviews of marital therapy and source materials cited in these reviews helpful (Alexander et al., 1994). In general, the four models of marital therapy most often tested in empirical studies are behavioral marital therapy, insight-oriented marital therapy, emotionally focused marital therapy (Greenberg & Johnson, 1988), and integrated systemic marital therapy. Reviewers have concluded that improvement rates are relatively consistent across all types of therapy and studies; only about 50% of treated couples are happily married at the end of therapy, and much research remains to increase the short- and long-term effectiveness of marital treatments (Alexander et al., 1994). The intervention strategies described in this section represent several communications, problem-solving, and intervention strategies common to behavioral and integrated systemic marital therapies.

Delivered within the context of MST, marital interventions should reflect MST treatment principles. That is, MST marital therapy should target well-defined specific problems, be present focused, address sequences within the marital dyad and between that dyad and other familial and extrafamilial systems, require daily or weekly effort (including homework), and so forth. The need to adhere to MST treatment principles is reiterated because practitioners new to MST and to marital intervention often revert to less structured supportive or insight-oriented therapies when the focus of intervention shifts from parent–child problems to marital difficulties. Anecdotal reports indicate that practitioners have greater difficulty maintaining action orientation, directiveness, and consistency when intervening in marital, rather than parent–child, interactions.

Setting the Stage for Marital Interventions

In light of the pressing nature of problems with antisocial behavior that characterize youth referred for MST, parents are typically focused on their child's problems rather than on possible marital difficulties. Thus, the MST practitioner often must take special care to obtain an explicit agreement from the couple to address relationship problems in the context of MST. Sometimes neither, or only one, parent indicates that parental disagreements or marital problems are an issue. In such cases, the practitioner must be able to articulate incidents and sequences of behavior that link marital problems to the child behavioral problems being targeted for treatment.

Having introduced the parents to the idea that marital problems may need to be resolved to attenuate behavioral problems in their children, the practitioner sets the stage for conducting marital treatment in the context of MST. The guidelines suggested by Henggeler and Borduin (1990) are often useful in this process. First, as is the case with MST interventions targeting parent–child, school, or peer problems, improving the marriage will require daily effort, "behavioral" homework, and sacrifice. Second, the couple and the practitioner are jointly responsible for the success of the interventions. The responsibility for designing and implementing appropriate interventions and for supporting the partners' efforts to change lies with the practitioner. Each of the partners is responsible for changing his or her own behavior. Third, to prepare partners to accept this responsibility, three suggestions regarding their engagement in marital treatment are useful:

1. The couple must emphasize mutual giving and cooperation (rather than competition).
2. The couple must learn how to resolve the conflict, resentments, or frustrations that occasionally arise (rather than letting them build up or become explosive).
3. Positive efforts made by each partner should be recognized by the other.

Facilitating Engagement in Marital Interventions

The practitioner begins the intervention phase of therapy by asking the couple to list several changes they would like to see in their relationship. Again, given the scope and intensity of youth behavioral problems that typically result in referral for MST, the couple may not be immediately able to respond to such inquiries. Alternatively, one partner may identify desired changes immediately while the other states that the marriage, although not particularly satisfying, is acceptable to him or her. In such cases, the practitioner may need to tie the marital issues back to the presenting problems (e.g., interparental inconsistency and arguments about discipline clearly contribute to Johnnie's staying out all night and getting into trouble), MST interventions that failed due to marital discord (only one parent administered consequences because the other left the house after an argument), or concerns about their child's current or future realities. Or, when a long history of negative interactions characterizes a marriage, the initial answers may take the form of a laundry list of complaints or a long wish list of desired changes that are unlikely to occur even in the best of worlds. Here, the therapist may need to respectfully point out that changes with respect to a small number of items on the list may significantly improve the experience of the marriage.

Throughout the course of marital therapy, the practitioner must attend to the "meta-level" messages about the relationship that partners convey to one another. That is, the practitioner must attend not only to the content of a statement but also to what the statement conveys about the speaker's perceptions, expectations, and feelings about the relationship. Put simply, what is said—the content of a statement—is only half of the message. How the message is said, both during a particular interaction and over the course of time, conveys important information about what the message means in the broader context of the relationship. The broader meaning of the message is the "meta-level" communication. The progress of therapy is often tied to the practitioner's ability to correctly interpret the meta-messages between spouses.

ADDRESSING MIXED MESSAGES

When the practitioner obtains evidence suggesting a partner is truly ready to leave the relationship, an individual interview may be necessary. Again, however, as is the case with parental proclamations indicating that the mother or father is "fed up" with a child, comments regarding a spouse's desire to end the marital relationship should be interpreted in the context of the family's typical interaction patterns. Is this a family in which threats of leaving are made often but never acted on? Do expressions of doubt follow particularly contentious parent–child or marital conflicts, long days at work, visits by in-laws? If, however, the practitioner obtains evidence suggesting that one partner has already begun the psychological process of leaving the marriage, an individual interview with that partner may be warranted prior to, or immediately after, conducting an interview with the couple about the possibility of undertaking marital interventions. During the individual interview, the practitioner should state directly that he or she senses that the spouse has significant doubt about the viability of the marriage. The practitioner should ask about the spouse's investment in marital therapy and in the marriage itself. During such an interview, the practitioner can help clarify mixed messages in a way that opens the spouse to considering marital therapy.

A spouse who is uncertain about his or her commitment to the marital relationship might use the "80% rule" (Henggeler & Borduin, 1990) to facilitate making a decision about whether to work on the marriage. That is, the partner should not expect to have 100%, or even 99% certainty about his or her commitment to the marriage as a prerequisite to making a decision. Instead, proceeding with the decision, one way or another, is worthwhile even if the spouse is only 80% certain that the marriage is worth saving or not.

PREDOMINANTLY NEGATIVE MESSAGES

When one spouse indicates that there is little likelihood he or she will remain in the marriage, and the therapist has determined that the marital or parent–child interactions sustaining behavior problems are related to this stance, the treatment goals established for the couple and for the family must be adjusted accordingly. On the one hand, developing joint marital goals is unjustified if one spouse is not likely to extend considerable effort on behalf of the marriage. On the other hand, when children have serious behavioral problems that require immediate attention, even the spouse who is leaving a marriage may need to change his or her behavior with respect to the partner so that parenting can be more effective. In such cases, the practitioner should help couples clarify the differences between marital and parenting functions and assist in enhancing the latter. Of course, the emotional distress that typically accompanies the ending of a marriage will complicate efforts to engage in collaborative parenting. Issues related to the continuation of parenting in such situations are discussed in the section on divorce.

Dealing with Negative Affect

Negative affect is easily generated and perpetuated in most couples with marital problems. The practitioner must help the couple interrupt the cycles of negativity that frequently occur in such marriages, and successful interruption of the behavioral sequences that constitute these cycles requires that partners learn and implement some basic skills. The following strategy, described initially by Henggeler and Borduin (1990), is useful in helping spouses to interrupt cycles of negativity and diminish the intensity and longevity of marital conflicts. The first steps toward helping couples interrupt sequences of negative interaction are listed here. Each partner must do the following:

1. Recognize that a negative behavior that is part of the cycle has been evidenced.
2. Inform the spouse that the negative behavior has occurred.
3. Explain the behavior and its corresponding meaning to the spouse in a nonattacking way.
4. Gain an understanding of the spouse's perspective regarding the negative behavior and the underlying circumstances that might have prompted the behavior.
5. Work out a mutually agreeable solution to the negative interaction.

Recognizing that a negative behavior has occurred requires that partners become aware of the precursors of conflict. Often, spouses describe a sense of "here we go again" when they describe their feelings during the early stages of a conflict. The cues that signal "here we go again" can be used by the spouse to stop the sequence and reflect on what exactly off the feeling of impending conflict. These cues (sensing "tension in the air," hearing a comment muttered under the partner's breath, etc.) should not be ignored. Neither should the cues provoke a critical reaction. Instead, partners need to learn that the cues represent an early warning system for an imminent conflict.

Informing the spouse that cues are sensed requires that the speaker communicate in ways that minimize defensiveness. Practitioners may need to teach spouses how to state concerns about a partner's negative behavior without blaming the partner. Helpful strategies include taking a "one down" position. For example, a husband might tell his wife that he feels that she is upset with him for some reason and that he is afraid that another conflict is brewing. The tone of voice and body language must be congruent with the one-down verbalization. When the couple recognizes that tension is beginning to develop, they should take a 5- to 10-minute time-out. A time-out is useful for two reasons. First, it breaks the couple's usual cycle of negative reciprocity. Second, each partner's willingness to take the time-out signals that he or she is able to put the relationship above personal interests. Couples should go into separate rooms during the time-out and try to understand the perspective of the other.

Immediately after the time-out, the couple should come back together to briefly explain their perceptions regarding the negativity in a nonattacking fashion. Explaining the nature of the perceived negativity is not the solution to the problem but can set the groundwork for a communication process that will help couples arrive at a satisfactory solution. When teaching couples to address their concerns in a more productive fashion, the practitioner will need to teach spouses to recognize the meta-level concerns raised by the conflicts.

Complaints about a messy house, for example, may actually reflect a spouse's fear that the partner does not care about him or her enough to help with household chores. Likewise, negative comments about the friend of a spouse may represent fear that the spouse is more interested in spending time with the friend than with the mate. To facilitate appropriate communication of concerns, the spouses must develop a more reflective approach to hearing one another's concerns. After years of interaction patterns lacking in such reflection, changing interaction patterns is often difficult and requires a good deal of practice. Thus, the practitioner should expect to engage the couple in within-session practice over the course of several sessions, and he or she should assign and expect completion of homework requiring daily practice between sessions (Principle 7).

After the couple explains their personal perspectives to each other, the central task is to demonstrate that each spouse appreciates the perspective of the other. Interpersonal conflict is exacerbated when one spouse perceives that the other is not listening to his or her point of view and does not appreciate his or her perspective. Partners with marital problems often devote their energy to developing rationales for their behavior rather than to understanding the mate's point of view. Shifting the pattern in which spouses do not listen to one another requires that each spouse use perspective-taking skills. Perspective taking requires that a person set aside his or her own view of a situation long enough to understand that another views the situation differently and the nature of that person's perspective. Again, in keeping with Principle 7 (interventions require daily or weekly effort), engaging couples in perspective taking usually requires that the therapist model the concept, provide multiple opportunities for practice within sessions, and assign homework that requires practice between sessions. In teaching perspective-taking skills, the therapist must consider the level of cognitive development that characterizes each partner. Individuals who think very concretely have great difficulty developing social perspective-taking skills.

The process of working out a mutually acceptable solution requires negotiation skills and the willingness to compromise. The practitioner must help spouses from a mode of dealing with conflict that emphasized "winning" to a mode in which conflict situations are resolved in ways that allow both spouses to feel that they gave as much as they received. The priority is placed on each spouse doing whatever is reasonable to make the other comfortable with the outcome. The practitioner's responsibility is to help the couple develop a cognitive set in which each partner can say "I believe I am right, but I understand my spouse's perspective, too." When couples can reach this level of cooperation, teaching negotiation skills is fairly straightforward. When a couple has difficulty compromising, however, the practitioner may need to serve as an arbitrator. In the arbitrator role, the practitioner helps each partner identify concessions he or she is willing to make. The arbitrator role, unfortunately, does not promote the long-term maintenance of therapeutic change (Principle 9) because the spouses are not learning to resolve issues themselves.

Changing Instrumental Relations

When marital conflict centers around instrumental issues such as household tasks, child-care responsibilities, and financial issues, the practitioner often needs to help spouses to develop shared expectations regarding one another's roles. In doing so, the practitioner should help partners to develop the cognitive set that marriage is a 50–50 proposition that requires equal effort, time, and energy from each partner. Although many couples will agree with this proposition, translating the concept into an equitable distribution of tasks often requires that a partner reconceptualize his or her ideas about the amount of effort he or she is required to devote to such tasks. Once reconceptualization occurs, desired behavioral changes must be defined so that they can be observed and monitored (Principles 4 and 8). Examples include doing the dishes three nights a week (as opposed to just "doing the dishes"), picking the children up from school five days a week, etc.

Spouses should be instructed to provide daily feedback to one another regarding their performance of instrumental tasks. Such feedback can occur at the end of the day, when they discuss their view of each other's efforts to change. Positive recognition is important because such recognition can help break the cycles of negativity described earlier. Daily feedback also helps to put "bad" days in perspective because couples have a more objective way of tracking how frequently bad days occur and can place their occurrence in the context of "good" days. Spouses should also receive accurate negative feedback about their performance. One useful technique for providing feedback is to have spouses use a "report card" or "grade" approach. Throughout the feedback process, the practitioner must be continuously and accurately informed of the spouse's efforts (Principle 8). Such ongoing feedback requires that spouses track one another's performance on paper, as is done when interventions designed to change the behavior of children are implemented.

Case Example

The Burke family was referred for MST after Jerry, age 14, was arrested for the third time and found to test positive for cocaine. Jerry was the youngest of three children; his 17-year-old sister was pregnant and finishing her GED, and his 20-year-old brother was unemployed and living at home. The Burkes were married for 20 years and abused alcohol and narcotics intermittently for the first 12 years of their marriage. Neither parent had used substances for 3 years at the time of referral. Ms. Burke attended Narcotics Anonymous meetings consistently, and Mr. Burke attended intermittently after repeated urging from Ms. Burke.

Assignments given early in treatment revealed that although the couple rarely openly disagreed or argued, they never spent time together without their children, Ms. Burke was unhappy in the marriage and believed that the family's goals for treatment (getting Jerry back into school, off cocaine, out of trouble with the law, and engaged in prosocial activities) would not be met if Mr. Burke did not participate. Mr. Burke, however, indicated that although the marriage was not ideal, he had made his peace with it and did not see the need for change. The therapist, unsure of the role of marital problems in the marriage, and having never conducted marital therapy before, proceeded with interventions targeting permissive parenting, monitoring of Jerry's whereabouts, mending fences with school personnel, and establishing expectations for household contributions to be made by the 17- and 20-year-olds.

Assignments that required participation from both Mr. and Ms. Burke were rarely completed, little progress was made, and Ms. Burke, increasingly frustrated with the lack of progress, began to doubt the therapist's competence. At this juncture, the therapist met with the couple and introduced the notion that marital interventions might be needed to help the couple help their children. For one week, the therapist met several times with the couple to assess the strengths and needs in their relationship (e.g., what first attracted them to one another, to what extent they still cared for one another, and whether they could engage in perspective taking and hear one another) putting previously implemented interventions "on hold." Thereafter, marital sessions were held twice each week, and sessions targeting parenting interventions and meetings with school personnel and neighbors were scheduled separately.

The therapist's early attempts to help the couple reach compromises regarding a new division of household labor failed primarily because neither individual felt the other appreciated his or her efforts. Thus, the therapist engaged the couple in perspective-taking exercises before and while attempting to help them reach compromises about instrumental issues. In addition, Ms. Burke complained that she needed more affection from Mr. Burke, while Mr. Burke complained that the couple had not had sex for over a year. In response, Ms. Burke complained that she was too exhausted to make love after spending all her energy on their children and family crises, and she suggested that she might have more energy if Mr. Burke did his fair share of parenting and supported her emotionally. The therapist quickly averted an argument, validated both partner's concerns, and added increasing intimacy to the intermediary goals. The couple agreed that going on a date might be a reasonable step toward increasing intimacy and agreed to make the first date one on which discussion of household tasks and child-related problems was not allowed and sex was not to be expected. The couple agreed to these terms and planned a date for the following Friday night.

On that Friday evening, the couple took their 17-year-old daughter along because she was distraught after an argument with her boyfriend. The therapist used this incident to illustrate the porous nature of boundaries between the couple and their children, revisited the date assignment, and established more specific terms of the date (no children allowed). Interventions related to permissive parenting, monitoring, and linking up with school personnel were reintroduced after the couple reached compromise agreements about the division of labor regarding household management and successfully went out on a date.

Marital Violence

When physical abuse occurs in a marriage, alterations in the usual approaches to marital treatment must be made. The practitioner's first priority is to ensure that the abused spouse will be safe when undertaking marital therapy. Similarly, the practitioner must take the perspective that the abused spouse is clearly the victim of violence. The abusive spouse needs to develop alternative skills to manage anger before the couple can be encouraged to engage in the steps outlined earlier regarding negative cycles of interaction. In many cases, the use of alcohol or drugs is associated with marital violence, and interventions need to be directed toward stopping drug and alcohol use. Both spouses may benefit from attendance at support groups for abused wives and for abusive husbands, which are available in many communities.

Enhancing Effective Functioning during and after Family Transitions

Families Affected by Divorce

When misconceptions about the divorce, inappropriate expectations about adaptation to divorce, or unsuccessful role negotiation contribute to the identified problems, several intervention strategies may be helpful.

1. The practitioner may need to educate family members about normative behavioral responses to divorce. Those normative responses vary in accordance with the child's age and level of development. Thus, for example, preschoolers of divorced families experience fears of abandonment by both parents more frequently than do school-age children, but even older children may need reassurance that both parents still love them.

2. To help fill the void in instrumental family functioning (e.g., house-

hold tasks), the practitioner can help parents and children develop reasonable expectations about the kinds of tasks that each child can perform, given his or her age and cognitive and physical capacity.

3. Previously effective parenting practices should be reinforced or reinstated, and the therapist may need to help parents develop new parenting skills to compensate for those previously implemented by the other parent.

4. The practitioner may need to assist parents in garnering the social and financial support required to sustain effective practices under what are often emotionally and practically difficult circumstances.

5. Practitioners may assist parents in renegotiating their relationships with their ex-spouses in ways that are conducive to coordinated parenting.

6. Finally, the practitioner may need to help the parent manage personal distress if that distress interferes with effective family functioning. Practitioners may find *Renegotiating Family Relationships* (Emery, 1994) a useful adjunct to the MST manual when working with families engaged in ongoing conflict and custody battles that are contributing to a child's behavior problems.

PARENT–CHILD SUBSYSTEM

Residential and nonresidential parents often have difficulties maintaining authoritative childrearing practices following separation and divorce. Emery (1994) identifies a specific and problematic pattern of parent–child interaction that may emerge after divorce as a result of parental guilt about the impact of the divorce on the child. In this pattern, the parent mistakenly attributes mild aberrations in a child's mood or behavior to the effects of divorce, rather than to normal influences. Such attributions can prompt parents to either minimize or focus excessively on negative child behaviors, attempt to appease the child, and relax appropriate parental disciplines. Consequently, a coercive cycle of parent–child interaction develops in which misbehavior that may have been punished previously is positively reinforced (e.g., appeasing the child), and parents are negatively reinforced for giving in to children's demands (i.e., parents experience relief from the child's negative behavior by giving in). As a result, children quickly learn the power of provoking parental guilt to achieve their aims.

If parents and children are caught in such a cycle, debating and gaining insight into the child's motivations (i.e., is the child being deliberately manipulative, or not?) are rarely useful. If the child's guilt-inducing comments and behaviors succeed in making his or her life easier because the parent fails to enforce rules or behaves more attentively, the child should be expected to continue such behaviors. Rather than take up issues of child motivation in such cases, the MST practitioner should help the parent to consistently enforce rules of conduct and provide support as the parent builds confidence in his or her capacity to manage guilt-inducing and problem behavior. Generally, such confidence increases as the parent experiences success in maintaining consistent rules in the face of the child's guilt-evoking comments or behaviors and as these behaviors decrease in frequency when they are no longer reinforced.

MST practitioners frequently use role-plays to ensure that interventions will be implemented successfully, but doing so is particularly necessary when parents face guilt-evoking complaints from their children. Divorced parents may harbor concerns about the child's love for and loyalty to him or her relative to the other parent, and such concerns sometimes present barriers to the parent's ability to exercise authority in the face of the child's comments comparing one parent with the other (e.g., "Dad doesn't make me do this"). When a parent has great difficulty "nonattending" to the content of the child's comments, the therapist might suggest that the parent focus on the behavior in question (e.g., the child won't clean up his room) rather than on the content of the child's comment (e.g., "Dad doesn't make me do this"). Although the child's comments may include realistic fears concerning conflict between parents, divided loyalties, and uncertainty about the future, such fears should be discussed at a later time, not during a parent–child interaction that revolves around limit setting, the completion of chores, and so on. Again, repeated practice, initially in the context of role-plays, may be needed to help the parent remain steadfast in effective parenting practices following divorce.

Finally, noncustodial parents who have contact with their children must be equally mindful of boundary issues. Disagreements between the parents, for example, should be addressed by the adults, not "through" the child. Similarly, noncustodial parents may try to compensate for the diminished amount of time they have with their children by planning special outings and activities each time the child visits. The practitioner may need to educate the noncustodial parent about the importance of engaging in everyday activities with children. That is, the important lessons of a child's life (e.g., caring for others, generosity, and the value of hard work) are learned through everyday behaviors rather than through trips to amusement parks. Although the noncustodial parent may feel that his or her limited time with the children provides little opportunity to convey such lessons, the therapist should encourage the parent to take a long-term perspective. That is, much can happen in the coming years, and, eventually, as the children reach late adolescence and young adulthood, decisions about with whom they spend their time will be theirs.

RELATIONS BETWEEN FORMER SPOUSES

When evidence clearly indicates that negative interactions between former spouses or the inability of former spouses to exercise interparental consistency contribute to a child's behavioral problems, the practitioner's overarching goal is to enable the divorced spouses to act in the best interests of their children despite difficulties in renegotiating the affective and instrumental aspects of their personal relationship. Recognizing that the renegotiation of intimacy and power between former spouses is an ongoing task, and one often fraught with emotional anguish and practical challenges, the practitioner should have realistic expectations of the parents when designing interventions. Emery (1994) observed that it is not necessary for parents to have an integrated, highly cooperative relationship to achieve the goal of redefining family relationships in a manner that will best promote children's well-being. Former spouses must, however, be able to make, keep, and renegotiate agreements about parenting tasks. Thus, the MST practitioner may have to help each parent devise acceptable means to communicate regarding such day-to-day issues as homework, doctor visits, birthday parties, and vacations. Similarly, visitation schedules should be agreed on and spontaneous violations of the schedule avoided for the children's sake. The practitioner should help the ex-spouses to resolve conflicts that directly involve and affect the children. Such resolution often requires conducting a series of individual meetings with each parent prior to, and sometimes instead of, joint meetings.

CONCRETE AND PRACTICAL CHALLENGES

Divorce may give rise to concrete and practical challenges, such as working longer hours to compensate for financial losses associated with the divorce, moving to a different dwelling following divorce, accommodating parent visitation schedules, and interacting with the legal system regarding divorce and custody issues. When divorce significantly reduces family income, the residential parent, typically the mother, may return to full-time employment outside the home or, if already employed, obtain a second job. Increased work hours may reduce adult monitoring of the children and negatively influence the mother's personal adjustment. The mother may also become isolated from her social support network when all her time is spent at work or engaging in child-care responsibilities, and social support is an important buffer against stress. Thus, intervention strategies may be needed to address the family's financial needs. In the short term, practitioners might help the parent to coordinate social services that will attenuate the family's financial needs. The practitioner may also need to help a parent navigate the court system to obtain adequate child support payments, although this legal process is time-consuming, stressful, and unlikely to address the family's immediate financial crisis.

ADDRESSING PARENTAL DISTRESS

When a parent's distress (grief, anger, anxiety) about the divorce interferes with his or her ability to parent effectively or to engage in appropriate communication with the ex-spouse about parenting tasks, the practitioner may need to provide emotional support before engaging the parent in strategies to parent or communicate more effectively. The practitioner should identify individuals who can help the parent grapple with the emotional and practical impact of the divorce and reinforce appropriate parenting practices. When the parent's friends or other adult family members provide instrumental support such as child care, the practitioner should ensure that these individuals refrain from discussing the ex-spouse, marital issues, and so forth with, or in front of, the children. When social support is needed but not available from adults in the indigenous environment (family, friends, coworkers), more formal sources of support such as church groups and community organizations like Parents Without Partners may be recommended to a parent. Prior to making such suggestions, however, the practitioner should be aware of, and attempt to address, potential practical (e.g., scheduling, transportation, and child care), social (e.g., discomfort with groups and concern about stigmatization), and cultural (e.g., religious and ethnic practices) barriers to increasing social support. Finally, if the distress precipitates depressive or anxiety-related disturbances or disorders, the MST practitioner implements the intervention strategies for these problems described earlier in this chapter and subsequently in Chapter 7.

Remarried Families

NORMALIZING STEPFAMILY EXPERIENCES

When the practitioner obtains evidence that unrealistic expectations about the family system (e.g., the expectation that the current family group is a recreated nuclear family) are contributing to behavioral problems, he or she may need to explain the developmental process of family reconstitution in terms that all members can understand. That is, the family may need to hear that it takes time to develop an identity as a family, that conscious effort is required to cultivate positive affective relationships and workable instrumental arrangements (e.g., who does which chores and how are money and time spent?), and that conflicts about preferred ways of doing things are normal. By reframing the thoughts and behaviors of the parent and children as natural occurrences in the development of a reconstituted family system, unrealistic expectations can be altered and a sense of cooperation among family members can be fostered.

When stepsiblings are housed under one roof, conflicts about the manner in which resources, affection, and time are spent on the various children in the household often occur. If such conflicts appear to contribute directly or indirectly to a child's behavioral problems, the practitioner should conduct a thorough assessment of the factors sustaining the real or perceived disparity.

If real and significant disparities do exist that are not inappropriate to the developmental needs of children of different ages (e.g., infants should receive more parental attention than adolescents), the practitioner should address the basis of these disparities with the parents. On the other hand, if the disparities are more perception than reality, such stepsibling conflicts should be normalized. Parents often hope, or even have the expectation, that children from different nuclear families will develop positive affective bonds with one another simply because their parents love one another and they all live together. The children, meanwhile, must adjust to changes in their relationship with the custodial parent while being asked to develop a new positive relationship with the stepparent and stepsiblings. Parents with unrealistic expectations about stepsibling bonding may need to be reminded that although they chose to marry, their children did not choose to have additional siblings. Although parents should develop and enforce rules for respectful behavior among all children in the household and encourage activities that might stimulate positive affective experiences among stepsiblings, parents should not expect the children to experience or express positive affection for one another initially.

CLARIFYING PARENTAL ROLES

When either lack of clarity regarding parental roles or inappropriate assignment of such roles contributes to the child's behavioral problems, the practitioner should arrange to meet with the marital partners without the children present. The purpose of the meeting is to determine whether the spouses have, overtly or covertly, agreed on the responsibilities each will have in caring for the biological and stepchildren, how they came to this agreement, whether differences of opinion emerged, how such differences were handled, and so on. Such meetings often reveal that little time and attention have been devoted to the negotiation of parenting issues, as the primary source of the spouses' concern was stabilizing the new marriage in the presence of children.

Generally, stepparents are more successful if they first establish a relationship with the child as a friend and assume the role of disciplinarian later. That is, a positive affective relationship should be established first, while the stepparent follows the biological parent's lead in enforcing discipline strategies (Hetherington & Clingempeel, 1992). This sequence of parenting tasks (i.e., first affective, later guidance) can be particularly difficult if the biological parent married, in part, to obtain help with parenting responsibilities. In such cases, the therapist should empathize with the biological parent regarding the many demands of single parenting, particularly when a child with serious behavioral problems is involved. The therapist should also, however, dispel the myth that the stepparent can and should become the primary source of parental control in the household. To accomplish this goal, the practitioner will most likely need to teach the biological parent effective parenting strategies, create opportunities to practice those strategies that afford the parent success experiences, and solicit the stepparent's support for the biological parent. The biological parent's belief that the stepparent should be a disciplinarian is not likely to be dispelled unless the biological parent is able to engage in effective parenting practices. The practitioner's task is to design and implement interventions that create such experiences.

Single-Parent Families

Many of the interventions for families affected by divorce are applicable to families headed by a single parent. When the intimate relationship of the single parent appears to contribute to the referral problem, however, additional interventions may be required. In these cases, interventions focus on clarifying parent–child and subsystem boundaries in much the same way as must occur in remarried families. In contrast with remarried or nuclear families, however, adults who have not (yet) made a commitment to a lasting relationship may have difficulty discussing such issues because doing so may require defining, constraining, or changing the developing relationship just when its novelty is most exciting.

If the MST practitioner obtains evidence that the custodial parent's involvement in intimate relationships alters family interactions in ways that contribute to a child's behavioral problems (e.g., the mother spends considerable time at her boyfriend's home, while leaving her adolescent in charge of the younger children), the practitioner seeks to help the parent to meet legitimate needs for adult intimacy, financial support, or assistance with parenting tasks in ways that do not radically alter the children's experiences. We have worked with several families in which a parent with a long-standing history of successive relationships was able to identify, with the practitioner's assistance, economic, emotional, and parenting needs that her various partners had helped to meet.

Case Example

Debbie was the 27-year-old mother of an 11-year-old son and 7-year-old daughter, each by different fathers. A former substance abuser, she was referred for MST following release from a residential substance abuse treatment program. During the previous 3 years, Debbie lived with several men who provided financial assistance and acted as surrogate parents to her children. At the first family meeting, Debbie introduced the MST practitioner to Al, a man she met in the treatment program. Debbie complained that her son Erwin would not mind Al, whereas her daughter "loved" him. Debbie's affection for Al and enthusiasm about his being a father figure for the children was immediately apparent to the practitioner. The practitioner empathized with Debbie's enthusiasm in terms that emphasized Al's value to her (e.g., adult intimacy and companionship) and deemphasized his value as a potential parent to the children. Over the next week, the practitioner gathered evidence via direct observation of family interaction and family responses to homework assignments that indicated the adult relationship was contributing to Erwin's behavioral problems. Armed with this evidence, but still validating Debbie's positive experiences of Al as an intimate partner, the practitioner was able to engage Debbie in a conversation in which she could begin to consider some ways in which involving Al so immediately and pervasively in her children's lives might be associated with the problems the family was experiencing. Next, a combination of interventions that involved obtaining child care, enrolling Debbie in a GED program so that she could obtain a job, identifying non-substance-abusing adults as sources of social support, and teaching parenting skills was implemented to enable Debbie to draw appropriate boundaries around her relationship with Al.

During the treatment, Debbie continued to defer frequently to Al for parenting help. Thus, the practitioner met with the couple often to (1) reinforce the importance of Al as a source of emotional support, intimacy, and companionship to Debbie; (2) establish and reinforce ground rules about his nonparticipation as a parent; and (3) assist the couple in discussing their plans for the relationship and what implicit or explicit agreements about financial support and parenting tasks were made between them. These discussions made both Debbie and Al uncomfortable, as they had agreed not to make a long-term commitment when Al moved in, each having "been burned" in previous relationships. Moreover, Al saw his financial support as tantamount to permission to parent, and Debbie implicitly agreed to this arrangement. In the end, Al moved out approximately 3 weeks prior to the scheduled termination of MST. In subsequent weeks, the practitioner worked daily to assist Debbie in practicing parenting skills, developing sources of social support, and obtaining public assistance to address concrete needs. It was not clear, however, that these efforts were sufficient to enable Debbie to draw appropriate boundaries around her adult relationships, as the practitioner was no longer involved in the case when Debbie met her next boyfriend.

5

Changing Relations with Peers

In this chapter
- The developmental importance of peer relations and the types of peer relations associated with antisocial behavior in youth.
- The role of family factors in the development of positive and problematic peer relations.
- Different methods of assessing the "fit" of peer relations with problems resulting in referral for MST.
- MST interventions targeting problematic peer relations.

Peer Relations and Development

Peer interactions and friendships provide an important context for the development of emotional, social, and cognitive competencies. The development of positive peer relations and friendships is an ongoing and increasingly complex task that begins in infancy and continues through adolescence and early adulthood. To effectively assess and intervene in the realm of peer relations, MST therapists should be familiar with the interplay of family, peer, and individual factors pertinent to the normative progression of peer relations at different developmental stages. A brief summary of this progression follows, but readers who have limited familiarity with research-based information about (1) the development of child and adolescent peer relations, (2) the interplay of peer and family interactions in development, and (3) the relevance of peer relations and family–peer linkages to positive and negative outcomes for youth may find reviews recently published by prominent researchers in the area instructive (see Bukowski, Newcomb, & Hartup, 1996; Cicchetti & Bukowski, 1995; Parke & Kellum, 1994).

Although friendship does not occur during infancy and toddlerhood, social behavior during the first 2 years of life progresses from smiling, seeking proximity with, and touching familiar (vs. unfamiliar) agemates to early signs of play behavior (e.g., imitating, showing, and offering toys). During the preschool years, social interaction with neighbors or preschool classmates takes place primarily in the context of coordinated play. The concept of friendship can begin to emerge at this age, though friendships are easily broken and reestablished from day to day and consist primarily of shared play activities. Interactions during the preschool years are important in teaching children skills for becoming acquainted, cooperating and sharing information about themselves, and dealing with such negative emotions as jealousy and rejection. These skills continue to develop through the first years of school, until middle childhood (around age 9), when it appears that friendships among same-sex peers begin to take on the characteristics of reciprocity, sensitivity to the other's needs, and genuine affection and love for one another. Some data suggest that the friendships of girls are more intense and fewer in number than those of boys. Nonetheless, this more mature form of friendship reflects the developing competencies of perspective taking and empathy and provides children with a means to experience trust, emotional support, and a sense of belonging. In early to middle adolescence, increases in self-disclosure, commitment, respect, trust, and similarities in attitudes and values become important components of friendship. Among girls, same-sex relationships become even more intimate. The transition to heterosexual relationships begins to occur during this developmental period as well, as some individuals initiate heterosexual relationships, with others following along until heterosexual groups socialize together periodically. The transition away from strong same-sex friendships toward the development of intimate relationships with members of the opposite sex most often occurs during late adolescence.

A variety of competencies developed in the context of social interaction between age mates are necessary to sustaining positive peer relations. Among these competencies are perspective taking, empathy, collaboration in activities and tasks, and initiation and reciprocation of interactions (see Bukowski et al., 1996; Newcomb & Bagwell, 1995). In general, youth who achieve positive status among their peers display these competencies across multiple social situations. The competencies, however, take different forms at different stages of development. For a preschooler, successful initiation of peer interaction involves first watching others play, then engaging in parallel play, and finally engaging in cooperative play. For a fourth-grader, a verbal invitation to play together would be an appropriate initiation move whereas for a seventh-grader, greeting a student and starting a conversation about a topic familiar to both would be appropriate.

Youth who have difficulty initiating or sustaining interaction and mutual give-and-take in relationships rarely achieve positive status with peers. Some such youth are simply neglected by their peers, while others are actively rejected. Research indicates that youth who are neglected appear to be rather inept in the context of social interactions whereas youth who are actively rejected often engage in aggressive and obnoxious behavior in social contexts. Youth who are neglected, socially isolated, and passive are at risk for subsequent internalizing problems, and youth who are rejected and aggressive in peer situations are at risk for subsequent externalizing problems, school failure, and delinquency (Asher & Coie, 1990; Hoza, Molina, Bukowski, & Sippola, 1995). In some cases, cognitive deficiencies and distortions such as those described in Chapter 7 contribute to inept or aggressive peer interactions. As well, physical attractiveness, hygiene, and conformity with peer norms for dress and appearance can influence acceptance among peers, though research indicates these factors are not as central as behavioral, cognitive, and emotional competencies to the development of positive peer and friendship relations. For any particular youth, however, problems with hygiene (e.g., dirty clothes and body odor), appearance (unusually tall, short, thin, or heavy, etc.) may be linked with negative attention from peers and increased self-consciousness, which, in turn, may lead to avoidance of, or conflictual, peer interactions.

As noted in Chapter 1, research consistently shows that problems in peer relations (e.g., association with deviant peers, little association with prosocial peers, and poor relationship skills) are strong predictors of antisocial behavior in youth. Moreover, many juvenile offenders commit offenses in the context of group activities (Hawkins et al., 1992), in which antisocial behavior is reinforced.

Linkages between Family Processes and Peer Relations

Longitudinal research highlights the synergistic nature of the relationship between family and peer processes from infancy through adolescence (for reviews, see Bukowski et al., 1996; Parke & Kellum, 1994). Both affective and instrumental aspects of parent–child interaction are linked with the quality of peer interactions. For example, several studies show that parental sensitivity to a toddler's affective cues and desires, engagement in arousing and physical parent–child play, and use of explanations and praise while engaging the child in developmentally appropriate tasks (e.g., simple puzzles) predicted positive peer relations in preschool and early grade-school years. On the other hand, unresponsive or directive responses to affective cues, low levels of parent–child play, and high levels of directive behavior during the child's early years predicted lower peer status in subsequent years. Researchers suggest that parent–child interaction that is playful and sensitive to the child's affective cues provides important opportunities for the child to learn how to encode and decode the social and affective displays of others, which, in turn, facilitates successful initiation and maintenance of child–child play and verbal interaction.

Overall, research suggests that parents influence their children's peer relationships in three primary ways (Parke, Burks, Carson, Neville, & Boyum, 1994):

1. Through the affective and instrumental qualities of parent–child interactions and childrearing practices.
2. As instructors or coaches regarding desirable behavior in social interactions (e.g., by suggesting that the child say hello or share a toy or that an adolescent offer a ride to an acquaintance).
3. As managers of their children's social lives, providing opportunities for social contact with children outside the family, and managing the interactions of peers when supervising such contact.

With respect to antisocial behavior, specifically, certain aspects of parent–child interaction (e.g., high conflict and low positive affect) and childrearing practices (e.g., harsh and inconsistent discipline, poor monitoring, and authoritarian, permissive, and neglectful parenting styles) are associated with youth involvement with deviant peers and antisocial behavior (see Chapter 1). Research also indicates, however, that positive family interactions can buffer or reduce the negative effects of deviant peers. For example, high parental monitoring and discipline skills attenuate the negative effects of youth involvement with deviant peers, and high levels of family support and involvement can reduce the influence of deviant peers on adolescent drug use and delinquency (Dishion, Patterson, Stoolmiller, & Skinner, 1991; Frauenglass, Routh, Pantin, & Mason, 1997; Mason, Cauce, Gonzales, & Hiraga, 1996; Poole & Rigoli, 1979). On the other hand, caregivers who do not allow their children to engage in age-appropriate activities or who are overprotective may stifle the adolescent's pursuit of appropriate levels of emotional and behavioral autonomy, which can interfere with the development of successful peer relations. As well, some parents may lack the knowledge that they play an important role in facilitating the positive peer relationships of their children.

Assessment

The overriding purpose of assessing the youth's peer relations is to enable the MST therapist and family to determine aspects of these relations that may contribute to or prevent further antisocial behavior. Pertinent aspects include the following:

1. Number and nature of acquaintanceship versus friendships.
2. Reputations of acquaintances and friends.
3. Social functioning of acquaintances and friends.
4. Intellectual functioning of acquaintances and friends.
5. Homogeneity versus heterogeneity of peer group (e.g., all deviant or rejected peers vs. some antisocial some prosocial peers). If the youth's peer interactions involve some positive and some negative peers, what are the settings and activities in which the adolescent associates with the deviant versus prosocial peers?
6. Sociometric status of the youth (i.e., well-liked, disliked, leader, loner, neglected, or actively rejected) and behaviors that appear to contribute to that status (e.g., aggressive, withdrawn, withdrawn when uncomfortable in social situations, and appropriately assertive).
7. Regarding the family–peer linkage, do the parents know the youth's peers and peer activities? Do parents express interest in the youth's activities? Despite adolescents' developmentally appropriate increases in peer, as versus family, activities, parents remain important sources of emotional guidance and support for adolescents, particularly with respect to issues such as education, jobs, and the future.

To gain a comprehensive picture of the strengths and weaknesses in the youth's peer interactions, the MST therapist should gather such information from direct observations of the youth in a variety of contexts involving peers and from interviews with family members, teachers, and the youth. Observations of interactions with peers should occur at home, in school (in class, at lunch, on school grounds), in the neighborhood, and at other sites in which the youth participates in organized or casual activities with other same-age, older, and younger peers. Information about the youth's peer relations might also be obtained from the youth's peers, parents of the youth's peers, coaches, and neighbors who know the youth and family.

Understanding Association with Deviant Peers

As noted in Chapter 1 and previously in this chapter, numerous aspects of family interaction can contribute to a youth's involvement with deviant peers, and the initial MST assessment of family functioning may provide preliminary clues regarding the contribution of such factors as family conflict, parenting style, and parental monitoring. Once involved with a deviant peer group, the youth's antisocial behavior is often reinforced via group collaborative participation in antisocial acts as well as peer support and acceptance for engaging in such acts. In light of the mutually reinforcing effects of deviant peers on one another, school, juvenile justice, and community efforts that place troublesome youth together in special classrooms, treatment groups, and community activities may exacerbate, rather than ameliorate, deviant behavior.

Often, youth referred for MST are placed in special classrooms or treatment groups. As noted by a group of leading researchers in understanding the determinants of delinquency (i.e., Elliott, Huizinga, & Ageton, 1985), it seems unreasonable to expect that a group of youth with behavioral problems will somehow generate prosocial values and group norms by interacting with one another. Indeed, the behavioral norms of antisocial peer groups typically run counter to the norms of society. Moreover, data also indicate that many delinquent youth are as closely attached to their deviant peers as are nondelinquent youth to their nondeviant peers (Elliott, Huizinga, & Ageton, 1985). Such youth are unlikely to voluntarily extract themselves from a deviant peer group.

Extraction from a deviant peer group may be particularly difficult for gang-affiliated youth. Although a discussion of the prevalence and composition of gangs and of the nature and outcomes of various juvenile justice and community-based prevention and intervention efforts is beyond the scope of this chapter, several findings from research in this area are relevant to MST treatment of gang-affiliated youth (see Howell, 1995).

- Many types of adolescent peer groups violate laws together but are not gangs.
- Gang membership is not stable, with nearly two-thirds of gang-involved youth remaining members for only 1 year.
- Previous gang members are able to develop prosocial peer associations following departure from the gang (Thomas, Holzer, & Wall, 1996).

The central implication of these findings for practitioners and families is that a youth's proclaimed or actual involvement in a gang need not be seen as an insurmountable barrier to the success of peer interventions. On the other hand, if serious threats on the life of the youth or family members ensue following efforts to extract the youth from a gang, these threats should be taken seriously by therapists, family members, and law enforcement officials and a safety plan should be devised.

Understanding Peer Estrangement or Rejection

When an adolescent is socially isolated, actively rejected, or simply neglected (left alone) by same-age peers, the therapist and family should assess which aspects of the youth's interpersonal behavior may be contributing to the lack of peer bonding and social isolation. If aggressive behavior appears to be the primary contributor to disrupted peer relationships, the therapist should ensure that family and family–school interventions are addressing all the factors that sustain the youth's aggressive behavior. If these interventions are being implemented but aggressive behavior continues, the therapist may need to assess the contribution of the individual factors discussed in Chapter 7, and implement interventions accordingly.

If, on the other hand, aggression does not appear to be a primary obstacle to the development of positive peer relationships, the therapist should work with the youth and family to identify which of several areas of interaction associated with successful peer relations may be problematic for the youth. In general, socially neglected or rejected youth often withdraw from social situations, have difficulty initiating and sustaining positive give-and-take in conversations, and act in ways that are not socially acceptable or valued by same-age peers. Withdrawal and failed efforts at maintaining social give-and-take often result in peer avoidance, which, in turn, minimizes the positive peer contact necessary for the unskilled adolescent to learn alternative prosocial behaviors. Socially awkward or intrusive adolescents also elicit negative responses from peers. Gradually, peers may develop a negative label for the adolescent and may ridicule or ostracize him or her. Such negative responses from peers feed into the cycle of negative experiences the youth has in the social world and inhibit establishment of the types of positive interactions needed to increase the youth's social appropriateness at each successive step in development.

Social rejection and negative labeling by peers can exacerbate the antisocial, awkward, or withdrawal behaviors of some youth in that peers may come to expect and selectively attend to inappropriate social behavior in a particular adolescent. When such negative expectancies occur, peers are less likely to notice and respond positively to the adolescent's prosocial behavior. In addition, because the social reasoning required to initiate and maintain friendships becomes more complex as children move from preschool to school-age to adolescent years (Bierman & Montminy, 1993), youth who have early difficulties in the realm of peer relations may be at greater risk of experiencing peer rejection or isolation as adolescents. The self-esteem of the awkward adolescent may be seriously compromised in such a situation, and negative peer feedback may exacerbate the adolescent's poor self-image, thereby contributing to further social isolation.

Interventions

Decreasing Association with Deviant Peers and Increasing Affiliation with Prosocial Peers

When the MST therapist and family find that association with deviant peers contributes to a pattern of antisocial behavior, interventions aimed at reducing the youth's affiliation with deviant peers and increasing his or her affiliation with prosocial peers are necessary. Such interventions rely on the therapist to help the parent to do the following:

- Monitor the youth's whereabouts.
- Increase parental contact with the youth's peers and parents of peers.
- Implement very unpleasant consequences when the youth contacts antisocial peers and positive consequences when the youth contacts positive peers.
- Facilitate the youth's participation in prosocial activities such as after-school sports and clubs, community-based sports and service organizations, church groups, recreation center activities, and after-school volunteer or paid employment.
- Help the youth identify areas of competence and interest, as talents and activities that may have been apparent during earlier years are sometimes eclipsed by involvement in antisocial activities, school failure, and involvement with the law.

The details of the intervention strategies will vary in accordance with the strengths of the particular youth, family, school, neighborhood, school, and community. In addition, interventions may vary as a function of the extent and intensity of the youth's association with the deviant peers. That is, some youth referred for MST have a mixture of prosocial and antisocial peers, others affiliate primarily with antisocial peers but have only done so for a relatively short time (e.g., less than a year), while others have been part of a deviant peer group for a long time and have minimal contact with prosocial peers.

PARENTS AS KEYS TO PEER INTERVENTIONS

Consistent with Principle 9, interventions to address problematic peer relations must be sustainable in the absence of the MST therapist. Thus, the five types of interventions enumerated previously all draw on parents or caregivers as key agents of change in the realm of peer relations. Parent figures are, or should become:

- Sources of monitoring and discipline strategies needed to reduce opportunities to affiliate with deviant peers.
- Experts in the interests and talents of their sons and daughters, even if these have been eclipsed by behavioral problems.
- Facilitators of exposure to community activities in which prosocial peers can be found.
- Liaisons with the parents of their child's peers.
- Adult supervisors, on occasion, of their youth's peer activities.

Moreover, fairly mundane practical activities can provide the parent with regular opportunities to observe and/or manage peer interactions. For example, a parent can transport several adolescents to and from the movies, to the mall, or to the ballpark; parents lacking transportation can recommend (or require) that the youth's friends meet at the family's home in advance of a scheduled bus departure or cab ride to an afternoon or evening event.

While assisting parents in taking a proactive role in rearranging the youth's peer ecology, several guidelines should be followed to increase the likelihood that this often exceedingly difficult task can be accomplished:

1. *Help the youth to see the disadvantages of associating with deviant peers.* Parents should engage the youth in conversations about the potential disadvantages of hanging out with the "wrong" peer group, particularly if the youth only recently began to affiliate with deviant peers and is experiencing some negative consequences as a result. If other individuals in the natural ecology of the youth and family, such as an uncle, coach, or neighbor, are more credible sources of information for the youth initially (because, for example, such individuals did not previously attempt to change the youth's peer affiliations, engaged in arguments about the peers, etc.), the therapist should encourage the parent to solicit the help of these individuals.

2. *Avoid berating, belittling, or insulting peers who are valued by the youth.* Parents should avoid berating, belittling, or insulting peers who are valued by the youth, as such interactions tend to fuel parent–child conflict and reduce the likelihood that the youth will cooperate. In addition, in light of the evidence that delinquent youth may feel as positively about their deviant friends as nondelinquent youth feel about theirs, the youth likely experiences some acceptance, bonding, and validation of self-worth when in the company of the very peer the parents are berating. Moreover, the youth feels compelled to defend his or her peers rather than consider the potential negative consequences of keeping their company. Thus, the parent should acknowledge that the youth has positive feelings about the deviant peer while focusing on the negative consequences to his or her life for affiliating with that peer.

3. *Prepare the parents for battle.* Given the power of peer relationships, parents must have the instrumental, emotional, appraisal, and informational support (see Chapter 8) of family members, friends, coworkers, and so on, prior to implementing interventions designed to minimize their child's contact with valued but deviant peers and increase contact with unfamiliar but prosocial peers. Even when such support is forthcoming, the therapist should be prepared to provide substantial assistance initially, taking phone calls at midnight when the youth does not return home, arriving on the scene when the youth does return and the parents try to implement a harsh consequence, and so forth. If, as occasionally happens, peer interventions require such extreme measures as tracking a youth's whereabouts when he or she is with

deviant peers who may temporarily house or hide the youth, the parents may also need to enlist the help of more formal community supports such as probation officers, community police, and social service staff (see the example of Tasha Cole in Chapter 4).

INTERVENING WHEN PEERS ARE MIXED

When a youth has some prosocial and some antisocial peers, the therapist and parents can attempt to steer the youth toward the former. For peers who are on the border between desirable and undesirable, from the parents' perspective, but who are regarded as close friends by the youth, the parents can set and enforce firm limits regarding their child's contact and interactions with that peer. The following example shows how parents can use indigenous resources to restructure their child's activities in ways that promote prosocial behavior.

Case Example. Shauna was a 16-year-old high school student whose perpetual truancy, failing grades, and late-night loitering resulted in referral to an MST program. She and her mother, Ms. Cummings, argued often but experienced some warmth and moments of mutual respect when they were not arguing. Shauna's 26-year-old brother, Ronnie, recently returned home from an inpatient substance abuse program, and Ms. Cummings asked him to monitor Shauna's whereabouts when she was at work. Shortly after his return home, however, Ronnie began to meet friends at a bar after work and the monitoring plan fell apart. Shauna continued to have periodic contact with two prosocial friends she had known since grade school but was hanging with a "rough" crowd she had met about a year before referral. One girl in the crowd, Anita, had recently become pregnant. Ms. Cummings forbade Shauna from having contact with Anita and encouraged her to call the two "old" friends, Lana and Mallory, but these admonitions and recommendations fell on deaf ears.

Because Shauna's peer relationships were a continuing source of mother–daughter conflict, the therapist helped Ms. Cummings to reduce her running negative commentary about Shauna's friends—in an attempt to reduce the fuel for this conflict. The therapist also encouraged Ms. Cummings to contact Anita's mother to request collaboration in detailing conditions under which Shauna would or would not be allowed to visit Anita (e.g., if a parent was at home, not when specific members of Anita's generally deviant peer group were present). Ms. Cummings instituted serious negative consequences for violation of curfew (which occurred most often when Shauna was with the rough crowd), and, with the therapist's advanced coaching, Ms. Cummings was able to discuss with Shauna her concerns about the possibility that Shauna was engaging in unprotected sex. Prior to this coaching, and following her discovery that Anita was pregnant, Ms. Cummings began to issue threats (e.g., if you ever get pregnant you'll be out on the street) and scare tactics (e.g., you'll get AIDS and die) in an effort to curb suspected (but not substantiated) sexual activity. These threats also escalated mother–daughter conflict and did little to achieve Ms. Cummings desired goals—learning whether Shauna was engaging in unprotected sex and preventing her from engaging in unprotected sex.

Next, Ms. Cummings and the therapist talked with Shauna about other ways of spending after-school time. Organized clubs at school held no interest for Shauna and were not open to her participation because of poor school attendance, but Shauna and the two "old" peers did hang out at a neighborhood beauty salon and enjoyed styling hair. To capitalize on this shared interest with prosocial peers (a strength), Ms. Cummings met with the parents of these friends and asked whether the one who knew the salon's owner would be willing to explore options for the girls to volunteer services (sweeping hair, etc.) several days per week. In return, Ms. Cummings offered to have the girls at her home after school on her day off from work. At the time of termination, additional strategies were being put into place to allow Shauna supervised access to male friends who were not part of the deviant peer group and to explore paid employment options that would become available in the summer.

INTERVENING WHEN PEERS ARE EXCLUSIVELY DEVIANT

When a youth is exclusively involved with deviant peers, the therapist and parent need to rearrange the youth's everyday ecology in ways that provide powerful positive reinforcers and negative sanctions to compete with the perceived benefits of affiliation with the deviant peer group. Again, the intervention strategies and guidelines articulated earlier should be attempted prior to making the decision to extract the youth entirely from a deviant peer group. This decision is usually made when three conditions are met:

1. Members of the youth's peer group do not have substantive participation in prosocial activities.
2. The group has an extensive history of participation in deviant activities, especially violent activities and drug abuse.
3. Parental attempts to structure the youth's behavior in ways that achieved changes in peer affiliation have been unsuccessful.

The following case provides an excellent example of the concerted effort by parents and others in the family's support network needed to disengage an adolescent from deviant peers.

Case Example. Corey Campbell was a 15-year-old male referred for MST following repeated arrests for minor thefts and vandalism, one arrest for drunken and disorderly conduct, and multiple suspensions from school. At home, Corey violated curfew and was verbally and physically abusive to his mother and younger sister. Corey and his friends spent most of their time after school and on weekends skateboarding on downtown sidewalks, smoking cigarettes, blaring a "boom box," and occasionally harassing merchants for free soft drinks and food. Corey was an average student until middle school, when he began to perform poorly, making C's, D's, and an occasional F.

Corey lived with his biological parents and a younger sister. Strengths in this family included the Campbell's long-standing marriage, Mr. Campbell's full-time employment, and parental concern about the children. Some aspects of Mr. Campbell's employment were also contributing to the problem, however, as he was out of town from 4 to 6 days per week as a teamster. During the initial family interviews, Mr. Campbell stated that he expected Mrs. Campbell to manage the household and children while he was gone, and Mrs. Campbell complained that she wanted more support from her husband. Mrs. Campbell noted that when she asked for his help, Mr. Campbell berated her because Corey demonstrated few behavioral problems in his presence and responded quickly when Mr. Campbell threatened to "use the belt" on his son. Mr. Campbell believed that his wife just needed to "toughen up" on Corey.

The MST therapist initially targeted parenting styles for therapeutic attention, as information gained from drop-in visits and additional interviews indicated that Mrs. Campbell was somewhat permissive whereas Mr. Campbell was very authoritarian. Interventions designed to change parenting styles, however, were only intermittently successful, and marital difficulties were identified as the major barriers to success. With success in marital treatment, the Campbells became more consistent in parenting, with Mr. Campbell calling nightly from truck stops to check on Corey, Mrs. Campbell being more demanding of mature behavior, and both parents agreeing on nonphysical consequences for rule violations that could be imposed in Mr. Campbell's absence.

In response to these changes, however, Corey began to use increasingly abusive language even when Mr. Campbell was present and began staying away from home more. After talking with the Campbells, teachers, and neighbors about Corey's acquaintances and friends, driving by the downtown hangout several times, and chatting with the policeman who walked the downtown beat, the therapist discovered that Corey's friends were beginning to exhibit gang characteristics, and that several youth had police records for such serious crimes as aggravated assault. In addition, the parents of several of these friends were themselves engaged in antisocial behavior (i.e., drug use and previous jail time). Moreover, the therapist learned that Corey had cut almost all ties with prosocial peers in the neighborhood over the previous 2 years, and the Campbells knew little about his current peer network.

After several interventions to increase parental contact with Corey's current peers and meet their parents failed, the therapist and parents determined that MST interventions should target removing Corey from his peer group. To initiate this plan, the family had to wait until Mr. Campbell had several consecutive days off, as the Campbells and therapist determined that Mrs. Campbell could not implement the plan without her husband's active support. In addition, the family arranged to have Corey's sister stay with a relative during the initial implementation phase, as they expected Corey might react violently to the plan. The initial steps of the plan involved the following:

- Taking Corey's skateboard away from him and allowing him to earn points to get it back by staying in school all day and coming home with a parent immediately after school.
- Picking him up immediately upon conclusion of the school day, or from wherever he was if he left school during the day.
- Preventing Corey from making or receiving calls or visits to any of his downtown buddies.
- Asking police to call the Campbells if they saw him with any of these youth.

Once home, and if he responded nonaggressively, the Campbells provided Corey access to the phone but only to make contact with a skateboard clinic or with youth in the neighborhood the family knew and whom Corey had severed ties with over the last year. Computer game privileges were similarly made contingent upon Corey's nonviolent compliance with getting a ride home and staying away from his downtown buddies.

To foster relations with prosocial peers, Mr. Campbell took Corey to the skateboard clinic where prosocial peers built and tested various skateboard courses under the supervision of a college-age male. In addition, the therapist and parents mobilized surrogates to take Corey to the skateboard clinic and to other community activities when Mr. Campbell was out of town, and Mr. Campbell continued to make nightly telephone calls to Corey from the road. Mrs. Campbell, in turn, remained assertive in her parenting practices even in Mr. Campbell's absence and also made use of neighbors and her brother to stand by her side when she anticipated that Corey might push a limit. In return for this support, she occasionally provided transportation for their children and baby-sat for one parent's toddler when Corey was at school. This plan had been in place for 4 weeks at the time of treatment termination, during which Corey left school only once to meet his pals downtown.

Socially Rejected or Neglected Youth

FAMILY INVOLVEMENT IN INTERVENTIONS

Socially rejected or neglected youth usually have deficits in various social skills and can benefit from interventions aimed at enhancing social facility. To increase the likelihood that the skills are learned and generalize to home and neighborhood settings, every effort should be made to include parents or caregivers in interventions to improve the social interaction skills of youth who are isolated, neglected, or rejected by peers. As with all MST interventions, the therapist should be aware of patterns of family interaction that may be contributing to the youth's problem interactions with peers. For example, the family itself might be socially isolated, or the parents might be socially anxious or relatively unskilled in social interaction. In addition, parents may not be aware of the important role they play in arranging opportunities for their children to engage in social interaction (by seeking out community activities, allowing peers to visit, providing rides to the mall, etc.).

If parent and family interaction patterns appear to contribute to the youth's problems with peers, interventions directed solely at the adolescent are unlikely to be successful. Thus, prior to and while implementing the individualized social skills training techniques, the MST therapist should effect intervention strategies to address the specific family factors believed to contribute to the peer problems. Presumably, for example, interventions to reduce verbal and physical conflict would be in place, the therapist would be working with parents to identify and access activities in the community that provide peer contact, and so on.

PEER INTERACTION INTERVENTIONS

Reviews of treatment programs for children and adolescents with social skills deficits (Bierman & Montminy, 1993; Forman, 1993; LeCroy, 1994) indicate that intervention approaches typically focus either on the individual adolescent or on peers in a natural setting such as a classroom. Within the context of MST, the therapist can implement individually oriented procedures with the youth at home while seeking opportunities for the youth to practice in the context of school and neighborhood settings in which same-age peers can be observed. The nature of the youth's social interaction difficulties or skill deficits and his or her level of cognitive development should be considered when identifying the specific targets of intervention. Common problems among school-age and adolescent youth include the following:

1. *Weak acquaintanceship skills.* Some youth have particular difficulties initiating peer interactions. They may be unsure how to approach others, what

to say to get a conversation going, or how to join a group. When children and adolescents resort to either obnoxious show-off behavior or anxious behavior (e.g., withdrawal, seeking sympathy, whimpering, and fidgeting), they may need instruction in positive methods of acquiring peer attention and engaging in peer interactions.

2. *Deficits in communication skills.* Communication skills become increasingly important for positive peer relations as children grow older. Youth with few friends often lack skills as basic as asking questions to initiate a conversation, telling about oneself, self-disclosing to promote intimacy and chumship, making suggestions, or giving advice to promote extended friendly interaction.

3. *Deficits in sharing and cooperation skills.* Many youth are not liked by peers because they do not play well—they cheat, have trouble sharing, and are generally no fun. Often these youth never really learned the principles of cooperation or how to balance a give-and-take relationship. Whether they are overly dominant or overly passive in peer interactions, these youth are basically lacking in the skills necessary for cooperative and reciprocal interaction.

4. *Deficits in problem-solving and conflict resolution skills* (described in Chapter 7). Deficits in the cognitive problem-solving abilities that mediate social interaction may reduce an adolescent's interpersonal effectiveness. When presented with interpersonal problem situations, socially unskilled youth may find it difficult to consider and appraise alternative courses of action.

To facilitate the development of social skills, the therapist and parent conjointly provide instruction in the particular skill to be learned, model the behavior, provide opportunities for the adolescent to practice, and give verbal reinforcement and corrective feedback after observing the practice. Therapists may find "Coping Skills Interventions for Children and Adolescents" (Forman, 1993) and "Social Skills Training" (LeCroy, 1994) useful resources with regard to specific techniques therapists and parents can use to model, teach, and help youth practice new interaction patterns with peers. Interventions should be explained to parent figures so that they can reinforce the newly developing skills and become involved in coaching the youth in the absence of the therapist.

Case Example. Dell Granger, age 15 years, resided with his grandmother, Ms. Evans, in a poor rural mountain community at the time of his referral for MST. Dell was arrested for theft of several gold chains at a strip mall near the high school he attended and tested positive for alcohol and marijuana at the time of the arrest. Although he was alone during the offense, Dell claimed his friends put him up to the theft. Dell refused to divulge the identity of these friends to the police, therapist, or grandmother. The therapist's interviews with his grandmother, schoolteachers, and shop proprietors indicated that Dell was a loner. Ms. Evans reported that Dell moved in with her when he was 11 years of age, and always kept to himself. She attributed this to his being new to the community and recently separated from his mother, who lost custody of Dell as a result of her serious substance abuse and neglect of him. Ms. Evans had not met any of his friends but said this was not unusual given that Dell was a teenager and the family's rural location made access to peers difficult after school hours.

After talking further with Ms. Evans, the therapist hypothesized that several practical and family factors contributed to Dell's social isolation and periodic association with deviant peers. The family's rural location and Ms. Evans's poor health, which limited her driving, presented concrete barriers to Dell's involvement in after-school activities. Ms. Evans had little knowledge about normative adolescent development, no inkling that Dell might be using drugs, and some misconceptions about Dell and his adjustment at school and with peers. These misconceptions were based on Dell's rendition of his life but not affirmed by any of the adults contacted by the therapist. Because Dell created little trouble for Ms. Evans, she presumed he was doing reasonably well at school, with which she had little contact, and believed that he had friends. In fact, Dell was doing C work in most classes, began getting D's during the semester of his arrest, had no real friends, and had two "fair weather" acquaintances who used him largely as accessories to their mischief. The gold chains, for example, were to have been delivered to the friends who, in turn, were to exchange them for alcohol and drugs, which they occasionally shared with Dell.

After establishing telephone linkages between Ms. Evans and the school, implementing interventions to increase her monitoring of Dell's whereabouts and drug use, and cultivating informational and appraisal support via increased phone contact with a relative in another town who had raised two sons and with her closest neighbors (nearly a mile away) with whom she had fallen out of touch, the therapist focused on Dell's peer relationship problems with Ms. Evans. The therapist observed Dell in class and on the school grounds and lingered at the strip mall after school and on the weekend to observe the groups identified by the proprietor and police as Dell's sometime acquaintances. The therapist observed that Dell was ignored by most students in class, largely neglected in casual situations (i.e., cafeteria and strip mall), picked on periodically for his appearance, and invited occasionally to join a group of drug-using peers at the mall. The therapist hypothesized that Dell's behaviors contributed in some ways to his relative isolation: He rarely looked up, rarely initiated interaction, did not seem to understand the humor in the normative adolescent banter of classmates, and wore his hair and finger nails longer than was customary for boys his age and responded defensively when others commented on his appearance.

Initially, Ms. Evans refused to believe the therapist's description of her grandson but agreed to accompany the therapist to obtain verification from teachers, the police, and the mall proprietor. Once the therapist made sure that Ms. Evans understood the importance of attending to Dell's peer relations, implementation of interventions began. Initial interventions targeted Dell's appearance, social behavior, and cultivation of interests or talents. With respect to the former, Dell's male shop teacher agreed to talk with him about his hair and fingernails and to invite him to become one of three students to share shop clean-up duty, under the teacher's supervision, several times a week. In addition, the therapist met with Dell every other day to implement individual interventions related to initiation and maintenance of peer contact and to generating alternative responses when ridiculed and invited to engage in antisocial activity. Ms. Evans was made aware of the objectives of individual treatment and of the practice homework related to each session, but in contrast with preferred MST practice, she was minimally involved in the individual sessions at Dell's request (i.e., he felt embarrassed by her presence for discussions related to peers). As therapy was ending, Ms. Evans arranged for the male relative with two grown sons to take Dell on periodic outings and was becoming familiar with community resources for males—an arena that was completely unknown to her prior to treatment. Dell had not yet developed a true friendship with a same-age peer. However, he was able to engage as an equal in interactions with the shop clean-up crew according to the shop teacher's report and therapist observation.

Barriers to Change and Strategies to Overcome Them

In our experience, barriers to the success of peer interventions occasionally arise for several reasons:

1. The parents are "on board" regarding the importance of peer interventions and their role in implementing them, but interventions are implemented incompletely or for too short a time to be effective.
2. The parents are not on board with the notion that peer interventions are essential or with their own importance in generating solutions to peer problems.
3. The parents themselves are engaged in antisocial behavior, which reinforces the youth's behavior and interferes with parental monitoring of peer relations.

4. Concrete or practical barriers (e.g., lack of transportation, minimal availability of prosocial community activities, and few informal social contacts) contribute to social isolation or affiliation with deviant peers.

Possible strategies to overcome these barriers are discussed next.

INCOMPLETE OR INADEQUATE IMPLEMENTATION

Inadequate implementation most often arises when parents are attempting to extract the youth from a deviant peer group. A common scenario is that the parents were inadequately prepared for battle and gave in when the youth "upped the ante" by, for example, running away or threatening violence. In such instances, the therapist and parents should review the support plan for the parents, determine where support broke down in ways that contributed to the parents abandoning the intervention plan, and design strategies to prevent the breakdown in the future. Moreover, if significant adults in other areas of the youth's life (e.g., teachers and chaperone at the recreation center) had not previously been part of the plan but can provide reporting (e.g., he left class with the tough kids today) or support functions, they should be approached. In addition, as noted in Chapter 4, the therapist and parents should ensure that the positive consequences for avoidance of negative peers and affiliation with prosocial peers are still salient to the youth, the negative consequences are powerful deterrents, and no familial (e.g., marital conflict, parental inconsistency, and parental drug abuse) or concrete barriers are interfering with the implementation of rewards and consequences.

LACK OF PARENTAL BUY-IN TO THE IMPORTANCE OF PEERS AND THE PEER–FAMILY LINKAGE

Some parent figures (like Ms. Evans, described earlier) simply are not aware of the importance of peer relations to positive development or of the important role families play in facilitating peer relations. Thus, throughout the ongoing MST assessment and treatment process, the therapist should be sure to obtain the parent's perspective on the contribution of peer issues to the referral problems and should have evidence linking the two if the parent is not able to see the connection (e.g., Dell steals and takes drugs only when he is with, or trying to please, certain acquaintances). Alternatively, some parents appreciate the importance of peer relations as a problem but are inexperienced in creating opportunities for their children or adolescents to socialize with others and in managing the interactions of the youths when they do socialize. In such cases, the therapist may need to help the parents identify developmentally appropriate activities for their sons or daughters and coach the parents in how to introduce and sustain involvement in such activities (including the mundane activities of providing rides or a gathering place at the home periodically). Finally, some parents may believe peer relations are important but experience themselves as unsuccessful in this arena due to social anxiety, depression, lack of time and resources, and so on. In such cases, individual interventions for the parent (see Chapter 7) should be undertaken prior to or concurrent with peer interventions.

CONCRETE OR PRACTICAL BARRIERS

When families have limited economic resources, the therapist and parent may need to request that entry fees for enrollment in community activities be reduced or waived, apply for scholarships or financial assistance from community organizations to assist with payment, or engage in informal bartering of one service for another (e.g., a parent agrees to bake for a drive to buy uniforms, and the child receives a uniform in return). Similarly, the youth may need to "make do" with clothing and equipment that is not brand new. Teens do not have to have the latest in designer athletic shoes, for example, to participate in a local basketball league, and parents should be wary of claims to the contrary. Some communities, particularly isolated rural communities and highly impoverished urban neighborhoods, offer relatively few organized recreational options for youth and rely more heavily on church, neighborhood, or informal social networks to provide activities for youth after school and on weekends. Although political and fiscal initiatives may be needed to alter the general landscape in these communities, the therapist and parent should work diligently to find out what youth in the community who are not engaged in antisocial behavior are doing after school and how to access those opportunities for their children.

6

Promoting Academic and Social Competence in School Settings

In this chapter
- The importance of family–school collaboration and the school context for promoting the short- and long-term adaptation of youths.
- Child, family, and school factors associated with children's academic and social functioning in school.
- Guidelines for interfacing with school personnel and for promoting parent–school collaboration.
- Strategies for overcoming barriers (e.g., high family–school conflict) to successful family–school collaborations.

The school is a major social institution that has a pervasive influence on child development (Swartz & Martin, 1997). As such, the school can provide a tremendous resource for the MST therapist, for example, providing opportunities to engage youths in prosocial peer activities and promoting the development of skills that will bear on the youth's future economic well being. Unfortunately, however, approximately 30% of the youths referred for MST in our various projects are not in school—having been suspended or expelled. Moreover, many of the MST referrals who are in school attend classes composed primarily of children with emotional disturbances or behavioral problems. Such classroom placements conflict with a primary goal of MST discussed previously—limiting youths' contacts with problem peers and maximizing associations with prosocial peers. Compounding these difficulties is the fact that the youth and their parents often have negative attitudes toward the school, and the school personnel often have similar attitudes toward the youth and their families. Such circumstances have contributed to poor school-related outcomes for youth with serious emotional disturbances (Knitzer, Steinberg, & Fleisch, 1990). For example, children with serious emotional disturbances have only a 36% high school graduation rate and high unemployment within 5 years after leaving school (Duchnowski, 1994). Such academic and behavioral difficulties present major barriers to the development of educational and vocational competencies that are crucial to the future functioning of youth presenting conduct disorder and other antisocial behavior. These barriers must be overcome to promote positive long-term outcomes for youth referred for MST.

The overriding goal of the chapter is to help therapists and parents develop interventions that "beat the odds" by empowering parents to advocate for and facilitate their children's school-related outcomes, thereby enabling youth to take advantage of the opportunities offered by school settings. This chapter provides an overview of the developmental significance of school settings and factors associated with school performance and provides guidelines for assessment of these factors, interventions aimed at enhancing school performance, and recommendations for addressing barriers to the success of these interventions.

The Developmental Significance of the School Setting

The school environment provides children and adolescents with a milieu in which they have the opportunity to experience a variety of social roles. For many young children, teachers are the first adults besides their parents with whom they have extensive contact. Some of these children find that patterns of behavior that are permitted by their parents can be problematic when used with their teachers. Such children must learn to make accommodations to different styles of adult control and affective interaction. For many young children, school provides their first extended contact with a stable group of peers. These children must learn strategies for gaining entry into peer-group activities, for responding to the friendly or unfriendly initiations of others, and for the development and maintenance of friendships. During the middle school and high school years, social roles become even more complex. Boys and girls often have most of their initial experience with the development of heterosexual relations within the school context. In addition, participation in clubs and organized sports provides opportunities to develop cooperative behavior, leadership skills, and friendships.

The school environment also has a strong effect on children's cognitive development and their subsequent vocational achievement. Children acquire strategies for learning in the classroom that can be used for the rest of their lives. Children who learn that significant personal effort provides substantive payoffs are probably more likely to continue such efforts during adulthood than are children who are not rewarded for their efforts or who are in a school context that does not demand significant effort. Moreover, based on the association between educational success and socioeconomic success, school performance can have a strong influence on occupational and career opportunities. The realization of such opportunities, in turn, has a pervasive effect on the quality of the child's adult life. For example, the status, prestige, and income associated with an individual's occupation affect his or her place of residence, choice of spouse and friends, and recreational activities. Thus, ideally, the school can provide a springboard for lasting social and economic competence.

Factors Linked with Children's Competence in School

Children's competence in school settings is associated with several broad factors. Because the vast majority of MST referrals have school-related difficulties, therapists must develop an understanding of these factors. Moreover, development of such an understanding is essential for therapists to determine the ecological fit of identified problems (Principle 1) and to design interventions that correspond to this fit.

Intellectual and Academic Abilities

Academic settings place a high priority on intellectual skills, especially verbal skills. Youth who possess high verbal skills are more likely to experience success in school and, consequently, are more likely to enjoy school and view academics favorably. On the other hand, youth with limited intellectual abilities will often find school to be a less rewarding environment. Few individuals enjoy spending time on activities that frequently lead to failure. Academic difficulties, therefore, often contribute to behavioral difficulties. Moreover, learning disabilities are often associated with both academic and behavioral problems (Sattler, 1992), though many youth with academic and behavioral problems do not have learning disabilities.

Mental Health and Psychosocial Functioning

As noted earlier, youth with serious emotional disturbances (and a high percentage of MST referrals qualify) have considerable difficulty achieving academic and social success in school. Children who present behavioral problems are not prized by teachers, administrators, or most classmates; and presenting such problems clearly interferes with the learning process and the ability to become involved in socially valuable school activities. Similarly, internalizing problems such as depression and anxiety often restrict both learning and participation in social activities.

Family Functioning

Family support and encouragement of children's academic and social performance in school is linked with better school-related outcomes. On the other hand, numerous family-related factors can attenuate a child's school performance. These include, for example, a chaotic family environment, parental psychopathology or drug abuse, high family conflict, negative parental attitudes toward school, a low value placed on education, and significant life stressors, such as poverty and physical illness.

The Learning Environment

Qualities of the teachers and school environment significantly influence children's social and academic competence as well as the prevalence of antisocial behavior in the school (Hawkins & Lam, 1987). Factors associated with low rates of antisocial behavior include school policies that are consistent and fair; student perceptions that the academic curriculum is relevant; accessible teachers; a strong, consistent, and effective principal; and the perception that students have a degree of control over their school experiences. Similarly, theorists (e.g., Polk, 1984) posit that antisocial behavior in school settings is exacerbated by policies that exclude "marginal" youth from such sponsored school activities as clubs, artistic groups, and athletics.

Family–School Linkage

The importance of the family–school linkage for child academic and social success is well documented (Fine & Carlson, 1992). Parents and teachers should have similar missions and goals: facilitating the optimal development of the child. On the parental level, these goals are facilitated by parental activities such as monitoring homework assignments and exam grades, having periodic contact with the teachers, supporting extracurricular school functions, and providing overt support for teachers' educational demands and goals. On the school level, teachers and administrators must endeavor to provide parents with regular feedback on classroom goals and the child's performance, maintain open lines of communication, and flex the scheduling of parent–teacher conferences to accommodate parental needs.

Assessment

As described by Schoenwald, Henggeler, Brondino, and Donkervoet (1997), the MST approach to the assessment of the fit of a youth's school-related difficulties consists of several steps:

1. Prior to contacting the school, the therapist elicits the parent's perceptions of how the aforementioned factors (i.e., youth intellectual abilities, youth emotional and behavioral functioning, family functioning, the school environment, and the family–school linkage) may be linked with identified academic and social problems. In addition, the therapist obtains the parent's and youth's views of the solutions that have been used to address these difficulties as well as their impressions of the success of these solutions.

2. Next, the therapist gathers similar perceptions from the school personnel who are involved with the youth, including, for example, teachers, administrators, coaches, guidance counselors, and so on.

3. The therapist integrates the multiple perspectives to develop rational hypotheses concerning the factors that are contributing to the identified problems as well as the strengths of the systems that may be used to facilitate change. Additional information may be needed from family members or school personnel to clarify inconsistencies or contradictions that emerged during the initial two steps. Moreover, as described next, educational testing may be used to gain a better understanding of how the youth's intellectual abilities and academic achievement are linked with the identified problems.

Intellectual and Academic Abilities

To determine whether a child's poor academic performance is a direct product of low intellectual abilities, the therapist should obtain at least two types of psychoeducational data: intelligence testing and achievement testing. As described next, a comparison of the child's ability with his or her actual achievement can provide an index of whether poor academic performance is commensurate with abilities. The therapist must remember that low achievement is a relative term, and that judgments about achievement must always be considered within the context of the youth's abilities and resources. Moreover, as few practitioners have the requisite training and experience in educational test administration, the therapist should consult qualified professionals (e.g., PhD in clinical psychology, EdD in testing) to administer and help interpret the results of the intellectual and achievement tests.

INTELLIGENCE TESTING

The youth's intellectual strengths and weaknesses should be examined through the administration of a well validated individually administered IQ test such as the Wechsler Intelligence Scale for Children—III (WISC-III; Wechsler, 1991). Therapists should avoid using results from group-administered IQ tests because knowledge of the youth's level of motivation during group tests is usually not available, and such information is essential to judging the validity of the resulting scores. As described by Sattler (1992), the reliability and validity of the WISC-III are well established for both white and minority children. An important advantage of the WISC-III is that it provides a meaningful profile of children's intellectual strengths and weaknesses. Factor-analytic research demonstrates that the subscales assess three primary dimensions of intellectual performance. The first factor, Verbal Comprehension, comprises the information, similarities, comprehension, vocabulary, and arithmetic subscales. Because of the highly verbal nature of most academic coursework, this factor is the strongest predictor of achievement in classes such as social studies and English. The second factor, Perceptual Organization, comprises the block design, picture completion, and object assembly subscales. This factor taps abilities that are nonverbal or analytical/mechanical in nature. The third factor, Processing Speed, appears to tap the child's ability to concentrate and maintain attention while processing information rapidly. This factor includes the coding and symbol search subscales.

ACHIEVEMENT TESTING

Achievement test scores are the second set of data that should be obtained when evaluating poor academic performance. The Wide Range Achievement Test—Revised (WRAT-R; Jastak & Wilkinson, 1984) and the Peabody Individual Achievement Test (PIAT; Dunn & Markwardt, 1970) provide the best validated measures of children's academic achievement (Sattler, 1992). An advantage of the WRAT-R is that the child is required to perform in a way similar to that required in the classroom (e.g., the child must actively calculate arithmetic problems). The multiple-choice format of the PIAT, on the other hand, greatly facilitates the testing of children with disabilities.

DETERMINING WHETHER ACHIEVEMENT IS COMMENSURATE
WITH ABILITIES

Once the child's intellectual skills and achievement levels have been assessed, determining whether the child is functioning at levels above, below, or commensurate with his or her intellectual abilities is possible. In making such a determination, a general rule of thumb is that the child's level of academic achievement in verbal subjects (e.g., spelling, English, civics, history, and science) should be consistent with the child's verbal comprehension skills. For example, a 10-year-old fifth-grader who has a 130 verbal comprehension IQ should be expected to achieve at an approximately eighth-grade level (i.e., mental age = IQ/chronological age; 13-year-olds are usually in eighth grade). Likewise, a 10-year-old with a 100 verbal comprehension IQ should be achieving at a fifth-grade level (i.e., mental age of 10 years), and a 10-year-old with an 80 verbal comprehension IQ should be achieving at a third-grade level (i.e., mental age is 8 years, and 8-year-olds are typically in third grade).

Returning to the main point of this section, poor grades and low achievement are often the direct result of low intellectual abilities. A 12-year-old seventh-grader with an IQ of 85 is going to have much more difficulty with academic materials than a 12-year-old seventh-grader with an IQ of 115. The former child will probably be achieving 1.5 to 2 years below grade level and will have approximately a C average in a typical public school. Thus, if one of the presenting problems for this child was low grades and the therapist determined that the child was achieving at a fifth-grade level, the therapist would probably conclude that the child's achievement was consistent with his or her abilities and that interventions seemed unwarranted. If, however, the child was earning F's in school, the therapist would investigate the situation further because the child was probably capable of earning higher grades. Similarly, if the child was found to be achieving at a third-grade level, such achievement would be below expectations and the therapist would need to consider the role of other variables associated with academic difficulties.

LEARNING DISABILITIES

By law, a learning disability can be designated when levels of achievement are not commensurate with intellectual abilities, and the discrepancy is not the result of "visual, hearing, or motor handicaps, of mental retardation, of emotional disturbance, or of environmental, cultural, or economic disadvantage" (*Federal Register,* 1977, p. 65083, §121a.5). As emphasized by Sattler (1992) and Taylor (1988), however, learning disabilities represent an amorphous category of childhood problems. Moreover, research suggests that these problems are multidetermined. Following Taylor's recommendations, therefore, the goal of a learning disabilities assessment is not to reach a "diagnosis" but to delineate the nature and extent of the problem and to suggest interventions that recognize the important roles that child factors (e.g., coping strategies, attitudes, and motivation) and parental and teacher support play in attenuating academic achievement. Hence, as suggested earlier in this section, the practitioner (and MST program) should have access to expert consultation from an educational professional who views academic difficulties from an ecological perspective.

Mental Health and Psychosocial Functioning

The fact that the youth was referred for MST indicates that he or she is presenting significant emotional or behavioral problems. Thus, the therapist should already be examining the social-ecological factors linked with these problems and identifying systemic strengths. When assessing the fit of identified problems with the school setting and vice versa, several points are pertinent:

• The cross-situational occurrence of identified problems has important implications for the design of interventions. For example, when problems are evidenced at home but not at school, or vice versa, the nonproblematic setting likely includes valuable strengths that can be harnessed to create change in the other setting. On the other hand, when problems are pervasive across settings, the therapist knows that significant attention should be devoted to developing cross-setting collaborations in the implementation of interventions that address needs in both settings.

• The therapist should evaluate the views of school personnel regarding any youth problems, perceived causes of these problems, attempts the school has made to ameliorate the problems, and perceived effectiveness of these attempts. Such an evaluation helps the therapist to make recommendations and design interventions that have credibility among school personnel (e.g., the therapist can avoid interventions that "failed" previously in the school).

• The therapist should assess, from multiple perspectives, the impact of the emotional or behavioral problems on academic (e.g., grades) and social (e.g., participation in after-school activities) outcomes as well as the impact of school personnel, policies, and so forth on the youth's psychosocial and educational functioning.

• If the youth is experiencing school-related difficulties, improving such difficulties should be incorporated into the goals of treatment. Depending on the specifics of the case, however, improving such outcomes may or may not have high priority early in treatment (e.g., in a context where the child's safety is at high risk from abuse at home, improving grades is a relatively low priority).

• School personnel can provide an extremely valuable and relatively "objective" perspective of the youth's peer relations. Whereas a youth might hide certain friendships from parents (e.g., friendships with gang members or drug-using peers) or pretend that he or she has closer peer relations than is the case, school personnel have excellent and ecologically valid opportunities to observe the youth's peer interactions. Thus, the therapist should ask educators about the youth's friends, focusing specifically on the reputations and competencies of these individuals. Treatment implications vary, for example, if the youth's main friends are well integrated into prosocial school activities versus frequently suspended or expelled (see Chapter 5 regarding peer relations).

- School personnel also provide information about how the youth typically interacts with adults who are in positions of authority. For example, does the youth respond with equal hostility to all authority figures, or do certain types of adult response styles evoke more appropriate behavior. Such knowledge can prove valuable in understanding the fit of problems.

Family Functioning

Because MST is fundamentally a family-based treatment model, the therapist should already be assessing key characteristics of the family system, as described in Chapter 3—including affective and control dimensions of parent–child relations, affective and instrumental aspects of marital or the caregiver's adult relations, parental psychosocial functioning (i.e., competence, drug abuse, and psychopathology), sibling relations, and so on. With regard to the youth's academic and social functioning in school, the therapist should determine how family functioning may be linked with identified problems in school. We have, for example, seen cases where children had sporadic school attendance because their single mother was too depressed or drug-involved to get them up in the morning in time to catch the bus. Similarly, we have seen cases where falling asleep in class or aggression with classmates is associated with high family conflict. Thus, as with aspects of the children's functioning in home and neighborhood settings, the therapist's task is to determine whether identified family difficulties are associated with identified problems at school.

The Learning Environment

A great deal of tact and sensitivity are needed in the therapist's assessment of the competence of school personnel and the capacity of the school to meet the needs of youth presenting emotional and behavioral problems. To accomplish this task, the therapist can ask a series of carefully framed questions within the natural flow of the discussion between the therapist and school personnel (i.e., teachers, administrators, and coaches). By adopting an attitude of helpful interest toward the youth's activities in school, the therapist can gather considerable information about the teachers' competencies and the quality of the school. The therapist should determine the following:

- How the class day is structured.
- The school's capacity to accommodate to individual needs of students (e.g., accommodations made for especially bright children, intellectually disadvantaged children, and children with behavior problems).
- How classroom disruptions, fighting, and illegal activities (e.g., selling drugs) are handled.

- How much contact teachers have with the children's parents, and how important the teachers regard such contact.
- The grounds for suspension and expulsion, and what actions are required for reinstatement.

The therapist should pursue lines of discussion that may yield additional pertinent information (e.g., is the curriculum demanding?), as needed.

Although the teachers have the most direct contact with the student, the educational tone of the school is largely set by the principal and his or her assistant. Many principals are superb educators and motivators who maximize teachers' and students' efforts, but others have essentially abdicated their leadership responsibilities. They fail to discourage teacher incompetence and laziness, permit students to engage in disruptive behavior, do not inform parents of truancy, and refuse to acknowledge serious problems (e.g., the sale and use of drugs) that are pervasive in the school.

One index of a principal's competence is his or her willingness to cooperate with responsible professionals who are not employed by the school system. Competent principals are usually very cooperative with professionals who are working with one of their students. Although the therapist's meetings with school personnel may represent an inconvenience for the school and may consume valuable time, these principals recognize that the professional's goal is to promote the well-being of the student and that this goal is consistent with the mission of the school. Moreover, successful principals are often pleased to "show off" their school. On the other hand, when the professional encounters considerable resistance from a teacher or principal, the therapist should attempt to understand the fit of the resistance in terms of practical constraints (e.g., demands for time from multiple outside agencies), temporal events (e.g., end-of-semester exams, or school-wide achievement tests), organizational factors (e.g., the school administration is not running the school as well as possible), and individual factors (e.g., an inexperienced teacher). If the therapist is cordial and persistent and expresses appreciation for the real or perceived barriers to cooperation articulated by school personnel, however, he or she can usually gain cooperation. Indeed, of the hundreds of school evaluations that we have either conducted or supervised, teacher/principal cooperation was flatly refused in only two instances.

Family–School Linkage

Parents' involvement in their children's schooling is an important determinant of academic achievement and psychosocial functioning in school. Therapists should assess, therefore, such parental involvement in school-related activities as the following:

- Monitoring homework assignments and exam grades.
- Setting aside a block of time and a quiet place for the child to study after school.
- Supporting extracurricular school functions.
- Implementing contingencies that are based on the child's efforts and performance.
- Providing overt support for teachers' educational demands, behavioral demands, and goals.

Parents do not need a high level of education to make valuable contributions to the child's progress in school. In fact, Stevenson and Baker (1987) demonstrated that mothers' involvement in their children's school activities affects the children's school performance independent of maternal educational status.

Therapists should also examine how school personnel enlist parental support for educational goals. Teachers can elicit such support by, for example:

- Periodically informing parents of their child's progress (rather than contacting parents only when problems emerge).
- Personally inviting parents to the school for conferences.
- Occasionally sending brief progress notes home with the child.

We know of several elementary school teachers, for example, who arrange to visit each child's family before the upcoming school year. Such teacher efforts communicate concern and caring to the parents and facilitate the development of open family–school communication. If academic or behavioral problems arise during the school year, the teacher and parents have already established a groundwork that will facilitate their ability to resolve difficulties. Although a high school teacher with 30 students in each of five classes cannot realistically visit the homes of his or her students, the teacher can initiate personal communication (preferably by phone) when needed to open lines of communication.

PARENTAL ATTITUDES TOWARD EDUCATION

Youth academic and behavioral problems can be exacerbated when academic success is not a high priority for the parents. Many parents do not appreciate the link between education and socioeconomic functioning. Several self-made and financially successful parents have told us, for example, that school is of minimal importance for their children because experience is the best education. Similarly, we have observed socioeconomically disadvantaged parents who, based on their own difficulties in school, have a negative bias toward school and show little interest in their children's education. Expecting a child to be interested in and excited about school when the parents are not is unrealistic. Much of the educational experience is hard work, and children rarely extend considerable academic effort in the absence of parental support and encouragement. Thus, therapists should identify parental attitudes toward the school and try to understand the bases of such attitudes.

PARENT–SCHOOL CONFLICT

Children's school performance usually suffers when conflicts develop between parents and school personnel. Such conflict can be linked with several circumstances, including the following:

- Miscommunications that can occur when parents and educators are of disparate sociocultural backgrounds (e.g., parents might feel intimidated by or resentful of the educators).
- Perceived insults or "putdowns" based on previous interactions between the parents and school personnel.
- The youth playing the parent off against the school (e.g., a youth who convinces his parents that the teacher does not like him and is discriminating against him).
- Parental perceptions that the school is not committed to meeting the needs of the youth.
- The perception of school personnel that the parent has little concern for the youth's performance or behavior in school.

Implementing School-Related Interventions

Setting the Stage for Successful Interventions

The therapist should follow several procedural and process-level guidelines when interacting with educational professionals such as teachers and principals. When the therapist observes these guidelines, most teachers and principals are very cooperative with the therapist's suggestions for school-based interventions. On the other hand, if the therapist ignores the guidelines, his or her suggestions may be resisted.

1. The therapist should respect the hierarchy and operating procedures of the school when initiating contact with school personnel. After obtaining a signed release of information from the parents, permission to talk with teachers and others familiar with the youth should be obtained from the office of the principal or assistant principal. In many schools, for example, the

principal wants to be informed of all contact teachers have with outside professionals regarding a student. In some schools, the assistant principal or a guidance counselor acts as the administrative liaison between the teachers and outside professionals. In such instances, the principal usually asks the therapist to contact the counselor to schedule a meeting with the teachers.

2. Support of the school hierarchy may prove to be crucial in the design of school-related interventions; thus, the therapist should endeavor to create a favorable impression at all levels of the hierarchy. During initial phone and face-to-face conversations, the therapist introduces him- or herself and the rationale for contacting school personnel. He or she should explain that the parents are concerned about certain problems that the youth is presenting and that the therapist would greatly appreciate any information that would assist in the development of effective treatment strategies for the youth. The therapist should stress that information from the youth's educators is especially valuable because of its relative objectivity. The therapist should not say or do anything suggesting that the school may have a substantive role in the maintenance of the child's behavioral problems, even if the therapist is almost certain that the problems are due to school mismanagement. If the therapist even implies that the child's problems are associated with such mismanagement, the educational professionals might become defensive and restrict the flow of information to both the therapist and the parents. In the face of perceived outside threat, most systems (family, school, governmental) respond by becoming less open.

3. During all interactions, the therapist should treat the educational professionals as equal-status colleagues who have particular expertise regarding children's functioning in school environments. Reflecting such an attitude, the therapist should meet school personnel who are knowledgeable about the youth at a time that is convenient for them. In addition, during meetings, the therapist should take a "one-down" position (e.g., conveying respect to the teachers in their role as experts on the child's education), emphasize the gathering of information, and avoid giving unsolicited advice and interpretations. If the child is disrupting the classroom or if the parents are not fully supporting the school's educational and disciplinary efforts, the therapist should empathize with these difficulties without appearing to "side" with the school against the parents, or vice versa. Thus, although the therapist aligned previously with the parents, he or she conveys sincere interest in the educators' perspectives on school-related issues, and the therapist needs to understand these perspectives to design effective interventions. The therapist should stress to school personnel that his or her task is to facilitate the attainment of mutually agreeable outcomes and that important goals from the parents' perspective are to ameliorate the child's behavioral problems and optimize the child's social and academic development. The goals of the family, therapist, and educators are essentially compatible.

4. If, during the conference, the educators request advice regarding the management of the child's behavior, the therapist should feel free to give whatever feedback is appropriate. The therapist might have some specific suggestions or might require additional information before making suggestions. In either case, the therapist should try to respond to the requests of school personnel. Finally, at the conclusion of the conference, the therapist should express appreciation for the teachers' and administrators' assistance and ask if those attending would be willing to assist the therapist in the implementation of interventions, if necessary.

Implementing Interventions

During the initial meeting with school personnel, the therapist should explain that requested assistance from teachers, coaches, and so on. will most likely take two general forms. First, the therapist would appreciate feedback from these individuals regarding the logic and probability of success of recommendations for school-related interventions. Such feedback and the therapist's flexible response to the feedback will enhance the school's cooperation with these interventions. Second, the therapist should ask if select school personnel would be willing to devote several minutes per day to assist in the implementation of therapeutic interventions. Because teachers and school administrators are generally underpaid and overworked, most will hesitate to devote an inordinate percentage of their time to the needs of one behavioral problem student. Hence, the therapist's recommendations for school-based interventions should require as little of their time as possible. In fact, parents should take most of the responsibility for school-related interventions (e.g., by implementing contingencies at home that are based on the youth's behavior in school). Such an arrangement fosters parental cooperation with the school and helps to ensure the school's continued support of treatment efforts.

After the therapist obtains the information needed to design the interventions and develops intervention plans in collaboration with the parents, the therapist should recontact the pertinent school personnel and set a conjoint meeting with the parents. During this meeting, the therapist and parents should provide a general overview of the presenting problems and of their proposed intervention plan. This overview can refer to family problems but should do so in only a very general way. For example, the therapist might indicate that the family is currently under a great deal of stress and that treatment is attempting to help family members cope with this stress. The therapist does not need to specify the exact nature of the stress (e.g., parental separation, incest, or alcoholism) but should attempt to elicit the school personnel's empathy with the family's overall situation. Thus, the therapist and parents should communicate that the family is actively attempting to resolve problems associated with the youth and hope to gain the school's cooperation in these efforts. Previously, school personnel may have viewed the parents' failure to seek professional help, in the face of serious problems, as an indication of their lack of support not only for the child but also for the school's efforts to educate the child.

The goals of the meeting between the therapist, parents, and school personnel, therefore, are to do the following:

1. Clarify that all parties have the youth's best interest at heart.
2. Explain the rationale (i.e., fit) of the proposed interventions to all parties.
3. Provide an opportunity to revise the proposed interventions, pending additional input from school personnel (assuming that any revisions are approved by the parents and therapist).
4. Delineate the exact responsibilities of each party vis-à-vis the interventions, with the parents assuming the bulk of the responsibility.
5. Develop a system for monitoring implementation and outcome of the interventions.
6. Develop a system for providing all parties with feedback regarding the outcomes.
7. Delineate strategies for revising the school-related intervention protocol, with the parents and therapists taking responsibility for such.

Assuming that the family and school collaborate successfully in the intervention planning and implementation process, the following types of interventions may be appropriate for addressing identified academic and social difficulties. Suggestions for overcoming significant barriers to planning and implementation (e.g., an obstreperous principal and an extremely angry parent) are presented at the end of this chapter.

Intellectual and Academic Abilities

When academic and social difficulties in school are associated with low intellectual abilities, several therapeutic issues may arise in regard to the family system, the child, and the school system. First, parents must learn to appreciate their child's intellectual strengths and weaknesses. For example, parents must reward and respect the child's maximum academic achievements (e.g., grades in the C range) to the same degree that they might reinforce a more intelligent sibling's highest achievements (e.g., grades in the A range). In meetings with the parents (where the adolescent is not present), the therapist can promote acceptance of the child's academic limitations by emphasizing his or her psychosocial strengths and how these strengths are often more strongly associated with successful adult functioning than is academic achievement. For example, perhaps the child is well liked by peers or has maintained a high level of motivation despite academic difficulties. The therapist might note that success in many occupations is determined more by motivation and strong interpersonal skills than by intellectual abilities. Likewise, qualities such as kindness, generosity, and a sense of humor are often more important than intelligence in the development of friendships and successful family relations. Many individuals who did not do well in school have rich and fulfilling lives as adults. Although the MST-referred youth may need considerable work to develop the aforementioned qualities of motivation and generosity, at least learning that the youth's poor academic performance is directly linked with low intellectual abilities helps to prioritize targets for intervention (e.g., less effort directed at raising grades and more effort at sustaining reasonable efforts and developing other skills).

With highly achievement-oriented families, the therapist should reframe the value of academic achievement. For example, a percentage of youth in MST programs come from homes in which the parents hold professional degrees, have high aspirations for the youth, and are frustrated by the youth's poor academic performance. When poor performance is linked with low abilities, the therapist might remind such parents that the developmental tasks of childhood and adolescence include more important goals than obtaining good course grades. The child might benefit more in the long run, for example, if the parents encouraged the development of close friendships with prosocial peers and the building of competencies in such diverse activities as athletics and the arts. Similarly, the parents should be told that their intense educational efforts may have an effect that is the opposite of the one intended. After several years of academic frustration and failure to achieve up to parental expectations, many children rebel in a potentially destructive manner. The primary task, then, is to determine how to capitalize on the youth's strengths to promote long-term vocational success (e.g., placing energy into developing a viable trade versus academic success).

A second focus of intervention may pertain to the child's attitudes and self-efficacy. In some cases, low-achieving children feel incompetent, especially if the family strongly emphasizes academic achievement. In a treatment process similar to that described for the parents, the therapist and parents should provide child with a broader view of his or her strengths and weaknesses. Although the youth might not be gifted intellectually, the therapist and parents should stress the significance of his or her emotional and interpersonal strengths. The youth should learn to be proud of these strengths and to value them highly. Moreover, the therapist and parents should emphasize to the youth that motivation and effort are extremely important strengths to cultivate. If, despite reasonable effort, the child earns a poor grade, it should not be viewed negatively. Instead, parents should reward the effort expended and help motivate the child to make reasonable efforts. In addition, energies of the parents and school personnel (i.e., coaches, club advisers, and teachers) should be devoted to identifying and developing strengths that can be used to promote favorable long-term outcomes (e.g., skills as a mechanic or skills as a salesperson).

The third focus of intervention pertains to the school context. Because the child with low intellectual abilities might fail more often than he or she succeeds, the teachers should be encouraged to reinforce the child's efforts rather than waiting to reinforce the successes. If the child's achievement is substantially below that of classmates, the child might also benefit from resource assistance, tutoring, and placement in classes that emphasize the youth's strengths.

Mental Health and Psychosocial Functioning

Assessment should have delineated how the youth's emotional and behavioral difficulties are linked with academic and social functioning in the school context and vice versa. If difficulties are evidenced at home but not at school, school-related interventions may be unnecessary. School personnel should be acknowledged for their skill in meeting the youth's needs and asked to help the parents track the effects of home-based interventions on the youth's behavior in the school setting (e.g., does an intervention in one setting have repercussions for behavior in another setting?). On the other hand, if difficulties are evidenced primarily in the school setting but not at home, the therapist should refer to subsequent sections, "The Learning Environment" and "Family–School Linkage," on intervening.

The most likely scenario, however, is that the youth presents difficulties across home and school settings. In such cases, the therapist's and parents' task is to develop a collaborative relationship with school personnel so that the same types of treatment goals and interventions developed for the home and neighborhood can be extended to the problems that school personnel identified in the school setting:

1. James was a 14-year-old juvenile offender who engaged in criminal activities and drug use with his friends in the neighborhood and frequently engaged in acting-out behaviors with his classmates at school. One focus of treatment was to severely limit James's association with deviant peers in the neighborhood while attempting to integrate him into athletic programs, as athletic skill was one of his strengths. Because he was in a self-contained class for emotionally disturbed youth at school, by definition, James was associating with deviant peers at school for 6 hours per day. The collaboration among the parent, therapist, and educators, therefore, aimed to (a) develop a plan for moving James to a regular classroom with well-specified steps and criteria for

accomplishing this goal; (b) in the interim, restructure his place in the special education class to minimize contact with the most deviant of his classmates (e.g., James was moved to sit nearest the teacher, and opportunities to integrate with nonproblem classmates were developed for certain academic subjects); and (c) use the strengths of the school to promote the overarching goal of reducing association with deviant peers. Here, athletics provided an excellent after-school prosocial activity, and a coach was included as a collaborator in the plan. Importantly, to increase the probability of successful engagement in after school activities, the parent and therapist provided support for the coach for handling difficulties that James might present in the athletic context.

2. Stan was a 15-year-old juvenile offender who specialized in stealing cars and behaving irresponsibly. At home, Stan lived well—coming and going as he pleased and helping himself to whatever resources (e.g., clean clothing and food) were available. At school, when Stan did attend, he often slept (having stayed out most of the previous evening) and rarely worked. As Stan's mother developed the support system and skills needed for her to regain parental authority, and as Stan's level of responsible behavior increased at home (e.g., meeting curfew and doing chores), plans were made in collaboration with school personnel to promote his responsible behavior in the school context. In this case, the primary interventions involved having Stan's teachers inform his mother daily of the extent of his responsible behavior (i.e., defined as staying awake and extending effort) on a 1–10 scale, and the mother implemented contingencies at home.

The theme of these cases is the same: parents and school personnel collaborating to provide consistent interventions for conceptually similar problems (association with deviant peers with James, irresponsible behavior with Stan) across home and school settings, with the parents assuming responsibility for the bulk of the work and the strengths of the systems being used to facilitate change (e.g., after-school opportunities for prosocial outlets for James and the development of maternal competencies for Stan).

Family Functioning

Unfortunately, many families referred for MST present such serious family-related difficulties that the development of family–school collaborations must be postponed until such difficulties have abated. For example, a single mother is addicted to cocaine, a youth is suicidal, or the children are being victimized. Here, the therapist's first priority should be to help family members cope with existing crises and to ameliorate serious family problems that compromise the safety of the children, as described in Chapter 3. Because the lasting success (Principle 9) of school-related interventions is predicated on caregiver support of and collaboration with the interventions, the therapist may need to delay the implementation of treatments in the school setting (though the therapist should not delay the school-based assessment, as obtaining multiple perspectives on child and family functioning is crucial to understanding fit [Principle 1]) until some stability in caregiving is achieved.

On the other hand, even in the context of serious family difficulties, the therapist should not delay certain school-related interventions. For example, if the youth is at imminent risk of expulsion, the therapist may need to intervene as the parent's proxy when the parent and family indicate they are not yet capable of advocating for the youth. The therapist must remember, however, that long-term outcomes for the youth will be driven by the therapist's capacity to build the competency of the parental caregiver to collaborate with school personnel. Thus, although expulsion from school may have been avoided at this time, the family's capacity to address future difficulties was not influenced. Similarly, when a caregiver faces multiple legal, employment, and family challenges simultaneously, or in the absence of requisite caregiver competence, the therapist may need to assume a larger than preferred role in making certain school-related interventions and decisions (e.g., should the child be retained a grade or placed in a special class?). Such treatment emphases, however, should never take priority over building the capacity of the child's natural ecology to make these decisions. In other words, the vast majority of the MST therapist's time should be devoted to developing family capacity (e.g., accessing psychiatric consultation for the mother with bipolar disorder and finding an alternative caregiver in the family's kinship network for the single parent who will not address his or her drug dependence) rather than to personally addressing identified problems at school or elsewhere—except when needed to avoid extremely deleterious outcomes.

The Learning Environment

Teacher incompetence and administrative indifference are not the types of problems that the therapist can ameliorate. Therapist and parent complaints to school administrators regarding such problems are likely to have little effect. Like most social institutions, school systems are highly resistant to change and do not respond favorably to protagonists from outside the system. Thus, when a child's psychosocial and academic problems are associated with the incompetence of school personnel, we rarely recommend that this issue be addressed directly. Such tactics are unlikely to achieve positive results and may result in subtle forms of retaliation against the youth.

We are not suggesting that the MST therapist never confront the educational system but that the decision regarding confrontation should be taken very seriously and should weigh the cost/benefit ratio of the possible outcomes. In serious situations (e.g., the youth is facing expulsion), the cost of inaction can be very high, and the therapist should support and encourage the parents to strongly advocate for their child's rights. In one such situation, for example, school personnel were attempting to expel a youth from school for a relatively minor infraction (though the youth had numerous serious infractions in the past) even though significant positive changes in home and school behavior had been made in recent months. The therapist gladly acted as an advocate on the youth's and family's behalf. In another case, a teacher was verbally abusive to an 8-year-old girl with serious emotional disturbance, the school was being unresponsive to the parents' request for corrective action, and the therapist, therefore, supported the parents' efforts to seek a legal remedy to the situation.

If the therapist and parents do not address school incompetence directly, what should the parents do when such incompetence is linked with their child's academic and social problems? The answer varies with the timing of the academic year:

• In the beginning of the school year, the therapist might provide the parents with strategies for convincing the principal to allow the child to change teachers—in an attempt to optimize child–teacher fit (Swartz & Martin, 1997).

• At the end of the school year, the therapist might advise the parents that it is too late to effect any substantial change and that energies should be devoted to ensuring appropriate placements for the upcoming school year.

• The situation is more problematic during the middle of the school year. In such cases, we typically recommend that the parents establish frequent contact with school personnel and attempt to make this contact as cordial as possible. The professed purpose of this contact is for the parents to assist school personnel in educating the youth. Three covert purposes, however, are that (1) periodic contact with the parents might encourage school staff to feel more accountable for their performance, (2) positive parent–school contact may lay the groundwork for improved efforts by school personnel or may provide the parents with a better case if they eventually choose to confront the school administration directly, and (3) frequent parent–school meetings may reduce the parents' anxieties and feelings of helplessness.

In rare instances, teacher incompetence is not an isolated phenomenon and, with the administration's tacit approval, a laissez-faire attitude toward education has been adopted by most of the school's faculty. In such cases, the only viable alternative is to enroll the child in a different school. Unfortunately, this alternative may present logistic and financial hardships for the family that are more problematic than the child's low achievement. Here, the therapist and parents may be forced to choose among several unsatisfactory alternatives. If the decision is made to stay at the same school, the therapist may help the parents link with parents of other students to obtain support in coping with a bad situation and problem solve together when possible. Increased social support and coping strategies may help buffer the negative effects of keeping the child enrolled in an inadequate school.

Family–School Linkage

MST therapists should encourage parents' involvement in their children's educational experiences. In many cases, the parents are already involved and may benefit from suggestions regarding the remediation of specific problems such as low child motivation or reading difficulties. In other cases, family members might not appreciate the significance of the family–school linkage. Here, the therapist can give concrete examples of the long-term effects of education on socioeconomic achievements. Specifically, for example, the lifetime earnings of high school graduates are hundreds of thousands of dollars higher than the earnings of high school dropouts, and a similar discrepancy exists between the lifetime earnings of college graduates versus high school graduates. Placing a dollar value on educational achievements helps to get the point across to most parents. In addition to enhancing parental appreciation for the benefits of education, the therapist must be prepared to recommend specific ways for the parents to foster their child's achievement and to facilitate family–school linkages.

FOSTERING ACADEMIC ACHIEVEMENT

To avoid embarrassment in educational situations that involve their children, many parents with little formal education either minimize the importance of education or avoid educational situations entirely. Teachers, in turn, often interpret lack of parental involvement as an absence of concern for the child's welfare. In fact, the low achievement of economically disadvantaged children is often attributed to family apathy toward education (Knitzer et al., 1990). In such cases, we emphasize to the parents that, in many ways, they can have a greater impact on their child's education than teachers by expressing high interest in the child's performance and supporting the child's efforts. Specifically, for example, the parents can do the following:

- Inquire about what the child learned in school that day.
- Ask to see the child's classwork.
- Inquire about test results and impending exams.
- Have frequent contact with the child's teacher.
- Sit near the child while he or she is doing homework.
- Express joy in the child's efforts and achievements.

The parents can also restructure home life in ways that promote education. For example, the parents can do the following:

- Establish a study hour during which all outside distractions (e.g., music, telephone, and television) are eliminated.
- Buy inexpensive used magazines and books for the children to read.

These aforementioned family-based interventions can have a greater impact on the motivation and achievement of low-achieving inner-city middle-school students than equally intensive school-based interventions (Rodick & Henggeler, 1980). In a well-controlled study, a random sample of the parents of low-achieving students were recruited to follow a program similar to that advocated by Rev. Jesse Jackson's "PUSH for Excellence" program. Parents and adolescents agreed to work together for approximately 1 hour per weeknight to enhance academic progress. During this time, the television, radio, and other distractions were kept to a minimum, and the parents shared any of a variety of high-interest readings (e.g., sports magazines and fashion magazines) or school-related tasks with their adolescent. In addition, the parents were encouraged to become more actively involved in monitoring their children's performance in school, completion of homework, and so on.

Results from a standardized test battery administered at a 6-month follow-up showed that the participants in the family-based intervention, in contrast with counterparts in three school-based intervention control groups, showed improved vocabulary skills, reading recognition, and reading comprehension. These results demonstrated two important points. First, parents who might seem apathetic toward education are often very willing to make changes to facilitate their children's educational achievement. It is noteworthy that all families in the family-based program were selected at random and agreed to participate in the project. Moreover, at the 6-month follow-up, more than half of these families continued the home-based interventions after the project was formally terminated. Second, these findings clearly show that parental involvement in the remediation of their children's academic and motivational difficulties facilitated academic gains. This remediation required a restructuring of the family home environment and the initiation of parental participation in the child's learning process using an approach that acknowledged and valued the parents' capabilities and emphasized the strengths of the families.

LINKING PARENTS WITH SCHOOLS

As noted earlier, a major cause of parental avoidance of the school system is that parents feel intimidated by the school context. We have observed that avoidant parents are often illiterate; they have low arithmetic skills and poor vocabularies. In addition, school personnel often use jargon and acronyms that are foreign to parents (and therapists!). In interactions with more highly educated school personnel, the parents' pride may inhibit revealing their lack of understanding regarding the teachers' communications and recommendations. The therapist may take several steps in promoting family–school collaboration.

1. Help parents to appreciate the importance of education for their children's future economic viability.
2. Help parents to appreciate the fact that they can have more powerful effects on achievement than teachers (Rodick & Henggeler, 1980).
3. Throughout the process of assessment and design of interventions, help to develop the collaborative capabilities of the parents (i.e., empowering the parents)—including the ability to advocate assertively for the child and to reinforce and support the school's educational efforts.
4. Help to identify and overcome any barriers to success (e.g., repeated sequences of negative interaction between parents and school personnel, parental anxiety and fear, and a teacher's bias).
5. During the assessment process, also set the stage with school personnel for family collaboration—by emphasizing the parents' true concern for their children's well-being and the family's current efforts to address identified problems. Thus, the therapist should be building positive expectations in the minds of the school personnel.
6. Prior to conjoint parent, therapist, and school meetings (as noted earlier in the chapter), prepare the parent for the meeting, role-playing, and practicing responses to the various items on the agenda developed by the parent and therapist.
7. During the meeting, be sensitive to the parent's connection with school personnel, and conclude the meeting with the specification of formalized linkages and communications between the parent and select educators (i.e., the collaborative treatment plan).
8. Monitor the subsequent success of the planned communications and help the parent to problem solve when difficulties emerge.

In general, then, the process of empowering the parent vis-à-vis the youth's school environment is similar to the process of empowering the parent to assume control of the home environment. Assessment aims to understand the fit of noninvolvement with the school. Interventions are strength focused, targeting well-specified goals. Outcomes are monitored constantly, and barriers to attaining outcomes are identified and addressed.

Barriers: High Family–School Conflict

Throughout this chapter, we discussed strategies for addressing several common barriers to developing strong family–school linkages. These barriers include, for example, severe family difficulties, ineffective schools, and parental embarrassment. Here, a significant and difficult barrier frequently observed for families of youth referred for MST is addressed: intense family–school conflict.

Occasionally, animosities between the family and school are so severe that the aforementioned recommendations for developing family–school collaborations are insufficient. In our experience, for example, youth referred for MST have assaulted and threatened teachers with homicide, and parents of MST-referred youth have assaulted principals and threatened school personnel with deadly weapons. In such situations, tensions run high and parents and school personnel, literally, cannot sit down together at the same table. Such circumstances clearly threaten the attainment of key MST goals: placing the youth on a favorable long-term trajectory with regard to educational and vocational functioning.

Before attempting to resolve intense conflict, the therapist and family should determine whether placement in a different school is a viable option. In weighing the pros and cons of such placement, factors such as geographic location, the quality of academic and vocational programs, and the possible amenability of personnel at that school should be considered. If transferring schools is a viable option, the therapist should help the parents to develop a collaborative relationship with the personnel in the new school, per the recommendations presented throughout this chapter. If, on the other hand, transferring schools is not a productive alternative, plans must be made to attenuate family–school conflict.

Resolving situations of intense family–school conflict to promote the long-term interests of the youth presents a major challenge for the MST practitioner—a challenge that tests his or her clinical skills. The therapist, however, has a unique set of strengths that can be used to attenuate family–school animosity. He or she (1) has experience resolving interpersonal conflict; (2) can be viewed as a neutral observer by both parties (at least to some extent); (3) has the clinical resources of the MST treatment team, supervisor, and consultant; and (4) has the administrative connections afforded by the MST project (e.g., a member of the school board on the project's community advisory board). The following guidelines are recommended for therapists confronted with intense family–school conflict:

1. Significant energy must be devoted to understanding the family's and the school's perspective on the conflict. The goal should be for both parties (parents and school personnel) to believe that the therapist appreciates and

empathizes with their viewpoint. In other words, the family and the school should view the therapist as their advocate.

2. When the therapist gains the trust of the family and school, and only after developing an alliance with both parties, he or she is in a position to gently challenge certain aspects of the family's view that the school is totally at fault and the school's view that the family is totally at fault. Challenging these views creates tension, but the therapist's task is to begin to help each party understand the other's perspective.

3. To facilitate such understanding, the therapist should emphasize the strengths of the respective systems and, again, align with each. For example, the therapist might indicate to the parents, "I spent 2 hours with Ms. Jones, Riley's teacher, and I truly believe that she cares about his best interests and wants the best for him. The problem is that she is afraid of him, afraid of you, and honestly feels that you don't care about Riley's education, though I know that's not true." At the same time, the therapist might indicate to the school, "You may find this hard to believe, but Riley's mom and dad have great hopes and dreams for his future and see education as a way of realizing those dreams. The problem is that they honestly believe that the school has discriminated against their son and are very angry about it, though I know that the school has gone out of its way to be fair in this case."

4. The therapist then searches for and accentuates common ground between the parents and school personnel. Common ground usually includes the desired social and academic behavior of the youth—well-behaved and performing satisfactorily.

5. When common ground is identified and at least some understanding of the other's perspective is gained, the therapist can begin to prepare the parties for a face-to-face meeting. Although the therapist will be tempted to serve as a go-between throughout the intervention process, such a role is not consistent with Principle 9. The time will come when the parents and school need to collaborate without the guidance of a therapist, and the present circumstance provides an excellent opportunity to practice such collaboration.

6. In preparing for the meeting, the therapist should role-play with the parents and discuss, as a colleague, the agenda with the school personnel. The therapist should set the behavioral guidelines for the meeting, stating, emphatically, that one item not on the agenda is determining who was at fault for previous problems. Such discussion is a "no win" situation and only leads to deteriorating communication between the parties. Rather, the focus of the meeting should be on developing a collaborative plan for addressing the youth's school-related problems.

7. With coaching and extremely close monitoring (e.g., interrupting and redirecting any "blaming" type of communication), the therapist will have placed the family and school systems in a position where collaboration is possible and the other recommendations in this chapter may be viable.

Case Illustration

A case example, borrowed from Schoenwald et al. (1997),[*] is used to illustrate key issues related to the assessment and delivery of school-related interventions from an MST perspective.

Jason, a 15-year-old ninth-grader, failed the ninth grade for his second time and was referred for MST. He had displayed significant behavioral problems since the age of 12 and had been suspended several times. Jason's troublesome behaviors at school included oppositional responses to teacher requests, refusal to follow through with schoolwork, verbal disruption of the classroom, repeated truancy, and occasional threats to teachers. Jason also fought with peers, and his best friends were a group of difficult children (i.e., children who would get in trouble for fighting, verbal abuse of the teacher, and oppositionality). Jason had recently been charged with vandalism.

Individual Factors

In assessing the fit between these behaviors and the total ecology (Principle 1), the therapist identified several aspects of Jason's educational experience that appeared to contribute to his troublesome behavior at school. A review of Jason's records, which included scores from intelligence and educational testing completed 2 years prior to referral, suggested that he possessed average intelligence and was capable of maintaining academic pace with his age mates. When educational testing data are not available, the MST therapist may recommend that testing be performed to rule out the possibility that significant intellectual deficits are interfering with academic performance, or to identify areas in which the child may require additional assistance. The therapist also determined, during the course of family, individual, and school meetings, that Jason's academic performance problems did not appear to stem from some type of psychological difficulty (e.g., anxiety, fear of failure, or trauma-related symptoms).

Classroom Factors

In talking with Jason's teachers, the therapist learned that Jason's behavior was somewhat manageable in some classrooms, and quite obstreperous in others. The therapist arranged to observe Jason in several classrooms, and found that his behavior was most obnoxious in the presence of a group of students who egged each other into frivolity, inattention, and acting out.

---

[*]Adapted from Schoenwald et al. (1997, pp. 199–202). Copyright 1997 by Lawrence Erlbaum Associates. Adapted by permission.

Jason's conflict with teachers occurred primarily when Jason was reprimanded for "cutting up" with his classmates. Thus, the therapist identified a consistent correlate of Jason's obnoxious behavior with peers and teachers, and on the basis of this evidence tentatively ruled out cognitive ability and psychological factors as major contributors to Jason's behavior problems.

Family–School Linkage

Next, the MST therapist began to develop an intervention plan in collaboration with Jason's parents and pertinent school personnel. At this juncture, the therapist found that communications between Jason's parents and the school had become quite contentious. Consistent with the MST emphasis on empowering families and facilitating long-term generalization of treatment gains (Principle 9), the MST therapist tried to forge a family–school alliance rather than proceeding with intervention plans from the position of go-between. As often occurs, the process of reestablishing productive family–school communications was met with significant reluctance on both sides. Parents and school personnel perceived one another as "responsible" for Jason's behavioral problems, which led to conflict and active avoidance of parent–teacher interactions. Moreover, parent–school contact occurred primarily around issues of discipline, suspension, or expulsion, which further reinforced a negative pattern of family–school interactions.

To lay the groundwork needed to develop a viable family–school collaboration, the therapist developed a premeeting role-play with Jason's father that mimicked the (real-life) situation in which the father was accused of being a "bad parent" and given unsolicited advice on how to raise his children. Through consistent practice (i.e., three sessions, on subsequent days, lasting 1 hour each), Jason's father was increasingly able to complete the role-played scenarios without overt displays of anger. He participated in two strategy planning meetings with Jason's teachers that included the MST therapist. In the second meeting, the MST therapist consciously limited her participation to allow the parents and teachers to arrive at mutually desired solutions.

Over the course of these meetings, problem areas requiring attention at school and home were identified. Initially, two intervention strategies were implemented; one targeted the negative influence of antisocial peers on Jason's classroom behavior, and the other focused on linking Jason's behavior at school with consequences at home. With respect to the first, teachers presiding over classrooms in which Jason exhibited significant behavioral problems negotiated seating arrangements so that Jason was detached from antisocial peers.

Connecting Behavior at School with Consequences at Home

A plan was developed in which Jason would receive significant consequences *at home* for his behavior *at school*. A positive report sent home by a teacher (i.e., active participation and lack of misbehavior) earned Jason a maximum of 30 minutes of Nintendo per evening. If Jason received a negative report, he was required to spend an additional 30 minutes studying and 30 minutes doing chores that evening. In addition to connecting consequences at home with behavior at school, the MST therapist worked directly with the family to identify barriers at home that might prevent Jason's completion of his homework. The family ensured that both a place and time for homework completion were provided during every evening. In addition, the family agreed that all televisions and radios would be turned off for the hour after dinner and the parents would read or work quietly during that time. This agreement presented a marked change for all family members (siblings included), as the family was accustomed to having the television on from morning until bedtime. Moreover, distractions were minimized and Jason's parents demonstrated, concretely, the value they placed on their son's academic performance. As the therapist expected, on the basis of initial and ongoing assessment of Jason's family and the subsystems that it comprised, issues related to parental management of the siblings' displeasure about the television policy surfaced, as did differences between Jason's parents regarding the best way to manage the siblings during the quiet hour. In consultation with the parents, intervention strategies designed to increase interparental consistency and parental capacity to effectively manage sibling relations were implemented.

Initially, the family–school interventions were quite successful, as indicated by reports from teachers, parents, and Jason (see Principle 8). However, despite teacher consistency in keeping Jason and his problematic peers separated, Jason and the peers found new ways to act up in class. Together with the therapist, the parents decided that Jason's mother (she was not employed outside the home at the time) would attend school with Jason, sitting beside him in each class in which he had trouble. By the beginning of the third day, Jason's level of discomfort with this arrangement was so great that he agreed to attend to his responsibilities more consistently and began to do so. In addition, the therapist and Jason's parents began to explore interventions to decrease Jason's association with antisocial peers in school (interventions implemented earlier in treatment had successfully reduced his involvement with antisocial peers after school and on weekends).

7

When and How to Conduct
Individually Oriented Interventions

In this chapter
- Individual factors as barriers to engagement or change.
- The assessment process and deciding on individual versus ecological interventions.
- Cognitive-behavioral interventions used with individual adults and youth in the context of MST.

The purpose of this chapter is to assist the practitioner in determining whether, when, and how to implement individual treatment for a parent or adolescent in the context of MST. Although some individually oriented techniques are subsumed within ecologically based intervention strategies (e.g., altering beliefs that sustain permissive or authoritarian parenting and role-playing a parent's negotiations with the school principal), the current chapter focuses on circumstances in which MST therapists engage in individual treatment with a family member on a continuous, albeit time-limited, basis.

In our experience, team (i.e., practitioner and clinical supervisor) decisions to pursue individual treatment with parent figures most often (1) pertain to problems that interfere with parental functioning, such as depression, anxiety disorders, and substance abuse; and (2) are made at two "ends" of the MST treatment period. These two ends are:

1. Early in treatment, if the parent figure's functioning is compromised so frequently or to such an extent that the practitioner is unable to

172

develop a working alliance, identify the parent's treatment goals, or engage the parent in making even minor changes toward a goal he or she has identified as important.

2. Well into treatment, when interventions targeting intrafamilial (parent–child, marital, kin) or extrafamilial (family–school, peer, neighborhood) interactions have been implemented inconsistently or implemented with poor results, and specific aspects of the parent's functioning are identified as critical barriers to implementation or success.

With respect to adolescents, four types of situations can warrant the implementation of individual interventions. These are:

1. When a youth continues to display serious aggressive or impulsive behaviors in one or more contexts (e.g., in the classroom, with certain peers, and with siblings) after systemic interventions have been consistently implemented by parents, teachers, and other relevant players in the youth's natural ecology.
2. When a youth with biologically influenced difficulties (e.g., ADHD, bipolar disorder, or clinical depression) is consistently taking appropriately prescribed medication and well-implemented ecological interventions are in place, yet, problems with impulsive or aggressive behavior continue to occur at home, in school, or with peers.
3. When the sequelae of victimization (i.e., physical abuse, sexual abuse, and criminal victimization) contribute to referral problems.
4. When intensive and comprehensive efforts to engage caregivers in changing parenting practices or other aspects of the youth's ecology are unsuccessful, efforts to overcome barriers to change are unsuccessful, and the adolescent will continue to live in a home in which the lack of favorable clinical change will exacerbate the identified problems.

For all but the last circumstance, the MST practitioner tailors empirically validated cognitive-behavioral interventions to the specific needs of the youth and engages relevant family members, teachers, and community members (e.g., youth group leader and coach, neighbor) in modeling, coaching, and reinforcing the new ways of thinking and behaving. In the fourth circumstance, a combination of cognitive-behavioral and supportive interventions for the youth is augmented with efforts to build relationships with one or more adults (e.g., relative, teacher, minister, and parent of a prosocial peer) who can provide needed nurturance and guidance for the youth on a consistent and ongoing basis.

Cognitive-Behavioral Therapies

Rationale for Use in MST

Several rationales underlie the selection of cognitive-behavioral interventions as a first choice for individual treatment in the context of MST. Cognitive-behavioral therapies:

- Demonstrate efficacy with depressive and anxiety disorders in adults (for reviews, see A. T. Beck, 1993; Chambless & Gillis, 1993; Hollon, Shelton, & Davis, 1993).
- Show promise with aggressive behavioral and social skills problems in youth when augmented with interventions engaging parents and teachers (for reviews, see Kazdin, 1994; Kendall, 1993).
- Are consistent with several principles of MST.

With respect to the latter point, cognitive behavioral interventions are present focused and action oriented (Principle 4); tailored to the level of cognitive development of the youth (Principle 6); evaluated from multiple perspectives (Principle 8); and, when applied with youth, require active parent or teacher support to assist with generalization to natural settings (Principle 9). In addition, the role of the cognitive-behavioral therapist as an active, directive, but flexible collaborator (J. S. Beck, 1995; Meichenbaum, 1993) is compatible with MST. In contrast with MST, however, cognitive-behavioral theory and treatment focus relatively little on the fit of behavior with interactions within and between multiple systems (Principle 1); are not explicitly strength focused (Principle 3); and, while engaging the parent in reinforcing particular cognitions and behaviors of the youth, do not explicitly empower families to manage multiple aspects of the youth's environment (Principle 9). Essentially, the targets of cognitive-behavioral interventions are narrowly focused relative to MST. Thus, within the context of MST, such interventions are used to address specific problems that present barriers to engagement or systemic change, or when changes in the ecology are insufficient to ameliorate aspects of individual functioning related to the referral problem.

Basic Concepts of Cognitive-Behavioral Therapies

Cognitive behavioral procedures focus on the nature of individuals' beliefs, expectancies, perceptions, and attributions about themselves and others and on the relationships between these cognitions and the individual's feelings and behavior. Cognitive-behavioral interventions emphasize cognitive information processing factors but also are concerned with changing the individual's overt behavior, particularly in the context of interpersonal interactions. Thus, the interventions consider the influence of others in the environment on the individual's thoughts, feelings, and behaviors.

Two constructs are central to most cognitive-behavioral interventions: cognitive deficiencies and cognitive distortions. Each represents a particular type of information processing problem, and research supports their relevance to difficulties in functioning associated with depression and anxiety in adults and children and with aggressive behavior in children. Individuals characterized by cognitive deficiencies demonstrate insufficient thinking in situations that require forethought prior to taking action (e.g., they act impulsively). Individuals characterized by cognitive distortions act in accordance with faulty thinking, as occurs with depressed individuals who see routine negative events as disasters or with aggressive teens who interpret inadvertent jostling in a line as intentional and hostile. From a cognitive-behavioral perspective, individuals—children or adults—with problems related to impulse control need treatment that provides them with skills to overcome their cognitive deficiencies, and individuals with symptoms of depression or anxiety need to have their cognitive distortions corrected so that they do not misinterpret their environment or their own actions (Kendall & Braswell, 1993).

A variety of clinical manuals on cognitive-behavioral interventions have been written. Practitioners who have limited familiarity with empirically validated cognitive-behavioral techniques may benefit by reading *Cognitive Therapy: Basics and Beyond* (J. S. Beck, 1995), which presents both the rationale underlying cognitive-behavioral interventions and concrete, step-by-step instruction in the use of common cognitive-behavioral techniques. In addition, worksheets to help the practitioner and client with each step appear throughout Beck's volume. The MST practitioner, however, may need to adapt these tools to the developmental and literacy level of the individual adult or youth, and to accommodate the demands of other MST interventions. Developmentally appropriate adaptations for youth are presented in *Coping Skills Interventions for Children and Adolescents* (Forman, 1993) and *Cognitive-Behavioral Therapy for Impulsive Children* (Kendall & Braswell, 1993). Additional MST supervision should also be obtained when implementing cognitive-behavioral interventions for the first time, as incomplete, haphazard, or inconsistent use of the interventions greatly diminish their effectiveness.

Individual Interventions with Parental Figures

Assessing and Addressing Barriers to Engagement and Change

On occasion, the MST practitioner is unable to develop a productive therapeutic alliance in spite of repeated efforts to locate and meet a parent figure, to understand the life of the parent and family through the parent's eyes, and to identify strengths of the parent and family. In such instances the therapist should assess concrete (e.g., long work hours, lack of child care, and inadequate transportation), systemic (e.g., marital, family, and kinship relations), and service system factors that may be linked with the difficulty to engage. With respect to service system factors, for example, practitioner behavior (e.g., failure to understand the parent's goals, inadvertent use of blaming language, and displays of frustration) and negative experiences with mental health, social service, juvenile justice, and education agencies should be examined, as such practitioner behavior and agency experiences may contribute to a parent's initial avoidance, skepticism, or rejection of MST (Federation of Families for Children's Mental Health, 1995). MST practitioners should bear in mind, therefore, the lessons the family offers regarding positive and negative experiences with other providers and clarify the nature of MST if misconceptions (e.g., the practitioner will blame the parents for the child's problems, can take the child away, or can have the child arrested) become apparent.

When systemic and ecological factors fail to account for barriers to engagement or therapeutic progress, barriers posed by individual factors are examined. In adult caregivers, depression, anxiety, ADHD symptoms, other treatable psychiatric disorders, recent or past victimization, and substance abuse are common candidates. When investigating the role of individual factors in the fit of presenting problems, *the practitioner's task is always to determine whether and how the factors constitute critical barriers to a parent's capacity to engage in MST.* To accomplish this task, the practitioner needs all of the following:

- Reliable evidence that the problem (depression, substance abuse, ADHD, anxiety) exists, which, in turn, requires practitioner familiarity with the hallmark symptoms of these problems.
- Observations or self-reports of interactions within the family and between the caregiver and other systems indicating that the caregiver is consistently unable or unwilling to make certain changes in behavior, even when she or he as sufficient knowledge, skills, and resources to do so.
- Evidence that the caregiver's failure to make the behavioral change helps to maintain or exacerbate the identified problems.
- Evidence that the psychiatric problem or substance abuse, as opposed to other factors (e.g., marital problems, practical needs, skill or knowledge deficits, and a history of adversarial relations with school officials) is a powerful predictor of the youth's identified problems.

Individual interventions should be designed only when the preceding criteria are met.

Depression

ASSESSMENT

As noted in Chapter 3, depression can interfere with caregiver responses to the affective needs of their children, to appropriate monitoring and discipline of the children, or to acquisition of social support. Along with the sad mood, adults with depression experience increases or decreases in sleep and/or appetite, lack of interest in usual activities (i.e., an avid bowler no longer bowls and a tidy homemaker stops cleaning) and loss of interest in sex. More severe depression in adults is associated with weight loss, hopelessness, helplessness, suicidal ideation, severe rumination with depressive themes, or psychosis (e.g., hearing voices, holding fixed irrational beliefs, and out of touch with reality).

Consistent with all aspects of assessment in MST, when a problem such as parental depression is identified, the individual and social ecological factors that maintain or contribute to the problem should be delineated (e.g., irrational thought processes, marital difficulties, realistic family problems, substance abuse, social isolation, trauma, and recent loss). In this respect, MST requires a broader conceptualization of the causes of depression relative to cognitive-behavioral formulations. Cognitive-behavioral interventions are implemented when distorted cognitions (negative self-talk and expectations of self and others, catastrophizing, etc.) contribute to the depression.

INTERVENTIONS

When symptoms of depression in the caregiver are identified as the most critical barriers to the development of a working alliance or to failed implementation of intervention strategies (e.g., newly established rules and consequences are enforced when the father is having a "good day" but not when he is having a "bad day" or a mother agrees to call the teacher daily but fails to do so because she does not "have the energy"), the practitioner should introduce the possibility that individually oriented interventions with the parent may be necessary. Because parents in families referred for MST are often focused on the behavior problems of the child, the therapist might need to explicate the linkages between suspected parental depression and the child behavioral problems (i.e., "When you can't get out of bed because you feel so sad, Jim is late for school, the teacher calls and complains, you feel even worse").

To address the identified multiple determinants of mild to moderate levels of depression, the MST practitioner often implements a sequence of verbal and worksheet-assisted techniques (see J. S. Beck, 1995). First steps typically involve helping the parent identify the connections between events, thoughts, feelings, and behaviors. Daily charts with columns representing events, thoughts, feelings, behaviors, and consequences of the behaviors are usually required to enable individuals to appreciate the strength of the relationships between what they tell themselves about events, how they feel, and what they do with how they feel (see Figure 7.1). Identifying the interrelationships among these aspects of experience constitutes a crucial step toward bringing automatic maladaptive thoughts (e.g., "This is a disaster; I'm no good") under the individual's control. Second, practitioners help clients develop and practice alternatives to counter maladaptive thoughts. For example, the therapist would help the parent who thinks, "This is a disaster," in response to a phone call from the principal, to (1) recognize that this automatic thought is a type of distortion that can be changed, and (2) generate alternative thoughts that better reflect the objective circumstances. The thought "This is a disaster" might be countered with "This is a problem." Third, just as feelings and behaviors that accompany maladaptive thoughts are logged on the daily chart, the feelings and behaviors that accompany such alternative thoughts should also be identified. For the parent chart represented in Figure 7.1, the thought "This is

BASELINE DAILY TRACKING SHEET

Event	Thought	Feeling	Behavior	Consequence
1. School's phone call	This is a disaster.	Sad, anxious	Hang up	Got no information. School-family strain increased.
	I can't handle this.	Hopeless, depressed	Lie on couch	Nothing else done.
2. Son walks in	You're a failure.	Hopeless	Withdraw	Son went out. Husband criticized (e.g., "What's wrong with you?" "Why didn't you do something?").

INTERVENTION DAILY TRACKING SHEET

Event	Thought	Feeling	Behavior	Consequence
1. Phone call	This is a problem.	Frustrated, "energized"	Stay on phone	Got information. Gave information.
2. Son walks in	He's part of the problem.	Angry	Gave consequence	Son complained. Husband supported me (e.g., "We have to do something").

FIGURE 7.1. Sample cognitive-behavioral tracking sheets.

a disaster" was accompanied by feelings of hopelessness and sadness, and by retreat to her room. Alternatively, the thought "This is a problem" was accompanied by annoyance and a feeling the parent described as being "energized" to do something about the problem. Initially, the parent said the annoyance and energy would have prompted her to stay on the phone with the principal and argue about the situation. The therapist pointed out the strengths in this alternative—that the parent would have engaged the principal rather than hanging up on him, and would not have felt as hopeless or sad—and the weakness—that arguing may not solve the problem but other approaches might.

After the parent is able to replace automatic thoughts across several clearly identified problem situations for several days in a row, the therapist and parent work together to increase the parent's repertoire of problem-solving skills. This process involves the following:

- Identifying the problem, desired outcomes, and strategies to attain the outcomes.
- Evaluating the costs and benefits of each strategy.
- Selecting a strategy.
- Practicing the strategy with the therapist and then in real-life settings.

Details regarding the problem-solving training process are presented in the section on individual interventions for adolescents. Although the therapist follows the same sequence of steps in working with adults, the content addressed in each step should reflect the specific problems in interpersonal interactions that arise for the parent. The process, however, of defining all aspects of a problem, establishing desired goals, and so on, is identical as with adolescents, as is the need for substantial practice in role-played and real-life situations. Together, these interventions provide ample opportunities for the parent to practice changing thoughts and behaviors, and for the therapist to monitor changes in the parent's cognitions and behaviors. Concomitant with the cognitive interventions noted in Chapter 3 and consistent with Principle 9, the MST therapist will also often help the parent engage in increased activity and develop indigenous social supports to build an ecological context that promotes long-term maintenance of therapeutic changes.

Anxiety, Posttraumatic Stress Disorder, and Victimization-Related Symptoms

ASSESSMENT

Social anxiety or phobia can impede the capacity of parents to garner social support or act on behalf of the social needs of their child (e.g., meeting parents of other children and taking the child to social, athletic, or church events). Practitioners should be sensitive to the possibility that adults with long-standing histories of relative social isolation may, in addition to showing signs of depression, have serious concerns about their ability to interact comfortably with strangers. Adults with anxiety disorders may appear ill at ease or experience physical discomfort in the presence of some or all people, situations, or places. This discomfort can directly influence how an individual structures his or her life (e.g., an adult who will only work the night shift because fewer people are on the job, or who avoids going to teacher–parent meetings because of social anxiety). The practitioner who suspects that a parent's anxiety is presenting a barrier to achieving treatment goals should assess the range of experiences, skills, and concerns the parent possesses with respect to engaging in social contact. The therapist's questions must be specific enough to facilitate the caregiver's ability to describe the aspects of situations that are associated with anxious feelings. Examples of such questions include the following: Are there places, people, or situations you avoid because you feel anxious when you think about or encounter them? Can you describe them in detail? Where are you when you become aware of being anxious? Who else is present? What are the others doing or saying? What are you thinking? What are you feeling?

Posttraumatic stress disorder, by definition, occurs as a sequela to a life event that is out of the ordinary and markedly distressing, such as natural disasters (e.g., fire, flood, tornado, hurricane, or earthquake), experiencing violence (e.g., assault, robbery, or rape), or witnessing of violence. Hallmark symptoms of PTSD are a heightened state of arousal (i.e., difficulty falling or staying asleep, difficulty concentrating, exaggerated startle response, and increased irritability), persistent reexperiencing of the traumatic event (i.e., through dreams, intrusive daytime thoughts, or a sense of reliving the event), and persistent avoidance of the scene of the trauma or reminders of the trauma. When practitioner observations or family member reports indicate that a parent consistently avoids a certain situation or becomes highly vigilant, easily startled, or particularly nervous in the presence of certain people, places, or other stimuli; the practitioner should arrange to meet individually with the parent to interview him or her about the symptoms. Again, such interviews should include questions about specific stimuli—people, places, events, sounds, smells—the individual avoids or becomes anxious about.

Victimization is a term that subsumes a wide variety of experiences (e.g., sexual abuse, physical abuse, domestic violence, and crime-related experiences) that can lead to symptoms of anxiety and PTSD. The short- and long-range impact of such experiences varies as a function of many factors, some of which are specific to the nature of the victimization (e.g., physical danger and perceived threat to life during the victimization, duration of the abuse, relationship to perpetrator, and response from others if and when disclosure occurred). Readers are referred to *A Clinical Handbook/Practical Therapist Manual for Assessing and Treating Adults with Post-Traumatic Stress Disorder (PTSD)* (Meichenbaum, 1994) for a very readable, well-annotated compendium of relevant research on the sequelae of various types of victimization for female and male victims (adult and child). Key findings from that research with implications for treatment are as follows:

1. No one symptom profile characterizes survivors of sexual or physical abuse, half of adult victims appear to suffer few negative effects, and even those who experience some negative effects also demonstrate considerable resilience in their lives.
2. Victims are not necessarily prone to repeating their own victimization. The intergenerational transmission rate of incestuous and abusive behavior is approximately 30%. Inept, neglectful, or abusive parenting practices emerge in roughly one-third of child sexual abuse victims, though another third may be vulnerable to the variety of social stresses associated with increased likelihood of becoming abusive parents (Oliver, 1993).

The implication of these findings for MST assessment of fit is that, for any particular individual who has been victimized, difficulties or symptoms in current-day living may or may not be related to the victimization. If problematic aspects of intra- or extrafamilial functioning are not related to past victimization, then treatments targeting the parent's past victimization will likely not result in resolution of the problems. Thus, as suggested earlier, the purpose of the assessment of past victimization is to determine not only whether it has occurred but how it affects sequences of interaction between family members and with extrafamilial systems (Principle 1) in ways that sustain clearly identified problems (Principle 4) that are targeted for change.

LAYING THE GROUNDWORK FOR INTERVENTIONS

Symptoms of anxiety, PTSD, and victimization are most effectively treated using exposure-based, cognitive, and social skills training techniques. Exposure-based treatments such as systematic desensitization and graduated exposure are designed to break the link between anxiety and the stimuli (i.e., certain types of interactions, objects, places, and people) associated with the anxiety. The cognitive-behavioral techniques introduced in the discussion of interventions for depression are used to target cognitive distortions, such as attributions (e.g., he gave me that look, and I know it means I sounded stupid) or beliefs that contribute to the anxiety (e.g., I could never do this, it would be a disaster). In social skills training, the therapist (1) describes in detail the target skills to be developed (e.g., introducing one's self to the child's teacher or to a parent in a church group), (2) models the skills, (3) provides ample opportunity for the parent to practice the skills in role-plays, (4) helps the parent to objectively evaluate his or her performance of the skills, and (5) provides necessary social support as the parent tests the skills in real-world settings. If the parent evaluates him- or herself too harshly, the therapist assesses the sources of the harsh evaluation. Often, automatic thoughts contribute to overly critical evaluations of newly learned skills. When this is the case, the therapist helps the client to identify and alter automatic thoughts contributing to the harsh evaluation. Thus, for example, the thought "If I don't say it perfectly, it will be a disaster" might be countered with "I do not have to say it perfectly to get a positive response." In addition, if negative evaluation continues in the face of objectively adequate performance, instituting the daily log-keeping process may be helpful. That is, the individual's automatic thoughts, and the feelings (increased anxiety) and behaviors (avoidance of the social situation) associated with them, should be tracked daily; and the therapist should help the client produce alternative thoughts, and track the feelings and behaviors associated with these thoughts, in and between the practice sessions.

The MST therapist and parent will together determine which aspects of individually oriented treatment can be safely and effectively undertaken in the context of MST and whether referral for additional treatment is warranted. A therapist should not undertake such treatment with a parent who is suicidal, actively abusing substances, currently being victimized, or experiencing other serious psychiatric difficulties. Such circumstances warrant referral to and collaboration with an ecologically minded psychiatrist (i.e., one who recognizes that problems in living have social and ecological causes).

If the parent is open to treatment, the MST therapist and parent should discuss the types of interventions known to be effective with the particular anxiety-related symptoms presented by the parent. To accomplish this task, the therapist should be familiar with the nature of treatments that have demonstrated effectiveness in ameliorating such symptoms, as described in Meichenbaum's (1994, pp. 330–339) handbook. Efficacious treatments focus on the following:

1. Alliance building and education about anxiety and victimization and its sequelae.
2. Assessment of the parent's symptoms, needs and strengths in multiple areas of living.
3. Bringing anxieties, acute PTSD symptoms (e.g., hypervigilance and reexperiencing), cognitions and beliefs under voluntary control through structured exposure, examination of beliefs, and mobilizing the parent's support network to bolster new beliefs and cognitions.

4. Helping the parent to reconnect with others at home, work, and in the community;
5. Training in "relapse prevention" to help clients anticipate, accept, and cope with possible setbacks.

If the therapist is unable to avail him- or herself of the type of information provided by Meichenbaum and additional clinical supervision to develop requisite clinical expertise is not available, referral to a practitioner with expertise in anxiety-focused treatment is warranted. In seeking such a referral, the therapist should assist the parent in locating a practitioner who engages in the empirically tested treatment approaches described next rather than in generic "talk" therapy, which has not been shown to be effective. In the treatment of trauma, be especially wary of therapists who insist that the client recover additional memories of abuse, as no evidence indicates that therapeutic techniques that focus on recovering memories of child sexual abuse are effective in comparison with interventions that primarily focus on the present (Beutler & Hill, 1992). If a referral is made, the MST therapist should, with the parent's permission, work with the referral practitioner and parent to ensure that progress is adequate and that the effects of the treatment are generalizing to the parent's functioning within the family. The information provided in this chapter should assist the practitioner and parent in assessing the extent to which therapeutic options available in the community embody the components entailed in empirically validated treatment.

If the parent declines the invitation to engage in individually oriented interventions with the MST therapist or with an outside referral, the therapist may temporarily drop the issue and continue implementing other intervention strategies and assessing the extent to which anxiety-, PTSD-, or victimization-specific issues continue to present barriers to change. Indeed, undesired treatment may even be harmful inasmuch as the stressful nature of exposure-based treatment may overwhelm the parent, which, in turn, may compromise the parent's ability to carry out her or his role.

INTERVENTIONS

Exposure-based interventions such as systematic desensitization, imaginal flooding, and prolonged exposure are effective in decreasing anxieties and certain PTSD symptoms (Foa, Rothbaum, Riggs, & Murdock, 1991; Foa, Rothbaum, & Steketee, 1993), and multicomponent cognitive-behavioral interventions that address trauma-related faulty attributions and beliefs, and the feelings and behaviors associated with them, have the greatest probability of being effective (Foa et al., 1993).

In *systematic desensitization,* the therapist asks the client, while deeply relaxed, to imagine a series of increasingly frightening scenes associated with the presenting anxieties or past victimization that fall along a continuum of least fearful to most fearful. The conceptual underpinning of systematic desensitization, as articulated by its developer, Wolpe (1961), is that relaxation and fear are two incompatible responses. When these two incompatible responses are repeatedly paired, fear is dispelled (Meichenbaum, 1977). Systematic desensitization consists primarily of three major components (Leitenberg, 1976):

- Constructing a graduated hierarchy of anxiety provoking scenes.
- Teaching deep muscle relaxation.
- Pairing anxiety arousing scenes with relaxation.

The first step in systematic desensitization is *constructing a graduated hierarchy* of anxiety-provoking scenes. Together, the therapist and client arrange the scenes in an order such that the first scene elicits minimal anxiety and the last scene evokes considerable anxiety. To rate the degree of anxiety provoked by each scene, the Subjective Units of Distress (SUDs) scale can be used (Wolpe & Lazarus, 1966). The scale ranges from 0 to 100, with 0 indicating complete calmness and 100 indicating extreme discomfort. After many anxiety-arousing scenes are described and noted on index cards, the level of anxiety produced by each scene is rated by the client on the 0 to 100 scale. A hierarchy is then constructed with approximately 10 units between each item, with approximately equal intervals between anxiety-provoking scenes representing equal increments of anxiety and SUDs scores ranging from 10 to 100 (Gambrill, 1977).

For example, a hierarchy of a mother who experienced past victimization by her father might resemble the following:

SUDs	Scenes
10	Seeing the shadow of her father outside her bedroom door.
20	Hearing her bedroom door open slowly.
30	Seeing her father standing inside her bedroom and slowly close the door. (Scenes 40 through 80 might describe the father coming toward the bed, the smell of his aftershave near her face, etc.)
90	Feeling her father pulling off her pajamas as she begins to cry.
100	Feeling her father force sexual relations on her.

The second component of systematic desensitization, *deep muscle relaxation,* requires that the therapist and parent physically meet in a quiet and private setting. If such a setting is not available in the home for the length of time required to achieve relaxation and engage in the desensitization process, the therapist may need to bring the parent to an office outside the home. Doing so may also require that logistical issues such as child care and transportation be arranged to allow for the parent's absence.

The following is an example (from Gambrill, 1977)[*] of deep muscle relaxation:

- Close your eyes. Get in a comfortable position. (*Pause*)
- Try to put all worrisome thoughts out of you mind and let your only concern be to let yourself go and become relaxed and comfortable. (*Pause*)
- As I mention each muscle group, give your attention to relaxing this group, remembering what it felt like when this muscle group was relaxed. Notice the feeling in each muscle as it becomes more relaxed. (*Pause*)
- Relax the muscles of your arms and hands and forearms up into your upper arms. (*Pause*)
- Just think about being calm and tranquil. (*Pause*)
- Picture yourself saying, "Just relax and be comfortable." (*Pause*)
- Signal me by raising your right index finger if these muscles feel completely relaxed. (*Signal*)
- Let this relaxation spread down to your eyes. (*Pause*)
- Focus on the difference between varying degrees of relaxation. Let you eyelids become more relaxed. (*Pause*)
- Each time you exhale, let your body become more relaxed. (*Pause*)
- [The therapist continues these instructions, directing the client's attention to the neck, back, stomach, legs, and feet.]
- Please signal me if your whole body feels completely relaxed and if you feel calm and tranquil. (*No signal*)

If the parent does not signal or if the parent reports a subjective anxiety scale rating (similar to a SUDs rating) above 20, the MST therapist should carry out additional relaxation. The level of deep muscle relaxation may be augmented by having the parent think of a soothing word, such as "calm," or of a peaceful landscape, such as a field covered with beautiful flowers (Meichenbaum, 1977).

If the parent signals and reports a subjective anxiety scale rating of less than 20, the third component of systematic desensitization, *pairing relaxation with the graduated hierarchy of anxiety evoking scenes,* is carried out. Here, for example, the client visualizes each scene of past victimization while in the relaxed state. For example, the first victimization scene, seeing the shadow of

---

[*]From Gambrill (1977). Copyright 1977 by Jossey-Bass. Reprinted by permission.

her father outside her bedroom door, is presented to the parent repeatedly coupled with instructions to relax until no anxiety is felt, or until the parent can readily reduce anxiety. When the scene no longer produces anxiety, the next scene on the hierarchy is introduced. This procedure is repeated until the client no longer indicates anxiety to any of the scenes on the hierarchy.

Prolonged exposure is a less distressing variation of flooding that differs from flooding in length of treatment sessions (60 minutes vs. 2 hours) and introduction to the exposure process via scenes from a hierarchy that evoke relatively low levels of anxiety prior to repeated exposure to more feared scenes. Therapists should not undertake the pure flooding protocol because it is not a graduated procedure, no attempt is made to keep anxiety to a minimum, distress may be significant, and no evidence indicates that flooding is more effective than desensitization at decreasing anxiety (Barlow, 1988). Prolonged exposure begins with situations from the client's hierarchy that evoke relatively low levels of anxiety. The client describes the scene in its entirety and repeats the scene several times for 60 minutes per session to facilitate habituation—the client's ability to describe the feared event without experiencing distress. Gradually, scenes that evoke increasing anxiety are described over and over until they can be described without distress. Prolonged exposure sessions are tape-recorded and clients are instructed to listen to the tapes at home at least once daily. As always, the therapist and parent should track very closely whether interventions are effective in terms of their impact on the target behaviors.

Some researchers note that prolonged exposure focuses too much on anxiety and not at all on the faulty attributions, beliefs, or expectations that are related to the anxiety and may be contributing to such symptoms as depression and difficulties with intimate relationships (Resick & Schnicke, 1992). Cognitive processing therapy (CPT; Resick & Schnicke, 1992, 1993) was developed specifically to address these potential shortcomings of exposure-based treatments, especially with regard to treating symptoms associated with victimization.

CPT is designed to identify and alter the faulty cognitions and attendant emotions that may emerge as a result of victimization. Both exposure and corrective experiences are seen as necessary to attenuate problems in living related to victimization, and the cognitive interventions provide the starting point for corrective experiences. The fundamental components of CPT are as follows:

1. Exploring, in a structured, focused manner, the meaning of victimization to the individual (what does it mean about me as a person that this happened; what does it mean about the kind of place the world is; what does it mean about the kind of god I believe in that this could happen, etc.).

2. Experiencing and understanding the connections between cognitions (e.g., "It was my fault, I deserved it"), feelings (shame, self-loathing), and behavior (isolating one's self).
3. Exposure through repeated writing of experiences and reading of written accounts. (This procedure would need to be adapted to accommodate the diversity of clients receiving MST, perhaps by using verbal or tape-recorded exposure to the traumatic events.)
4. Challenging "stuck points," where beliefs that existed prior to the victimization collide with beliefs that developed because of the victimization experience (previctimization belief, "I can trust most men"; postvictimization belief, "I can trust no men").
5. Challenging beliefs about five areas of living potentially compromised by the experience of victimization—safety, trust, power, intimacy, and self-worth. From an MST perspective, challenging beliefs would occur only if compelling evidence showed that parent difficulties in any of these areas affected the identified problems and family's efforts to change.

A complete description of the treatment and adaptations likely to be necessary for implementation of CPT within MST is beyond the scope of this chapter. Thus, prior to implementation of this approach, the practitioner and clinical supervisor should become familiar with the CPT treatment process by reading the manual written by Resick and Schnicke (1993), bearing in mind that the objectives of the treatment protocol and the sequence in which interventions are delivered should be retained, while other aspects of the treatment protocol (e.g., duration and frequency of sessions and specific form of the homework assignments) should be altered to accommodate the particular strengths and needs of the parent and the other MST treatment-related activities in which the family and therapist are engaged. Promising alternatives to CPT (still multicomponent and cognitive-behavioral) that rely less on extensive written assignments and complex charting tasks are currently being tested with diverse populations (Najavitz, Weiss, & Liese, 1996).

Serious Psychiatric Disturbances

Sometimes families referred for MST are affected by more serious disturbances such as severe clinical depression accompanied by psychotic features, bipolar disorder in a parent, or schizophrenia in a relative. As noted in Chapter 3, when psychiatric symptoms of a parent or family member are severe, the practitioner works with the family to identify an ecologically minded psychiatrist who will collaborate closely with the practitioner and family members in the process of providing any needed psychopharmacological treatment. In general, the responsibility for providing psychosocial aspects of treatment remains with the MST practitioner, unless homicidal, suicidal, and floridly psychotic behavior on the part of the parent requires hospitalization. In such cases, however, the practitioner remains responsible for understanding the nature of treatment being provided to the family member, assists the family in obtaining needed information from professionals treating the family member, and designs interventions and engages community resources that will increase the family's capacity to cope with what may turn out to be a chronic and difficult problem.

Attention-Deficit/Hyperactivity Disorder Symptoms in Adults

ASSESSMENT

In some families, a parent figure with no apparent psychiatric problems, substance abuse, or significant limitations in intellectual functioning seems unable to organize his or her life and the lives of the children. For example, although the parent may seem to have sufficient knowledge, skill, and motivation, appointments are missed and school-, work-, and treatment-related tasks are rarely completed. Such difficulties are often a function of concrete or practical factors (e.g., having appointments with multiple agencies) or other ecological factors (e.g., work schedule and low instrumental support). When interventions to address ecological factors and skills deficits fail to produce change, however, the practitioner may need to investigate whether symptoms of ADHD contribute to the fit of the apparent difficulties.

If the difficulties emerged relatively recently and are not associated with changes in lifestyle (new stepfamily formation, taking a second job, new boyfriend, having a child formerly in placement return home, etc.), an appointment with a physician is recommended to rule out illness-related causes (undetected stroke, adult onset diabetes, high blood pressure, etc.) or the side effects of medications prescribed for health problems. If the problems are long-standing, the practitioner should meet with the parent individually to investigate the nature of the difficulties and to gather evidence to support or rule out the possibility that the parent suffers symptoms of ADHD.

Research conducted over the past decade led to new conceptualizations of ADHD that have implications for effective management of its symptoms in adults and youth. A prominent researcher suggests that the hallmark features of ADHD—impulsivity, decreased attention and concentration, and excessive non-goal-directed motor activity—are the result of a core deficit in the individual's capacity to delay responding to a stimulus or event, and that this core deficit continues to plague some individuals through adulthood (Barkley, 1990). Among the symptoms of ADHD in adults that can be explained by this conceptualization are the following:

- Poor sense and utilization of time, especially difficulty anticipating the future and, therefore, engaging in activities needed to prepare for the future (e.g., arranging in advance to be picked up by a coworker at the car repair shop before taking the car in for repairs).
- Deficiencies in organizational skills.
- Forgetfulness.
- Excessive emotional reactivity.

INTERVENTIONS

The major implication of Barkley's conceptualization is that ADHD interferes with the performance of skills at the appropriate time and setting, rather than representing a failure to acquire the appropriate response or skill. That is, the difficulty lies in when to do something, not how or what to do. Over time and life-course development, the fundamental inability to delay responses may interfere with positive educational, vocational, and interpersonal adjustment, as such adjustment requires the ability to anticipate the future and to organize resources to meet multiple demands. Thus, adults with ADHD may be at increased risk for marital conflict, late or inconsistent performance on the job, inconsistent parenting efforts, and other behaviors construed by society as demonstrating a lack of personal responsibility.

Given the theory that the fundamental deficit driving ADHD symptoms lies in the when, rather than the how, of behavioral performance, treatment should involve restructuring natural settings (home, office) in ways that will affect behavior just before and while the behavior is to occur. For example, if a calendar of appointments for each child is kept at home but not in the parent's locker at work, the father with ADHD will be less likely to bring his son to the doctor on Tuesday afternoon. The MST practitioner's task, then, is to help the parent to set up daily structures that will remind him or her to perform tasks designed to meet the treatment goals. For example, Don, who has ADHD, and Vera determined in their marital session that Don should wash the dishes after dinner and be available to help their son complete his homework on Tuesday and Thursday nights. A two-word note, "dishes, homework," was written in session, and Vera agreed to place this note on Don's dinner plate for the first Tuesday and Thursday of the intervention.

Substance Abuse

Chapter 3 presented information regarding the assessment of parental substance abuse, during the discussion of individual factors that contribute to a caregiver's difficulties changing parenting, marital, or community interactions. As noted in that chapter, multicomponent behavior therapy (MBT; Higgins & Budney, 1993) and its predecessor, the community reinforcement approach (Sisson & Azrin, 1989), demonstrate effectiveness in treating adults with cocaine dependency. Because MBT is theoretically and clinically compatible with MST, the integration of these two effective intervention models may prove valuable in the development of treatments for an extremely challenging population—drug-abusing and -dependent parents. Such an integration is currently being examined in the context of a quasi-experimental study of substance-abusing parents of young children (see Chapter 9), and we hope that the integration of MST and MBT will prove effective. Here, key features of MBT are described to help the MST practitioner conceptualize the determinants of parental substance abuse and design interventions accordingly.

MULTICOMPONENT BEHAVIOR THERAPY

The treatment theory underlying MBT is based on a behavioral understanding of drug dependence and conceptualizes drug use as reinforced by both the pharmacological effects of the drug itself (e.g., the "high") and contingencies in the user's ecology (i.e., family, vocational, educational, social and recreational) that support drug use and discourage abstinence. This conceptualization has significant empirical support (see Higgins, Budney, & Bickel, 1994) and differs from other perspectives on drug dependence (e.g., disease model, self-medication model, and moral model), which have little or no empirical support.

   Like MST, MBT interventions are individualized and present focused and target well-defined problems with behavioral and ecological interventions. An individualized treatment plan is based on a functional analysis of the client's substance abuse. That is, the client is taught to identify all stimuli, or "triggers"—people, places, time of day, smells, sights, sounds, activities, moods, and thoughts—that lead to and reinforce substance use. Using this information, the triggers (e.g., the car of a friend who uses), drug-using behavior (e.g., snorting cocaine), positive consequences of use (e.g., feeling exuberant—usually short term), and negative consequences of use (e.g., work, financial, and family problems—usually longer term) are identified. This information is used to design individualized interventions that restructure the client's ecology to eliminate or reduce exposure to ecological triggers (e.g., enrolling in job training and developing non-drug-related social activities) and change self-statements and beliefs that serve as triggers (e.g., "I can't make it to work without a hit"). The lifestyle changes must incorporate activities engaging and reinforcing enough to compete with the powerful reinforcing effects of drug use. Such lifestyle changes are composed of many small steps that are taught by the therapist, practiced with the therapist in office and real-world settings, and actively supported by a significant other who collaborates in treatment. Throughout the treatment process, swift detection of substance use via monitoring of urinalysis results is coupled with immediate dispensation of concrete (e.g., points toward vouchers to be exchanged for a desired activity or product) and social reinforcers or with the withdrawal of such reinforcers.

INTEGRATING FEATURES OF MBT INTO MST

MBT-informed enhancements to MST specific to the treatment of adults include the following:

- Swift and ongoing detection of drug use and abstinence via therapist monitoring of urinalysis results.
- Dispensation of positive reinforcement for abstinence.
- Immediate loss of reinforcement for drug use.

A fourth critical component of MBT has long been and remains a primary focus of MST interventions for adults and youth engaging in substance abuse. This component emphasizes modification of the drug user's social ecology so that the amount, intensity, and satisfaction of reinforcement from prosocial activities is increased to compete with the reinforcing effects of drugs (Higgins & Budney, 1993).

Prior to the aforementioned study testing the integration of MBT with MST, a study that we hope will set a new standard for treating drug-abusing parents, MST interventions focused on using family strengths to rearrange the environment in ways that attenuated drug use. Two examples illustrate MST interventions for parental substance abuse from an earlier MST perspective (i.e., without linking contingencies to the results of frequent drug screens). In the first example, parental substance abuse was successfully targeted and ameliorated; in the second, interventions targeting the substance abuse were only partially successful, but other marital, family, and concrete obstacles to effective parenting were addressed and the youth's problem behaviors decreased.

Case Example 1. The first example pertains to the Keane family, which is composed of Ms. Keane and four children ages 11 to 16 years. The children's father had been in prison for 4 years at the time of referral. The 16-year-old son's drug use and delinquent activity prompted the referral, though the 13- and 14-year-old daughters were also truant and suspended from school. The family's strengths included Ms. Keane's love of her children, desire to see them succeed in life, part-time employment as a maid in a motel, and social support network. Among the weaknesses were a permissive parenting style, partly a result of lack of knowledge and skill as well as marijuana-induced lethargy; lack of transportation, which restricted employment options; crowded housing and financial woes; and Ms. Keane's frequent marijuana and alcohol use, which was supported by women friends in the neighborhood. After the initial MST assessment, the therapist identified several ways in which the marijuana use, specifically (as opposed to the other factors listed earlier), interfered with family functioning and described these to Ms. Keane. In addition, the therapist obtained detailed information about when, with whom, and where the use occurred as well as the short- and long-term consequences of use. This information was used to design intermediary goals that included decreasing Ms. Keane's marijuana use, decreasing contact with her drug-using friends, developing sources of social support that did not involve drugs, finding full-time employment to increase income, decreasing afternoon visits with drug using peers, and increasing satisfaction with another arena of her life.

Because the collaborative relationship between the therapist and Ms. Keane was very strong, the mother was willing to report drug and alcohol use to the therapist daily. The therapist, Ms. Keane, and the children constructed a reward and punishment system in which fines were levied for each incident of marijuana or alcohol use and points were earned for each day of abstinence. The points were traded for an activity of Ms. Keane's choosing. Thus, although urinalysis was not conducted, detection of drug use occurred quite consistently via reports of multiple respondents (i.e., mother, children, and drug-using peers). In other cases, the therapist may have asked the parent to agree to the drug screen plan and would have arranged with the local substance abuse or public health agency to obtain such screens frequently and at low or no cost.

In addition, job hunting increased Ms. Keane's exposure to non-drug-using adults and eventually resulted in full-time employment, albeit earning minimum wage. Prior to seeking employment, however, the therapist and Ms. Keane completed applications together, and the therapist helped Ms. Keane purchase secondhand clothing appropriate for job interviews and transported Ms. Keane to her interviews. Early in treatment, the therapist helped Ms. Keane learn to detect her son's substance use, but swift delivery of consequences and rewards was hampered by her own substance abuse and permissive parenting style. Thus, interventions to develop an authoritative parenting style and to deliver immediate rewards and consequences for her son's substance use and affiliation with drug-using peers (the most powerful predictor of his drug use, as with many adolescents) were implemented when reductions in Ms. Keane's drug use were achieved.

Case Example 2. In the Dillard case, the delinquent activity and school suspensions of two sons prompted referral for MST. The Dillards were married for 20 years and had four children, ages 20, 18, 14, and 13 years. The 18-year-old, her 2-year-old daughter, and the two younger boys were living at home. Strengths in this family included both parents' love of their children and desire to see them finish school and cease criminal activity, the parents' long-standing marriage, Mr. Dillard's steady employment as a laborer, and Ms. Dillard's housekeeping and cooking talents. The weaknesses included insufficient monitoring of the youths' whereabouts, inconsistent discipline practices, long-standing marital problems, and Ms. Dillard's chronic alcohol use. The latter interfered specifically with her ability to monitor the children during evening hours, as Ms. Dillard met neighbors on the corner almost every evening after dinner to have a few drinks. Ms. Dillard responded to school requests for meetings about her sons' misbehavior (a strength), but sometimes appeared at the school with alcohol on her breath (a weakness). Mr. Dillard worked primarily the day shift but was often asked at a moment's notice to stay for a second shift. The couple did not believe their marital problems could be resolved but emphatically stated that they would not divorce for religious reasons. Mr. Dillard saw his wife as a good cook and homemaker who loved her children, and Ms. Dillard viewed him as a decent provider for the family.

The therapist was unsuccessful in attempting to persuade Ms. Dillard to consider altering her drinking behavior or in convincing other family members (Mr. Dillard, the 18-year-old daughter) to join the therapist in this attempt. In light of the failure to address the mother's substance abuse directly, the therapist implemented several interventions designed to bypass the problem. The therapist helped Mr. Dillard develop the assertiveness and negotiation skills needed to talk with his supervisor about obtaining advanced notice of second shifts and the consequences of declining the extra shift (Mr. Dillard was legitimately concerned about job security). To increase monitoring of the boys, the therapist convinced Ms. Dillard to stay home one additional night per week, to stay home until Mr. Dillard came home, or, when necessary, to ask the 18-year-old daughter to monitor the boys in exchange for daytime baby-sitting for the 2-year-old. The couple agreed on rules and consequences related to the boys' homework, peer activities, and curfew. In addition, Mr. and Ms. Dillard met their sons' deviant peers and the parents of these peers to discuss solutions to the boys' auto theft activities, and Mr. Dillard began to take his sons to the city gym one morning per weekend if they did their homework during the week, as monitored through a daily report exchanged by the teachers and Mr. Dillard. Although a preferable outcome from the perspective of the therapist would have been decreasing Ms. Dillard's drinking significantly, the family met its goals—decreased truancy, increased homework completion, decreased association with deviant peers, no contact with juvenile justice, and increased contact between father and sons.

Individual Interventions with Youth

Many youth referred for MST due to serious antisocial behavior engage in impulsive and aggressive behaviors that result in negative consequences to themselves and others. Usually, these behaviors diminish in frequency and intensity when ecological and systemic interventions are implemented. In some cases, however, impulsive or aggressive behaviors continue to emerge and cause negative consequences for the youth or others, even in the context of favorable changes in the youth's social ecology. In such cases, the practitioner and family should take stock of the MST interventions in place to ensure that they are targeting all factors contributing to the fit of the impulsive or aggressive behaviors (Principle 1) and are being implemented consistently by all key players in the ecology (parents, teachers, neighbors, etc.). Often, an important aspect of the social ecology is inadvertently omitted from the treatment plan. However, when ecological interventions are comprehensive and implemented consistently but problem behavior continues to surface, individual adolescent characteristics should be examined as significant contributing factors.

Assessing the Fit of Social Cognition with Problem Behaviors

Research on aggressive and impulsive youth indicates they experience some distortions and deficiencies in social cognition that contribute to their aggression. Aggressive youth, for example, pay more attention to aggressive cues in the environment, attribute the behavior of others to hostile intentions even when that behavior is neutral (distortions), come up with fewer verbally assertive (deficits) and more physically aggressive solutions to social problems, and are more likely to label arousal as anger rather than as fear or sadness (Kendall, 1993).

Practitioners new to MST often have experience with a variety of "anger management" curricula that focus on interventions to help contain aggressive responses once they occur. These practitioners sometimes list anger management as an intermediary goal and "teach him to walk away" or "count to 10" as intervention strategies to achieve this goal. From an MST perspective, and with respect to what is known about social cognitive processes, such goals and intervention plans are likely to fail because they (1) do not address the sequence of interactions that led to the angry or aggressive outbursts, and

(2) overlook the role of cognitive distortions in the sequences of events punctuated by verbal or physical aggression. Jim, for example, often angrily threatened to "pound" his brother Sam whenever he used an item belonging to Jim. As it turned out, Jim perceived Sam's behavior as intentional stealing and his anger and threat to pound Sam as reasonable retaliation. The usual MST approach to a problem such as one family member using the belongings of another family member without permission would be to develop family consensus regarding rules for such behavior with consequences for violations. If such family interventions were not effective at curbing Jim's aggression with his brother, however, individual interventions helping Jim identify and correct his attributions about Sam's behavior would be considered. Interventions targeting family interactions and cognitive distortions, therefore, provide opportunities to prevent angry or aggressive outbursts rather than relying solely on helping the youth and family members to manage the anger and threatening behavior after it occurs.

Cognitive-behavioral interventions, therefore, involve the MST practitioner and youth in collaborating to think through and behaviorally practice solutions to the specific interpersonal problems targeted for change. The main objectives of the individual sessions are to identify and address those distortions and deficiencies that compromise the youth's ability to develop, choose, and implement solutions to interpersonal problems—distortions and deficiencies that result in negative outcomes for the youth or others even when ecological interventions are in place. Cognitive-behavioral interventions to accomplish these aims generally draw on four classes of strategies (Kendall, 1993): (1) modeling, (2) role-play exercises, (3) behavioral contingencies, and (4) self-monitoring and self-instruction.

A fifth strategy, problem-solving training, combines all these strategies to teach individuals to engage in a sequential and deliberate process of solving problems that arise in social interactions. The therapist implements these strategies in the context of individual sessions and actively engages the parents and teachers in anticipating and reinforcing (using behavioral contingencies and verbal praise) the changes initiated in individual meetings with the youth. To this end, the therapist describes to the parent the specific skills being modeled, taught, and practiced in individual sessions and asks the parent to watch for and concretely reinforce instances during the day in which the youth has tried to use the skill. To assist the parents in this effort, it may be useful to make a chart that identifies the target being addressed during a particular week's worth of individual sessions (e.g., describing a problem in terms of situational details; connecting the events, thoughts, and feelings the youth had in the situation; or identifying all possible strategies to solve a problem) and the types of behaviors that demonstrate the youth is trying to develop the skill.

Problem-Solving Training

When aggressive or impulsive behavior is associated with a failure to think before acting, or to think enough before acting, problem-solving training can be an effective means of helping adolescents think for themselves and act in a nonimpulsive manner on the basis of that thinking. The essential steps of most problem-solving approaches (for a sampling of approaches, see Forman, 1993; Kendall & Braswell, 1993) are to (1) identify the problem, including all relevant emotional (feelings in the situation), social (who is present, what is the social context), and environmental aspects of the problem situation; (2) determine the youth's goals in the problem situation; (3) generate alternative solutions; (4) evaluate these solutions; (5) choose, practice, and implement a plan for the solution; and (6) evaluate the plan, and redesign as needed. Before using these strategies, however, the therapist must assess the youth's level of cognitive development (Principle 6). With younger children and teens with poor cognitive abilities, a behavioral approach that taught the child how to use the steps would be preferred to extensive analysis of how the problem-solving process works. With more mature children and adolescents, the therapist can facilitate generalization of skills by including more work on the reasons the problem solving process can be effective.

STEP 1: DESCRIBE THE PROBLEM

The main objectives of this first step are to describe (1) the youth's problem in terms of real situations that occur in his or her life; (2) the situational details and what happens over time in the situation; (3) the thoughts, feelings, and behaviors the youth experiences as the situation unfolds; and (4) the characteristics of the situation that make it a problem. The MST therapist has ample observations and reports from others of real situations in the youth's life that exemplify the problem. Using these exemplars, the therapist and youth can describe the problem in terms of *antecedents,* or what happened prior to the situation; *behaviors* of concern, or what happened during the situation; and *consequences,* or what happened immediately and longer term following the problem situation. The therapist helps the adolescent identify the interrelationships between thoughts, feelings, and behaviors as they arise over time in the problem situation so that the youth can become more aware of his or her own impact on problem situations. For example, the therapist asked Pete, who was repeatedly suspended for verbally threatening teachers, to think about the last time he "got in trouble" with a teacher at school. The therapist asked Pete to describe where he was in the classroom, what he was doing, and who he was with when the teacher called his name. The therapist then asked him to describe what he said and did, what the teacher said and did, what thoughts were going through his head at the time, and what feelings he experienced during each verbal exchange with the teacher. With this information about the behaviors, feelings, and thoughts Pete had during each step of the argument, the therapist pointed out the relationship between his thoughts ("The witch has no right, I'll show her"), feelings (anger, humiliation related to being "picked on" in front of peers) and the statements he made that "upped the ante" in the argument to the point where suspension was ordered. The therapist also helps the youth identify what makes this problem a problem, that is, what negative consequences are experienced either by the others or themselves (e.g., aggressive outbursts directed toward authority figures led to my expulsion at school and arrest in the neighborhood, and most adults do not like me because of these problems).

STEP 2: DETERMINE THE GOALS

In this step, the therapist focuses on goals—basically, given a problem situation, what is the outcome to be achieved. The criteria, discussed with the youth, are that goals should be assertive (i.e., reflecting the feelings or opinions of the youth without being aggressive or passive) and should consider both improving something (e.g., increasing days in a regular classroom vs. an in-school suspension classroom) as well as decreasing something (e.g., teachers stop sending the youth to in-school suspension).

STEP 3: GENERATE ALTERNATIVE SOLUTIONS

This step is "brainstorming," and the goal is to have the youth, with or without assistance, generate a list that includes solutions that might actually work and options that would probably lead to negative consequences. Criteria for brainstorming are as follows: (1) no idea is evaluated until the list is complete; (2) the list should include realistic, unrealistic, and funny options; and (3) aggressive, assertive, and passive options are required. The therapist should emphasize having fun and encourage the teen to ask others—especially those who are socially desirable—for help generating options.

STEP 4: EVALUATE THE SOLUTIONS

Once the list is developed, the therapist asks the youth to evaluate each option. Only assertive options can be considered acceptable. Thus, the youth is instructed to cross out the aggressive options (e.g., punch out someone's lights). Passive options are a bit more acceptable in some situations, especially with authority figures. For each option, possible consequences, both immediate and long term, for others as well as themselves, are listed and then discussed. After consequences for each solution are noted, the youth and therapist should evaluate their relative merits.

STEP 5: CHOOSE A SOLUTION, DESIGN AND PRACTICE A PLAN

Next, the therapist reviews the relative strengths and weaknesses of the solutions with the youth and helps him or her design a plan. All positive options should be considered. Either one or a combination of positive options can be used for the plan, which should be described in behaviorally specific terms (e.g., who does what, when, and where?). If talking with another person is necessary, the goals of the conversation should be identified (e.g., What do you want to say to the other person given your set of assertive goals?). Developing and practicing sample scripts may be helpful. Even without a script, role-played practice, and plenty of it, with praise and constructive corrective feedback, must precede *in vivo* implementation of the plan.

STEP 6: IMPLEMENT THE PLAN

The therapist helps the teen to implement the plan at a particular date, and all details are discussed. In some instances, the therapist goes with the youth and provides support, though, in the long run, youth need to learn this set of skills so that they can accomplish all steps on their own (Principle 9). Again, the therapist elicits the support of the parents in encouraging the youth and in checking with others to see whether the youth has been able to execute the skills *in vivo*.

If the plan does not work the first time, the therapist helps the youth to reevaluate and redesign the plan. Such reconceptualizations require that the youth develop the skills to objectively evaluate his or her performance. To facilitate this process, the therapist should model and encourage the use of self-monitoring statements that are specific and objective (e.g., "I didn't use assertive statements") rather than global and distorted (e.g., "I'm a total failure"). Finally, if the plan is successful, the therapist encourages the youth to describe the bases for the success and emphasizes internal attributions for positive outcomes (e.g., "I was appropriately assertive and convinced the teacher to give me another chance").

Addressing Cognitive Distortions

A variety of techniques can be used to identify and help change the nature of the cognitive distortions associated with aggressive or impulsive behavior in youth. A useful starting place for the therapist is to understand what the youth "takes in" in a social situation. Does he or she tune in to hostile or negative cues in the environment much of the time? Does the youth interpret behaviors that may be neutral, or mildly negative, as being motivated by hostile intentions? Is a sidelong glance perceived as an invitation to fight? Therapists can obtain information about the youth's perceptions and appraisals by accompanying the youth to a variety of settings that afford opportunities to watch people interact, such as a mall, fast-food restaurant, or public basketball court. Once in the setting, and having identified individuals interacting in some way, the therapist asks the youth to respond to such questions as the following: "Why do you think the guy is tapping his fingers on the counter?" Responses could range from "He's bored" (neutral, probably not distorted) to "He's getting ready to chew out the cashier" (possibly true, possibly a hostile attribution, depending on the specifics of the situation). Other questions might include the following: "How do you think he's feeling? What do you think he'll do next?" The practitioner then overtly verbalizes his or her appraisal of the situation, various solutions, and possible consequences of different solutions. Role-plays, en route to and from observation posts, and at home during individual sessions, are necessary to enable the youth to practice making alternative interpretations of cues observed in social situations.

When distortions such as hostile attributions generalize across different types of people and situations, they can become attitudinal biases. For example, some juvenile offenders may believe that their parents, their teachers, and the police are "out to get them." The posture, tone of voice, and other subtle or overtly hostile behavior they exhibit on the basis of this distorted cognition, and the feelings of anger, persecution, or hostility associated with the attribution, in turn, often evoke hostility from peers and adults. This hostility then serves to reinforce the adolescents' belief that others are biased against them. In such circumstances, the adolescent must learn that his or her body posture, tone of voice, and behaviors contribute to this cycle of hostile interactions. To promote this understanding, the therapist might use a variety of perspective-taking exercises, including Socratic methods that enhance the youth's appreciation of the other person's perspective. For example, the therapist might encourage the adolescent to consider how his teacher felt when, in front of the class, he challenged the teacher's competence and authority. The therapist might ask the adolescent a number of different questions such as "What is the teacher's job? How do you think the teacher took your behavior? What choices did the teacher have in responding to you? How would you respond if you were the teacher and a student smart-mouthed you in front of the entire class?" In essence, the therapist attempts to teach the adolescent that, in many situations, his or her negative attitude and behavior force adult authorities to respond in a punitive fashion. Adolescents who are able to understand the connection between their behavior and the responses of others, are then capable of learning how to "play the game." If obnoxious behavior evokes punitive responses from adults, it follows that respectful and considerate behavior should evoke favorable responses from adults. When attempting to alter the adolescent's attitudinal biases, the therapist should help parents make changes in the family, school, and peer systems that will reinforce the youth's progress.

Victimization-Related Symptoms

Research on the mental health impact of physical and sexual abuse on children counters much of the clinical lore that prevails in the mental health community (e.g., all abused children require treatment and all behavioral problems of children who have been abused are caused by the abuse). Key findings (for reviews, see Beitchman et al., 1992; Kendall-Tackett, Williams, & Finkelhor, 1993) relevant to treatment are: children who are abused may experience a broad array of adverse short- and long-term mental health difficulties, or they may experience no apparent difficulties; symptomatology differs across developmental levels; and characteristics and context of the abuse (e.g., perpetrator's use of force, threats, and weapons; duration and frequency of abuse; and lack of parental support upon disclosure) are related to victim symptomatology. Thus:

1. Child abuse cannot be substantiated by the presence or absence of any particular behavior in a child.
2. Therapists cannot assume *a priori* that victims of abuse require mental health treatment.
3. When victims present mental health problems, these problems may or may not be the result of abuse (i.e., the problems may be linked with difficulties that preceded the abuse or have no relation to the abuse).
4. Assessment should consider the context and characteristics of the abusive incidents when evaluating the impact of abuse on the victim.

ASSESSMENT

In keeping with MST principles, information about the nature, impact, and aftermath of the abuse and its disclosure on the youth and family should be obtained from multiple sources. These sources include the victim, parents, family members, relatives and other individuals in the youth's ecology. As well, information from the courts, police, and children's services agencies should be obtained with the family's permission. Such information is needed to understand the extent to which the abuse itself, versus other factors (e.g., changed interaction patterns within the family, reactions of friends, removal of the child or a perpetrator from the home, and a courtroom ordeal) may be contributing to the behavioral or emotional problems in question.

The practitioner should prepare to obtain information from the victim by talking first with the parents, as enlisting parental support increases the victim's comfort in disclosing the details of the abuse. The practitioner should be prepared to describe for the parents the rationale for discussing the abuse at this juncture in treatment—that the purpose of the discussion is to facilitate development of interventions that will attenuate the youth's distress or problem behaviors. The therapist should also assuage concerns the parent or youth might have regarding the possible negative consequences of talking about the abuse. When discussing sexual abuse with an adolescent, a structured approach to obtaining details is likely to increase the quality of information obtained and reduce the duration of time needed to obtain the information. Meichenbaum's (1994) handbook, referenced in the discussion of adult victimization, provides some guidelines regarding sensitive and direct methods of questioning youth about abusive experiences.

INTERVENTIONS

MST treatment strategies for problems experienced by children and adolescents who were victimized reflect the same breadth, diversity, and logic as MST interventions with nonabused children and adolescents presenting behavioral and emotional difficulties and their families. Thus, it is anticipated (and recommended) that interventions addressing other aspects of the fit of the identified difficulties (family, school, peer, practical issues) will be in place before abuse-specific interventions are implemented. When abuse-specific interventions are undertaken, they are targeted toward symptoms of anxiety (e.g., avoidance of reminders of the abuse, intrusive memories, hypervigilance, and fears) or self-deprecating thoughts related to the abuse that contribute to depression. As with adults, behavioral approaches that involve controlled exposure to the anxiety-provoking stimuli and cognitive-behavioral techniques addressing faulty beliefs (e.g., that the victim was responsible for the abuse) have the greatest probability of success with youth, though they must be geared to the developmental level of the youth.

Youth experiencing anxiety related to memories of the abuse may benefit from learning strategies to reduce the physiological arousal associated with anxiety. *Anxiety management* techniques such as controlled breathing (Craske & Barlow, 1990) and deep muscle relaxation (Deblinger, 1995; Ollendick & Cerny, 1981) can be taught to the parent and youth simultaneously, with the expectation that the parent will practice with the youth and reinforce practice and use of the technique. Therapists unfamiliar with these techniques, which require step-by-step implementation and close tracking of the youth's physiological and subjective distress, should review the example provided for treatment of adults earlier in this chapter and familiarize themselves with texts that tailor these techniques to youth (Deblinger, 1995; Ollendick & Cerny, 1981). Additional MST clinical supervision should be obtained prior to and during the implementation of these techniques.

When implemented with children and adolescents, *graduated exposure* involves having the youth recapitulate the abusive incidents by beginning with situations that evoke lower levels of anxiety, followed by slightly more anxiety-provoking situations. This technique is used only when the youth is protected from further victimization and if the parent is supportive of the youth's disclosure. The parent should participate in treatment sessions conducted with preschool or school-age children. When treating adolescents, the therapist, parent, and youth should determine together whether the parent's presence during exposure would be experienced as supportive or intrusive by the adolescent.

Developmentally tailored *cognitive techniques* can be effective for youth who make incorrect assumptions about who is responsible for the abuse or concerning what the abuse means about them (e.g., being bad or damaged goods), others (e.g., "All men are bad"), their physical health, or the world (e.g., "It's a bad place if this can happen to me"). Thirteen-year-old George, for example, who was sexually abused by an older male neighbor, feared that he was homosexual and going to die from AIDS as a result of the abuse. Because the practitioner knew little about the caregiver's (grandfather) knowledge and beliefs about sexual abuse or AIDS, she discussed these issues with grandfather before arranging for the him to help her counter George's beliefs that he was a homosexual and would contract AIDS. Before engaging parental figures in interactions designed to help children overcome incorrect attributions, practitioners should ensure that parental figures hold appropriate assumptions and beliefs about responsibility for the abuse (i.e., the perpetrator is responsible) and have an accurate view of the victim (e.g., as a child or adolescent who has experienced a traumatic event rather than as damaged goods). Once this is accomplished, the practitioner and parent together investigate the youth's beliefs about the abuse and help her or him overcome inaccurate or inappropriate beliefs. For example, the therapist and parent may ask if the youth ever believed the abuse was his or her fault and, if the child says "yes," inquire as to what made the child feel this way. In George's case, the grandfather forbade George from going near the perpetrator's home on learning of the abuse. George interpreted this prohibition as a punishment and felt that he deserved the punishment because the abuse would not have happened if he had not gone to the neighbor's house. Initially with the therapist present, and subsequently on their own, George's grandfather countered these erroneous (but understandable) beliefs and assured George that he was not responsible for the abuse. Similarly, with the aid of the therapist, the grandfather countered other erroneous beliefs that George held about sexual orientation as a consequence of the abuse.

ADHD in Youth

ASSESSMENT

The antisocial behavior of some youth is exacerbated by ADHD; on the other hand, many youth with ADHD do not engage in serious antisocial behavior (Kendall, 1993). Thus, as with all behavioral problems, practitioners should assess the fit of ecological and individual factors with referral problems before designing interventions to help parents and teachers manage behaviors that may be associated with ADHD.

In many cases, families have already obtained a psychiatric evaluation that confirms a diagnosis of ADHD, appropriate doses of stimulant medications (e.g., Ritalin and Cylert) have been prescribed, and the youth and family are able to ensure that medication is being taken as prescribed. In other cases, a family physician, school nurse, teacher, or principal has "diagnosed" the youth with ADHD, a prescription for stimulant medication has been obtained, and that prescription may or may not be dispensed regularly or even needed. In such instances, the therapist should explore the parent's understanding of the diagnosis, medication, and relationship with the prescribing physician. If a lack of information or confusion about these topics is apparent, the therapist should ask the parent's permission to contact the physician and establish a working relationship between that person, the parent, and the therapist. If adequate information or such a relationship is not attained after significant effort, an updated evaluation, preferably from an ecologically minded child psychiatrist, should be obtained. As is the case when facilitating successful meetings between caregivers and individuals in other systems (e.g., schools, child service agencies, and health department), the therapist should work with the parent and psychiatrist to ensure that communication between the two is clear, that technical terms are understood by the parent, and that the MST therapist (rather than psychiatrist) is taking the clinical lead with respect to the psychosocial (as opposed to biological) interventions. This recommendation applies, in fact, any time a youth already on prescription medication for ADHD or any other difficulty bearing a diagnosis rendered by another professional is referred for MST.

INTERVENTIONS

The conceptualization of ADHD introduced in the section on adult interventions is used to guide MST practitioners' understanding of the fit of ADHD with presenting problems in youth. To recap, that conceptualization holds that the hallmark symptoms of ADHD—impulsivity, decreased attention and concentration, and excessive non-goal-directed motor activity—can be explained by a fundamental deficit in the ability to delay responses to stimuli. The major treatment implication of this conceptualization is that the ecology of the youth—at home, in the classroom, in a locker the student uses daily, etc.—should be structured to provide cues for performance of certain skills just before they are to occur. Such restructuring of activities is entirely consistent with the ecological emphasis of MST, and, thus, concrete behavioral cues should be readily integrated into ongoing parent–child and family–school interventions.

In restructuring the ecology to better meet the needs of children with ADHD, practitioners might provide parents with practical tips that appear in the easy-to-read newsletter *The ADHD Report* (Barkley & Associates) or in *Attention-Deficit Hyperactivity Disorder: A Handbook for Diagnosis and Treatment* (Barkley, 1990) and the accompanying clinical workbook (1991). Providing bibliotherapy on ADHD (i.e., providing reading materials), however, is never a substitute for direct interventions that help parents and teachers to restructure the youth's environment at home and school. Moreover, if reading materials are used, they should be gauged to the cognitive and literacy level of the parents.

Case Example. Wanda was the single mother of Michael, age 9 years, and Belinda, age 4 years. Michael was referred to MST for disruptive behavior (including fights) in class and because he was failing the second grade. Wanda and the children had been living in the two-bedroom trailer home of her boyfriend, Bob, and his 14-year-old son, Ed, for 1 year. Prior to moving in with Bob, the family had lived in a homeless shelter for 6 months after Wanda left an abusive husband (a strength). Michael and Belinda slept in Ed's room when Ed stayed with his mother (half the week), and on the foldout couch in the living room when Ed stayed with his father. Because Michael had been aggressive and "bouncing off the walls" since his preschool days, Wanda sought help (a strength) from a pediatrician, who issued the diagnosis of ADHD and a prescription for Ritalin. Following a comprehensive MST assessment of the multiple factors contributing to the fit of Michael's aggressive behavior and school failure, initial priorities for intervention were identified. The therapist assisted Wanda in (1) obtaining an updated diagnosis and prescription, if such was deemed necessary, from a psychiatrist who would collaborate with Wanda and the MST therapist; (2) asking the school to conduct IQ and achievement testing to assess capacity-related contributions to Michael's failing grades; (3) implementing strategies at home that were used with some success at school to help Michael focus on and complete tasks; and (4) rearranging the home environment to create stability of sleeping arrangements regardless of the 14-year-old son's whereabouts.

Of specific interest in this section are the techniques used to structure Michael's home environment to facilitate focused behavior and task completion, two problems that appeared to contribute to his classroom disruptions. First, a space in the corner of the adults' bedroom was designated, with a colorful sign made by Michael, as his study space during after-school hours. The bedroom became (as noted by a sign and closed door) an adults-only space after dinner. Second, during a meeting with Michael's teacher and the therapist, Wanda learned that Michael loved individual attention and could complete short tasks if the teacher praised him very often. Unfortunately, the demands of the classroom prevented her from doing this consistently. The teacher demonstrated her check-in technique for Wanda, and the two women determined that the teacher would send Michael home with half-completed assignments which Wanda was to help her son complete for 3 days. Wanda used an egg timer to remind herself to check on Michael's progress, initially every 5 minutes. As it turned out, more frequent checking was needed—Michael responded best when Wanda checked in after he completed each item. Third, points were accumulated for each interval in which progress was made, and a reward—free time on his bike—was given at the end of the assignment. Fourth, during Michael's homework time, the television was turned off, and phone calls were answered by Bob or not answered if Bob was not home. Finally, bedtime and morning routines were established and followed regardless of Ed's presence or absence. Thus, Michael's clothes, book bag, and lunch ticket were put in the same place on the kitchen counter every night at bedtime, even when he slept in Ed's room.

Shortly after treatment began, it became clear that the makeshift sleeping space was inadequate for the children and cramped Ed's style on his nights at home. Thus, the therapist asked Wanda and Bob to meet to discuss housing options. She introduced the topic by acknowledging that making decisions about housing options would likely require that the couple address their long-term plans, and that those plans had implications for both the housing decision and with respect to the nature and extent of each adult's parental role with the other's children. The couple met with the therapist several times to discuss these issues and determined that Wanda and Bob wanted to try to "make a go of it." Thus, the couple began searching for a larger trailer. At the same time, additional parent-teacher interventions were developed to apply rewards and consequences at home for Michael's disruptive behavior at school and to match as closely as possible the techniques the teacher and Wanda used to focus Michael's attention on task completion.

Finally, information about ADHD can sometimes be used to help shift parental attributions about the nature of the child's problem (e.g., the parent believes the child is willfully bad when, in fact, some of the disruptive behavior at home and school is related to the ADHD). On the other hand, the practitioner must be a critical consumer of any information passed on to the parent and should be aware of the myriad lecturers, workshops, and lore-filled booklets that may contain more misinformation than good information. Essentially, the volumes by Barkley (1990) and Kendall and Braswell (1993) can be useful resources for professionals. The accessibility of these volumes to parents, however, will vary with the parents' literacy levels and available time to read and translate fairly technical volumes into action.

Youth Refusal to Cooperate in Treatment: When and How Does It Matter?

Throughout this volume, numerous recommendations are made regarding the engagement of parents, families, school personnel, and agency colleagues in working alliances. In essence, the key principles of engagement pertain to having the individuals collaborate fully in setting treatment goals, easing burdens of service accessibility, emphasizing the strengths of the individual or system, providing "hope" (quickly fortified by evidence that some interventions are successful) for favorable outcomes, and holding the therapist, supervisor, and provider organization (vs. the family, teacher, or outside agency) accountable for engagement. Although engagement of the youth can facilitate treatment gains, such engagement is by no means necessary if the full force of the ecology can be rallied to support treatment goals. Indeed, while the behavioral problems of the youth result in referral for MST, the majority of the therapist's efforts are directed toward changing the youth's ecology. Thus, individual treatment with the youth is generally pursued as a last resort and is attempted only when all other ecological changes are consistently implemented, significant behavioral problems continue, and these behavioral problems are clearly linked with a particular attribute of the youth (e.g., ADHD, attributional bias, and poor problem-solving skills).

In some cases, the procedures described in this chapter are helpful adjuncts to systemic interventions, and behavioral problems targeted for individual interventions begin to decrease when they are implemented. In other cases, the youth refuses to cooperate with individual treatment, but the therapist and parents are able to identify additional systems strengths that can be used to manage or contain the behavior. In still other cases, no matter how hard a parent or therapist might try, a youth will absolutely refuse to cooperate with any intervention, including individually oriented interventions. In the vast majority of such cases, the youth perceives that he or she has everything to lose and little to gain by cooperating. For example, a youth who, prior to the implementation of system-level changes effected by parents, teachers, and key individuals in the neighborhood or community, was allowed to skip school, use drugs with his or her friends, and have no household responsibilities, may persist in his or her efforts to escape newly developed monitoring, sanctioning, and reward mechanisms at home and school. Assuming all contributing systems factors are assessed and addressed with effective interventions, the first line of defense in such situations is to shore up support for the parents and help them to close all loopholes in the community that might support the youth's antisocial behavior, as described in the example of Tasha in Chapter 4. If the youth continues to engage in serious antisocial behavior that puts him- or herself or others at risk of harm, the therapist, parents, individuals who provide the parents with support, and staff of participating agencies (e.g., juvenile justice and education) may decide together to allow the youth to "take the lumps" associated with the problem behavior. That is, the parents may decide not to advocate for their son or daughter at the school board's expulsion hearing or may have the youth arrested for drug use. In light of the serious consequences of such decisions (e.g., termination of the youth's educational opportunities in the public school system or a jail sentence), they are only to be made in the most dire of circumstances, and there should be no illusion that the decision will result in the youth's "learning a lesson" about the seriousness of his or her behavior (e.g., contrary to popular belief, no evidence shows that incarceration "scares" youth into changing their behavior; indeed, evidence clearly indicates that youth released from programs designed to shock them into changing continue to reoffend).

When supporting a decision to remove a youth from school or to send him or her to an out-of-home placement, caregivers and the community are acknowledging the possibility that the youth's future social and economic competence may be seriously compromised, and parents may need assistance in coping with the potential loss of hope such a decision represents. In the best of such circumstances, ecological changes made during MST treatment benefit the siblings of the referred youth and may assist parents in dealing with the challenges presented by the referred youth in ways that preserve effective family functioning.

8

Family Linkages with Community Supports

In this chapter
- The importance of informal and formal supports to family functioning.
- The factors that influence the development and maintenance of positive social support networks.
- A framework for assessing and enhancing families' informal and formal supports.
- Barriers commonly encountered in helping families build their social support network and strategies for overcoming these obstacles.

Developing and maintaining close interpersonal relationships and community ties are crucial in helping families raise children. When children manifest serious antisocial behavior, families face extraordinary pressures to meet the multiple and changing needs of their offspring, often with few or diminishing resources (social supports, money, time, etc.) (Marcenko & Meyers, 1991; Oswald & Singh, 1996). Coupled with systemic (i.e., marital problems and family transitions), concrete (i.e., subsistence wages and inadequate transportation), and personal difficulties (i.e., psychiatric disorder and drug abuse) often experienced by parents in such families, the practical challenges of raising children with serious behavioral problems can seem overwhelming. In light of the importance of close interpersonal relationships and community ties to family functioning, *the development and maintenance of social supports are major goals of MST.*

Role of Social Supports in a Healthy Family Environment

The African adage "It takes a village to raise a child" is an apt description of the resources required to meet children's basic needs for nurturance, guidance, and protection. These resources are highly diverse and include finances, information, nutrition, health care, housing, time, care for dependent family members, emotional support, accurate feedback, and so on. Many of these resources are accessed through close interpersonal relationships and community ties (i.e., friends, neighbors, and extended family), or what social scientists refer to as "social supports."

Importantly, *robust social support networks* (i.e., high-quality support from extended family, friends, coworkers, neighbors, and community organizations) are strongly associated with favorable family functioning and capacity to promote prosocial behavior (Harrison, Wilson, Pine, Chan, & Buriel, 1990; Reiss & Price, 1996; Vondra & Belsky, 1993; Weisz & Tomkins, 1996; Wellman & Wortley, 1990). Families with robust social support networks have access to more resources, and the availability of resources predicts differential responses to changing environmental conditions and traumatic events (Hobfoll, 1991). That is, having resources can help families cope with the challenges of raising children as well as buffer the negative effects of periodic misfortunes. For example, when a single mother with five children required hospitalization for surgery, the children were able to continue living at home, attending their own schools, and engaging in community activities because grandmother moved into the family's home to care for the children, neighbors provided transportation needed to buy groceries and household supplies; and church members and parents of the children's friends transported the children to school and other community activities.

Types of Resources Provided by Social Supports

Social support is a multidimensional construct that encompasses four main types of support (Quick, Nelson, Matuszek, Whittington, & Quick, 1996; Unger & Wandersman, 1985).

1. *Instrumental* support, such as financial assistance, helping with housework and child care, and borrowing a neighbor's car.
2. *Emotional* support, for example, expressions of empathy, concern, love, trust, and caring.
3. *Appraisal* support, which provides affirmation or feedback (e.g., "You did the right thing by punishing Jamie for getting expelled from school, even though he is angry with you; hang in there").

4. *Information* support, for example, "The Piggly Wiggly has the best price on baby formula."

Rarely are all types of support provided by single members of the support network. Some members are used for one type of support (e.g., a favorite relative for emotional support when feeling down), whereas other members are used for other types of support (e.g., a neighbor who always knows where to get the best buys in town). Thus, as noted previously, families benefit from having access to a broad array of support resources.

The Continuum of Social Support Resources

The family's social support network can range from informal, proximal relationships (extended family, friends, neighbors, coworkers) to more distal formal relationships with personnel of public (e.g., Department of Juvenile Justice and Department of Social Services) and private (e.g., YMCA and My Sister's Place) entities. Access to a broad range of supports is important because families of children presenting serious antisocial behavior often have multiple needs that might profit from a robust social support network (e.g., a neighbor to help monitor the adolescent after school, a friend for the parent to relax with, a coach who will go the extra mile to engage the child in prosocial activities, a church to provide prosocial outlets for family members, and state agencies to tap for financial resources such as Medicaid benefits and welfare). Indeed, contemporary scholars and advocates for children's services argue that children with extraordinary needs often require a range of services at varying levels of intensity commensurate with their level of disturbance across different settings (see Stroul & Friedman, 1994). Thus, MST practitioners must be knowledgeable about the full range of potential informal and formal resources available in the community.

Consistent with the MST emphasis on ecological validity (Principle 9), however, *all efforts should made to develop and tap family resources at the proximal end of the social support continuum* before moving to the formal end. Obtaining social support in an ecologically valid manner provides several advantages:

- Informal supports are more likely than formal supports to meet the immediate needs of the child and family. For example, the family's most pressing need may be for $50 to fix the car's carburetor so that the children can be transported to child care. The money may be more readily available from a family friend than from public or private agencies operating under categorical funding schemes that earmark services for narrowly defined needs (e.g., social skills training groups for children) but do not have flexible funds.

- Informal sources of support are often most pivotal in helping families achieve complex goals. For example, unemployed persons more often find jobs through informal networks than from formal sources such as employment agencies (e.g., Rife & Belcher, 1994).
- Informal supports are more likely to provide resources that are timely and easily accessible. A mother is more likely to obtain emotional support from a family member or neighbor at 2 A.M. than from a probation officer or mental health worker.
- Most important, and consistent with Principle 9 (maintain generalization of treatment gains), informal supports are more likely to be sustained following treatment than formal supports. Resources from formal support systems are susceptible to discontinuation due to changes in public policy, funding, political climate, and staff turnover.

Although a system of informal indigenous supports is preferable to a formal system of external supports provided by state or private entities, at times the needs of some children and families exceed the functional capacity of the informal system. Consequently, the therapist and family must be able to access resources available from formal sources of support at the point that informal supports fail to meet the child's and family's needs. Nevertheless, even as formal supports are accessed, the therapist and family should be working together to build the capacity of the informal and proximal support network.

Factors Influencing the Development and Maintenance of Social Support Networks

The development of social support networks is influenced by contextual and individual factors (Cochran, 1993). Contextual factors include those ecological, cultural, or social forces that promote or constrain the development of social relationships. For example, an ecological factor that may constrain the development of social relationships is living in a high-crime neighborhood. Because "fear of crime" restricts normal human interactions and movement, living in such a neighborhood may help to explain the fit of a family's social isolation. Similarly, contextual factors in a parent's workplace can affect the pool of individuals eligible to become part of the parent's social network (e.g., a parent who is the night watchman at a convenience store vs. a teacher's aide at a neighborhood elementary school). Personal factors that affect the development of social support and social networks include personality characteristics, attractiveness, time and energy, social and cognitive skills, self-esteem, and socioeconomic status. For example, a parent who is extremely critical of others has great difficulty developing and maintaining close interpersonal ties.

Once established, several factors maintain social relationships. For present purposes (i.e., treatment of families with antisocial youths), the most important of these factors is *reciprocity*. Reciprocity refers to the giving and receiving of tangible and emotional resources that is predicated on the expectation of a return or quid pro quo (Uehara, 1990). That is, the individuals in the relationship give as much as they receive (Unger & Wandersman, 1985). Embedded within this definition of reciprocity is the notion of equity, which refers to explicit or implicit rules regarding what is a fair exchange. The treatment implications of this notion are substantial: *To maintain social supports for the long term, families who receive support (e.g., borrowing money or a car and having a shoulder to cry on) must reciprocate.* Therefore, the therapist who helps a family to develop a social support network must make sure that the family is giving back in ways that reinforce the givers. Otherwise, unilateral giving will be short-lived.

Social Isolation and Social Networks as Sources of Stress

The absence of social supports, *social isolation,* is a significant risk factor for a host of psychosocial problems (House, Landis, & Umberson, 1988), including domestic violence, child abuse and neglect, and mental health problems. Several pernicious effects of social isolation on family functioning have been identified. Social isolation can do the following:

- Adversely affect parent–child emotional bonding and effective parenting. For example, Wahler (1980) found that multistressed mothers were more likely to interact coercively with their conduct-disordered children during times of sparse social contact with members of their social support network.
- Attenuate treatment generalization and the maintenance of therapeutic gains (Wahler, 1990).
- Limit the pool of potential resources available to a family.

Finally, therapists must remember that social networks are not necessarily supportive per se. Social networks can also stress families in ways that adversely affect parenting. For example, duress from unpleasant interactions with spouses, friends, neighbors, therapists, or social service personnel can have negative effects on parent–child interactions (Wahler & Hann, 1987).

Assessment of Informal and Formal Family–Community Linkages and the Factors Influencing Those Linkages

MST assessment of all aspects of the youth's ecology is an ongoing, reiterative process conducted from the beginning to end of MST treatment; thus, community linkages are assessed from the point of referral to MST and assessment continues throughout treatment. The primary purpose of the assessment of family–community linkages is to identify those factors in the family's social ecology that influence the development of informal and formal networks, which, in turn, influence the functioning of family members either positively (grandfather supports parental discipline efforts; neighbors help to monitor the children's after-school activities) or negatively (neighborhood children can readily make money by selling drugs; family court mandates iatrogenic services for the youth). Assessment of the strengths and weaknesses of family–community linkages is integrated with the corresponding MST assessment of other systems (family, school, peer) to provide a comprehensive understanding of the fit of the identified problems with the youth's and family's social ecology. This fit guides the design of the initial MST interventions as well as subsequent assessment and interventions until the targeted outcomes are attained.

Proximal, Informal Supports

The MST practitioner can gain an appreciation of the family's informal support (and nonsupport) network by taking several straightforward steps.

1. Ask family members to identify friends, neighbors, coworkers, church members, or extended family that "help" the family when needed. For example, the therapist can ask, "Who would you go to if you needed $100 right away?" "If you couldn't pick your children up from school, how would you get them home?" "When troubles really get you down, who makes you feel better?" "Who do you go to for advice about your kids?"

2. Identify the type(s) of positive support (instrumental, emotional, appraisal, information) that each of the identified individuals provides. In item 1, for example, the first two questions address instrumental support, the last two, emotional support.

3. Determine how the family reciprocates the support received from each member of the network who provides positive support and determine together if such reciprocation is equitable.

4. Finally, specify the individuals in the social network who stress family members and ascertain the nature of the stress. Remember that the

same individual in the social network can both provide positive support (e.g., financial assistance) and increase stress (e.g., belittling the parent for needing the financial assistance). Also, sources of support and stress can vary for different family members. For example, a negative peer may be a source of emotional support for the youth but a source of stress for the parent.

Formal Supports

Formal supports pertain to the family's relations with individuals employed by agencies or entities that provide resources or services. Importantly, the therapist must remember in the assessment of formal supports that the family's relationship with child serving agencies is rarely reciprocal. That is, the family receives more than it gives, which exacerbates the hierarchical structure of the family–agency relationship. The agency has the power because it controls the allocation of the resources, and the family is not a consumer in a true sense. The influence of genuine consumers comes from their capacity to affect the well-being of organizations by refusing to interact with the organization in ways that affect the organization's viability (e.g., by not buying poorly constructed widgets and not shopping at the store that discriminates). With regard to economically disadvantaged families involved with child-serving agencies, however, such "boycotting" of services can have a negligible impact on the organization and a potentially negative impact on the family (e.g., failure to receive services). Indeed, the omnipotence of agencies responsible for children's services is one variable that prompted systems reform efforts to provide more family-focused services and consumer advocacy efforts to enhance agency responsiveness to the needs of children and families. Despite such efforts, however, the hierarchy between agencies and families remains, and this reality requires that the therapist take a different approach when assessing a family's formal, as versus informal, supports. Therapists should determine the following:

1. The agencies that are involved with the family, and the family's key contact person(s) at each agency.
2. The nature of the agency's involvement ("Why is the family involved with this agency?"), and whether the involvement is legally mandated (e.g., youth in the juvenile justice system and family involved with child protective services) or voluntary.
3. The family's view of the benefits versus costs of continued involvement with the agency.
4. The therapist should touch base with the identified contact person at any agencies that have legally mandated involvement and other

agencies from which the family wishes to continue receiving services. Essentially, the therapist should let the agency representative know that he or she is working with the family and that any recommendations, from the perspective of the agency, would be welcomed.

Throughout the assessment process, the practitioner must remember that an ultimate goal of MST is to *empower* families to address the inevitable difficulties of raising children. Thus, information obtained during assessment should lead to plans to decrease the role of hierarchical formal supports while increasing the role of more equitable informal supports.

Therapist Knowledge of Agency Stakeholders

The MST therapist and his or her colleagues possess much information about the service agency ecology that can be useful in the development of productive family–agency linkages. For example, although some families are aware of the inner workings of agencies or of local politics affecting them, others are not. MST therapists and program administrators, on the other hand, should investigate the strengths and weaknesses of various agencies in the community, of key staff within them, and of the relations between those agencies. That is, therapists and program administrators should be able to make sense of, or understand, the fit of what appears to be more or less helpful behavior on the part of various community agencies (and their staff) with respect to the particular family. To understand the fit of family–agency relations that may impact the outcome of the case, the therapist may need to gather information about intra-agency contingencies and external pressures that influence the behavior of agency professionals with whom the family interacts. Such information might include the following:

- The modus operandi of the agency (goals, objectives, operating procedures), which can inform how (e.g., specific procedures to be followed or forms to be completed) and to whom (e.g., front-line staff or direct supervisors) requests concerning the family are directed, leading to speedier reviews, less frustration, and more collegial relations.
- Beliefs (90% of juvenile offenders are drug abusers, boot camps are the best solution for chronic juvenile offenders) that are faulty and/or based on poor information; attitudinal biases (e.g., what can you expect from those ghetto kids and their families) of key personnel.
- Structural or systemic factors that support or interfere with effective agency functioning (caseloads are increased or reduced due to staff turnover, policy changes, or budgetary scrutiny from the governor's

office; staff wages are notoriously low; a particularly effective or ineffective director is named to the agency, etc.).

- Agency conditions that facilitate or interfere with positive transactions between the family and agency. For example, agency personnel's level of cultural competence contributes to their capacity to interact effectively with persons of different ethnic backgrounds.

Individual and Contextual Factors Affecting the Family's Informal and Formal Supports

The therapist must be mindful of individual and contextual factors that can influence the family's informal and formal supports. Individual factors can include the following:

- *Personality characteristics* (emotional stability, sociability, temperament, trust). For example, parents who are outgoing and energetic will have less difficulty developing support networks than counterparts who are more sanguine, introverted, or suspicious.
- *Cognitive skills.* For example, attributional biases (e.g., "If I ask for help they will think I am weak") can adversely affect interpersonal interactions, whereas strong problem-solving skills can be used to facilitate the development of support networks.
- *Resources* (e.g., time and energy). For example, a single mother of five working full time may have difficulty finding the time and energy needed to develop and maintain close relations with friends and neighbors.
- *Individual psychopathology or substance abuse.* For example, prosocial neighbors and church members may have little desire to provide social support to a drug-abusing parent or may stop visiting a clinically depressed parent who does not "cheer up" during the visit.

Contextual factors affecting the family's informal and formal supports can include the following:

- *Social or cultural mores regarding social contact and interactions.* For example, in some drug-infested communities, socializing outside with neighbors may lead to harassment by drug dealers who do not want their "transactions" observed.
- *Neighborhood stability.* For example, communities with transient populations are likely to have a weak sense of community and low levels of neighborliness.
- *Poor transportation.* The availability of transportation limits the geographic range from which social supports can be developed.

- *Child-care availability.* A parent has difficulty engaging in supportive activities outside the home with friends and neighbors if child care cannot be obtained.

In summary, the assessment of a family's linkage with community supports includes (1) identification of existing informal and formal supports with a corresponding evaluation of the advantages and disadvantages of each linkage, and (2) review of the individual and contextual factors that influence the family's transactions with informal and formal supports. The integration of such information should provide an understanding of the fit of any problems identified regarding the family's support network. Again, the therapist should remember that the point of building strong support networks is to promote the maintenance of therapeutic gains (Principle 9).

Linking Families with Social Supports

An ecologically based continuum of social supports ranges from individuals such as friends and neighbors to civic and religious organizations to business and governmental agencies. The skilled MST practitioner can facilitate the use of multiple components of this continuum to help families to develop strong and diverse social support networks. Assuming that barriers to obtaining support are not substantive, linking families to informal and formal systems of support is a two-step process of (1) identifying available social resources and (2) preparing families to interface with identified resources.

Identification of Informal Supports

Even in the most troubled and disadvantaged communities in the United States, social support resources can still be identified. Consistent with an ecological focus, the therapist moves from the identification of proximal to more distal sources of support.

- *Neighbors* can provide rich sources of support for a family. Neighbors, for example, are often part of MST treatment plans for monitoring youth when parents are working.
- *Work-based relationships* may be one of the few opportunities that parents have for peer interactions. As noted by Crouter and McHale (1993), "Informal friendships among coworkers may be an important setting in which parents seek advice and are exposed to norms about childrearing" (p. 184).
- *Community caretakers and gatekeepers* are individuals who invest time and energy improving the community and can provide rich

sources of informational and sometime instrumental support. Such individuals typically work through local churches and tenant associations and in neighborhood watch programs. Community caretakers and gatekeepers can be identified by asking community residents, "Who do you respect and go to when you need help or advice?"

- *Neighborhood organizations* such as neighborhood watch groups, parent groups (e.g., tough love programs), tenant associations, local businesses, churches, sororities and fraternities, the NAACP or Urban League, 4-H clubs, Rotary clubs, labor unions, and advocacy groups may also provide social resources for families. Almost any organization that has public service as one of its missions is a potential source of social support.

Identification of Formal Supports

Helping families obtain needed resources begins with knowing what is available in the community or knowing how to learn what is available. MST therapists and administrators, therefore, should be informed about federal, state, and local resources and initiatives in their community that are designed to help families of children with behavioral problems. At the federal level, several offices administer programs for children and their families, including the Department of Agriculture (e.g., the food stamp program), the Department of Health and Human Services (e.g., Head Start Bureau), and the Department of the Interior (e.g., the Housing Assistance Program). At state and local levels, programs and initiatives can be identified by the types of services they provide. Services often accessed by MST therapists include mental health treatment, social services, educational supports, health care, substance abuse treatment, vocational training, and recreational opportunities. Therapists should remember that agencies often have multiple and overlapping services. Thus, for example, therapeutic foster care is often provided through juvenile justice, mental health, and social welfare authorities.

Three useful places to start accumulating information on formal resources are the telephone directory, advocacy groups, and local professionals. Telephone directories often have federal, state, and local programs and agencies listed under the services they provide (e.g., education, recreation, and mental health), typically in the "Blue Pages." National advocacy groups, especially those with local affiliates, are a rich source of information on programs designed to help children and families. Because advocacy groups often have a lobbyist working on their staff, they are generally aware of local programs and initiatives that have been funded. In addition, advocacy groups often have lists of contact persons at various agencies and information on applicable laws that govern the behavior of agency personnel. For example, the Federation of Families for Children's Mental Health, a consumer advocacy group established by parents of youth with serious emotional and behavioral disorders, has databases on local resources including parent support groups, parent contacts, and various programs that are available in the community. Finally, local professionals (e.g., social workers, teachers, psychologists, and psychiatrists) can be a good source of information on formal resources.

Creating Family Linkages with Supports

Identifying potential informal and formal supports is the first step toward building the support network. Families and therapists may have difficulty cultivating such supports, especially when resources are scarce. To increase the probability of gaining the cooperation of identified supports, families and therapists should follow several guidelines.

FOLLOW STANDARD PROCEDURES

For socially isolated parents, developing an increased pool of eligible supports is the primary focus. Increasing the number of persons eligible for a parent's informal social support network involves two steps. First, the parent must be in a position to meet others. Likely places to meet others include neighborhood and civic groups (e.g., tenant associations and YWCA) and church groups. Attendance and active participation in community activities is also likely to increase the pool of eligible supports (e.g., Neighborwood Watch). The second step involves ensuring that the parent has the repertoire of social skills needed to seek out and benefit from increased exposure to others. If a parent lacks appropriate behaviors and skills, the therapist must devote time to the development of such skills (as outlined in Chapter 7). Thus, as with all MST interventions, the therapist must determine the barriers to, for example, engaging in a pleasant conversation with a fellow church member. Interventions are then designed to address these barriers using the parent's strengths.

When interfacing with formal sources of support, parents and practitioners must learn and follow normal agency operating procedures (at least until the time that personal contacts allow the family to bypass some of these procedures). Most formal organizations have a set of explicit or implicit procedures that govern how things get done. Explicit procedures include who to contact and how (e.g., phone calls, letters, facsimiles, and in person), available appointment times, and cancellation and rescheduling procedures. Generally, parents can obtain information on agency procedures from any of the following:

- Agency brochures or pamphlets.
- Agency personnel (e.g., a receptionist can inform the parent of require-

ments, such as paper work, that must be completed before face-to-face contact is scheduled).
• Extended family, friends, neighbors, coworkers, and so on, who have had experience with the agency.

Implicit rules include the protocol of manners and mutual respect that should accompany interactions. Formal agencies often control scarce resources and gatekeepers have discretion regarding who receives these resources. Thus, therapists and families, as described subsequently, should endeavor to create positive relations with those who control the resources.

INTERPERSONAL PRESENTATION AND ATTITUDE

Building a positive informal support network is not an easy task. Reasonably competent individuals must be identified in the parent's social ecology, and the parent must have or develop the ability to engage these individuals in a mutually satisfying quid pro quo. Behaviors that are respectful, emotionally positive, and giving are more likely to gain the cooperation of informal supports. Thus, the therapist may need to help the parent develop and implement a plan to engage a particular source of support. The basis of this plan would be to determine the ways in which the parent's needs and resources might fit with the possible needs and resources of the support source (e.g., an elderly neighbor would love to have someone visit regularly or cook a meal, and the parent needs someone with whom his or her adolescent can check in after school). In addition, the parent and therapist must "match" the behavioral styles of the parent and support source. Individuals are more responsive to those who are "more like them."

When contacting formal sources of support, first impressions are very important because they influence present and future agency responses to the parent and family. Consequently, a parent's initial (and subsequent) meeting with formal sources of support should be characterized by respect and appropriate deportment and decorum. That is, the parent must dress and behave in a manner consistent with the mores of the setting. For example, meeting with a judge requires formal behavior and dress. When such standards are violated, a judge is less likely to respond in a manner consistent with the parents' and therapist's goals. Consequently, therapists may need to prepare family members for interactions with agency personnel from whom they desire resources and favorable decisions. Several straightforward steps include the following:

• Discussing and role-playing appropriate behavior and dress.
• Observing others skilled in interacting with agency staff, preferably in the naturalistic setting.

- Asking extended family, friends, neighbors, coworkers, and so on about useful strategies.

Obtaining resources may sometimes require that parents and therapists behave in ways that are inconsistent with how they feel. Many individuals balk at acting in a manner inconsistent with how they actually feel (e.g., smiling and cooperating when they are angry and resentful), especially with an agency professional who has annoyed or harmed them. Although the professional may have made a mistake, parents and therapists who compound the mistake by responding with anger and hostility toward the professional are less likely to achieve their desired goals. Few benefits result from the development of adversarial relationships with professionals who control the resources. Consequently, parents and therapists should learn to incorporate the following in their interactions with resource gatekeepers:

- Focus on the goals (e.g., obtaining resources).
- Take a "one-down" position when necessary (i.e., humbling oneself).
- Look the gatekeeper directly in the eyes, smile, and use positive reinforcement (e.g., compliments).
- Send formal evidence of appreciation (e.g., a thank you card or a drawing by the child).

Addressing Barriers to the Development of Social Supports

In light of the serious problems experienced by the vast majority of youths and families referred for MST services, the development of positive informal and formal supports is rarely as straightforward a process as described previously. Therapists and families may find progress blocked by any number or combination of obstacles, and these barriers can often be grouped into the following categories:

1. *Individual*: very low cognitive abilities, social skill deficits, parental drug abuse, parental psychiatric disorder.
2. *Family*: high levels of conflict, marital discord, criminal attitudes and behavior of family members, lack of resources.
3. *Neighborhood*: high crime, low economic base, poor public transportation, high rate of transience, low percentage of property ownership.
4. *Family–agency linkage:* poor match with agency culture and mission.
5. *Agency–MST linkage:* poor match with agency culture and mission.

The purpose of this section is to describe several common barriers encountered by MST practitioners working with family–community/agency linkages and to provide suggestions for overcoming these obstacles.

Individual Barriers

Significant individual-level barriers to developing effective social support networks include parental drug abuse, severe mental illness, social skill deficits, and very low cognitive functioning. Because these difficulties can present barriers to successful adaptation in virtually all aspects of functioning (e.g., marital relations, parent–child relations, family–school interface, and employment), they have been addressed in earlier chapters. Hence, if an individual-level variable is interfering with the development of social support, the therapist is referred to sections of this volume that address that variable.

Family Barriers

The development of positive social support networks can also be hampered by several characteristics of the family, including high levels of conflict (e.g., neighbors avoid the family because the police must often be called to quiet family disturbances), marital discord (e.g., the couple allows marital conflicts to spill over into their work environments, upsetting coworkers and supervisors), criminal attitudes and behavior (e.g., family members routinely steal items that neighbors leave in their yards), and a lack of family resources (e.g., financial, time, and energy). Aspects of marital and family relations that might impede the development of social support networks are described extensively in Chapter 5 and 4, along with suggestions for overcoming these barriers. This section attends to a common barrier experienced by disadvantaged families referred for MST—lack of instrumental and financial resources.

As the MST therapist guides the caregivers in implementing action-oriented interventions (Principle 4) that require daily or weekly effort (Principle 7) to reach overarching goals, barriers to accomplishing these tasks will quickly become apparent. When obstacles emerge, the therapist's central tasks are to do the following:

1. Determine how identified barriers fit the family's social network and community context.
2. Collaborate in the design of strength-based solutions to overcome the barriers (Principle 2).
3. Implement the solutions with special consideration given to factors affecting the long-term maintenance of clinical change (Principle 9).

Therapists must note the particular importance of Principle 9 when conceptualizing interventions that involve agencies and the community. Historically, and in contrast with the clear emphasis of MST, community-based treatments emphasize the connection of the family with formal and distal systems of support, such as parent support groups, agency-sponsored "big

brothers," or federal financial aid. MST, on the other hand, strongly emphasizes the development of interventions that tap more indigenous or proximal
supports. Informal supports are more likely to promote empowerment of
families and to continue to be accessible after treatment ends. Therefore, the
therapist should help the family to access or develop resource capacity from
within their family, extended family, or circle of friends and neighbors. If, and
only if, such sources of social support do not exist and cannot be developed
despite the well-targeted and concerted efforts of the therapist and family, the
therapist should assist the family in pursuing local community resources that,
preferably, are not associated with local or state government. This search
should begin with more proximal local organizations, such as churches,
recreational centers, schools, and community groups. Only when all local
avenues of support have been tapped should the therapist move to more formal
agency-based sources of assistance.

The following case provides an example of developing and using indigenous supports to prevent an out-of-home placement.

Joe Smith was a 13-year-old boy who lived with his mother and older
sister in government-subsidized housing in a high-crime neighborhood. Joe
was referred to the MST program by juvenile court because he was at
imminent risk of incarceration due to chronic delinquent behavior. Ms. Smith
reported that helping Joe stay out of trouble was her main treatment goal.
Assessment revealed that Joe's delinquent behavior was linked primarily with
a lack of parental monitoring, which in turn, allowed him to associate with
deviant peers. Thus, the therapist helped Ms. Smith to develop a system to
monitor her son's whereabouts, minimize his interface with deviant peers, and
provide differential contingencies for improved versus antisocial behavior. To
promote access to prosocial peers, Ms. Smith agreed to allow her son to play
football, as Joe enjoyed playing football and knew several prosocial peers on
the team. Ms. Smith was "on board" with the treatment plan and seemed
motivated to work toward the goal of reducing her son's criminal activity.

Several days after the initial implementation of the interventions, the
therapist checked with the mother, youth, coach, and teachers (Principle 8) to
assess preliminary outcomes. Ms. Smith, unfortunately, had not been able to
effectively implement the monitoring system or apply the behavioral consequences. A close evaluation of the barriers to implementation revealed that
Ms. Smith lacked the social support, time, and financial resources needed to
carry out the treatment plan that was developed in collaboration with the
therapist. Consequently, the therapist decided to conduct a more complete
assessment of the family's support network to gain a better understanding of
the failure to implement. In terms of financial resources, Ms. Smith worked
two 25-hour-per-week jobs at minimum wage and without benefits (e.g.,
health insurance) to support her family. Despite having two jobs, Ms. Smith

was barely able to pay her bills and was unable to afford the fees required for Joe's football equipment and transportation. Moreover, as Ms. Smith worked 50 hours a week, she had difficulty finding time to carry out the treatment plans. Compounding the problem, Ms. Smith's social support network consisted of a mother who was elderly and medically ill and a sister recently diagnosed with schizophrenia. Thus, at best, Ms. Smith found herself supporting rather than being supported by her social network. Given these barriers, Ms. Smith's difficulty in closely monitoring her son, implementing the behavioral contingencies, and transporting him to prosocial activities was fully understandable and reflected a significant lack of instrumental support.

To progress in achieving the ultimate goals of the case (i.e., reduce crime and prevent incarceration), the therapist and Ms. Smith developed a series of intermediate goals that targeted the identified barriers to implementing the aforementioned interventions. The initial intermediate goals required Ms. Smith and the therapist to (1) find someone to help monitor Joe's whereabouts after school and ensure that he attended football practice and (2) figure out a way to finance Joe's football expenses. When working to help Ms. Smith overcome these barriers, the therapist first explored proximal resources such as her family and friends. By carefully assessing the support potential of each of these individuals, the therapist was surprised to learn that Ms. Smith had a brother who lived nearby. Although Ms. Smith and her brother did not communicate often, they were on friendly terms, the brother seemed prosocial, and he liked Joe. The therapist also learned that Ms. Smith had friends at church whom she had not mentioned previously because she "did not want to burden them" with her problems. After discovering these potential supports, the therapist worked with Ms. Smith to better understand her reasons for not accessing their assistance on her own. She discovered that Ms. Smith had "just drifted away" from her brother over the past few years because of her busy schedule and their lack of shared interests. Ms. Smith had not considered her brother a resource because she saw him infrequently and, similar to her church friends, did not want to "give him her problems." On the one hand, the therapist saw this negative attribution of support-seeking behavior as a potential barrier to intervention implementation; on the other hand, the therapist recognized the strength (desire to be self-sufficient, to engage in relationships as an equal rather than as a bother) in the statement.

Viewing Ms. Smith's reluctance to be perceived as a bother and desire to engage others as an equal as a strength, the therapist then facilitated Ms. Smith's development and implementation of a plan that would ensure that everyone was reinforced in some way for their assistance (thus reducing the possibility of being perceived as a bother and increasing the possibility of being seen as an equal). Ms. Smith first met with the football coach to determine when and where practices would be held and what would be required of Joe in terms of money, equipment and time. She then talked with

Joe about these needs and how to best meet them. Next, Ms. Smith and Joe approached her brother together and worked out an arrangement in which Joe's uncle agreed to drive Joe home from practices and promote his involvement in the sport. In return, Joe promised to help his uncle, a painter, paint houses 1 weekend day each month. Ms. Smith located an after-school, teacher-supervised study hall that Joe agreed to attend on days that he did not have football practice. The church readily committed to be Joe's financial sponsor for the football team. In return, Ms. Smith became actively involved in one of the church's mission projects two Sundays per month after services.

Thus, through reorganizing her informal social support network to make better use of resources within the family's natural ecology, Ms. Smith was able to overcome the initial barriers to the successful implementation of interventions with her son. Moreover, by reorganizing and mobilizing the family's informal support network, the costs of treatment services were minimized and the probability that treatment gains would be sustained following treatment termination was enhanced.

Neighborhood Barriers

The family's neighborhood can play a very important role in shaping the life of the family and the actions of its members. As described in Chapter 1, several well-researched models of juvenile delinquency and drug use demonstrate that neighborhood environment can attenuate or contribute to youth antisocial behavior above and beyond the impact of family, peers, and school. As such, the neighborhood has the potential to provide positive social support (e.g., neighbors willing to monitor the behavior and safety of local children and crime watch) as well as contribute to youth behavioral problems through negative support (e.g., neighborhood norms that sanction drug use, drug distribution, domestic violence, prostitution, and unemployment).

When neighborhood-based barriers interfere with the attainment of treatment goals, the MST therapist should assess the neighborhood both in terms of its strengths and weaknesses. A useful beginning is to ask the parents about the informal networks that exist within the community (Unger & Wandersman, 1985). Because the parents of youth presenting serious antisocial behavior might not be connected with prosocial neighborhood networks, the therapist might also talk with the owners of local businesses (i.e., the corner store manager or hairdresser), the resident assistants of the housing development, or pastors in area churches. These people often have access to, or are involved in, informal social networks that can serve as informational and instrumental resources for families. When linked with certain informal networks, for example, a parent may be able to find low-cost, quality child care for a young child or information about summer job possibilities for an adolescent. Importantly, informal neighborhood resources are usually free of cost and should continue to be accessible to the family long after treatment ends.

The informal neighborhood network is a strength that can be utilized by the therapist and family, but even the most disadvantaged of neighborhoods often have additional strengths and potential resources as well: parks and recreational centers for after-school and weekend activities; schools with after-school activities (e.g., clubs, sports, arts, and drama); churches with youth groups; and community policing, where specific law enforcement officers are assigned to specific neighborhoods.

Specific individuals within community settings should also be viewed as potential resources: a teacher may agree to tutor a youth after school, a church member may transport a teen to practice, and a business owner may mentor a youth in exchange for helping around the store.

To summarize, when neighborhood-based barriers interfere with treatment outcome, the therapist should assess the neighborhood and surrounding community to identify informal social support networks and community strengths. The following case example demonstrates how the identification and utilization of neighborhood strengths greatly facilitated favorable outcome in a difficult case.

Andrew was a 14-year-old violent offender who lived with his mother and five siblings in a crime-ridden neighborhood. In assessing the fit of Andrew's antisocial behavior, the therapist acquired considerable evidence that Andrew's aggression was exacerbated by boredom, a lack of structure for his free time, and easy access to deviant peers who lived in the surrounding community. Although Andrew's mother was willing to increase her efforts to monitor and discipline his behavior, she needed assistance in monitoring his neighborhood activities, and Andrew was greatly in need of community-based activities to structure his time.

To better understand the neighborhood's informal support network, the therapist spoke with Andrew's mother about people in the community that she perceived as informational resources. Per the mother's suggestion, the therapist visited the manager of the corner convenience store with the mother to ask about potential resources in the neighborhood (e.g., "Who in the neighborhood might be interested in reducing crime and helping youth?"). By conducting such interviews, the therapist discovered two potential resources: a policeman assigned to the community who seemed genuinely interested in helping problem youth and the manager of a car repair shop located nearby.

Eventually, the therapist and caregiver put into place a plan in which the neighborhood policeman would report Andrew's whereabouts in the community to the mother, which greatly facilitated her ability to monitor and provide appropriate reinforcers and punishments. The manager of the car repair shop agreed to allow Andrew to help in his garage, thereby providing structure and a prosocial activity to diminish Andrew's boredom and free time. To recipro-cate, the mother sent a letter to the policeman's sergeant commending his work and periodically baked pies for the garage manager. Thus, a community-based intervention was used to meet the therapeutic goals of monitoring Andrew's behavior and providing more structure.

Barriers Pertaining to Family–Agency Linkages

When a therapist encounters barriers associated with the family's relations with an agency (e.g., mental health, juvenile justice, and social welfare), the understanding of fit requires that the therapist be knowledgeable about the internal workings of the family and of the agency. Particular attention should be devoted to factors that influence the agency's ability to be responsive to and empowering of families.

AGENCY MISSION AND CULTURE

When agencies are not being responsive to or empowering of families, two frequently encountered barriers should be explored in an attempt to understand the fit of this difficulty. The first potential barrier is the *formal mission* of the organization, including the rules and structure supporting day-to-day efforts to accomplish its mission. Often, the fit of the family–agency stalemate highlights differences between the goals of the family (and MST therapist) and the goals of the agency. Thus, although the family's mission may be to keep their children at home and out of trouble, the mission of the social service agency may be to ensure that the youth and community are safe, and the agency may perceive sending youth home as counter to that mission. By understanding the legal mandate, procedural rules, and organizational guide-lines that constrain the agency, the therapist can avoid wasting time and energy on interventions that require a change in state policy and focus on more manageable issues, as illustrated in the following case.

Child Protective Services removed a 10-year-old boy from his mother's home because he was being sexually abused by her boyfriend and was presenting conduct problems. The boy was terminated from six different out-of-home placements (one inpatient, four foster care, one group home) during his first 6 weeks of placement, and, consequently, his conduct problems were worsening as the lack of stable placement continued. One of the family's goals, therefore, was to quickly find an acceptable placement for the boy, preferably with a member of the extended family (i.e., kinship foster care) in or near the neighborhood where the family lived. A concomitant goal was for the therapist to provide the boy and "foster parents" with the resources needed to ensure the success of the placement. Although the family and therapist located a home with the boy's aunt that was appropriate and safe for the child, the custodial agency was reluctant to utilize this resource. A meeting with the agency case manager revealed several barriers to placement with the extended family. The first and largest barrier pertained to rules and procedural guidelines that constrained the agency from changing the placement quickly. Other barriers included the case manager's large caseload, which affected her ability to process paper work quickly, and the agency's lack of knowledge about the comprehensiveness and intensity of MST home-based services. Although the therapist was not able to have an impact on the first barrier (i.e., rules and regulations), she could address the remaining barriers. The therapist, therefore shared information about the boy and family, thus facilitating the agency's understanding of the case; shared information about the MST program and noted, in light of that information, that she could easily take on activities construed as case management services (taking the boy to appointments, enrolling him in the school near the extended family member, dealing with Medicaid paper work, etc.) for the boy, thus reducing the case manager's workload and allowing her to complete the paper work more quickly. Finally, by interfacing frequently with the case worker throughout the course of treatment, the boy's placement in a family-based setting was expedited.

A second frequently encountered barrier to family–agency collaboration is the *culture* of the agency. Agency culture refers to the group's informal perception of its mission or role. Importantly, the informal perception of the agency's mission may differ dramatically from the formal or official mission of the agency. For example, the official mission of a local middle school is to educate all children, yet the culture of that school was to exclude youth with severe behavioral problems from school. When the therapist has a sense of the "culture" of an organization, he or she should next determine the possible bases of the culture. In the case of the local middle school, the culture of exclusion was supported by several factors: Teachers were overwhelmed with work, were not trained to work with behaviorally disturbed youth, were not supported by school administrators when attempting to work with problem youth, and were afraid they might be harmed by the youth. The fear of harm was elevated by an incident in a nearby county where a teacher was murdered by a student. By understanding the underlying bases of an agency's culture or informal perception of its mission, the MST therapist can begin to help the caregiver to develop interventions that overcome these barriers. In the case of this middle school, the therapist and caregiver provided the teachers with an "empathy-inducing" appreciation of the family's circumstances and efforts to improve their lives, expressed appreciation for the teacher's willingness (as reluctantly forthcoming as it was) to work with the child despite her workload and developed a behavioral intervention plan that placed most of the responsibility on the caregiver, offered 7-day, 24-hour availability for crisis consultation, and established a safety plan.

FAMILY CONTRIBUTIONS TO FAMILY–AGENCY DIFFICULTIES

Family or caregiver factors can also play a role in family–agency difficulties. In addition to those individual (depression, parental drug abuse) and family (social isolation) barriers to productive family–agency collaboration discussed previously, many families are unable to advocate effectively for themselves. The most common reasons for such difficulties are lack of education about how to obtain appropriate services, history of hostile interactions with the agency, for example, in a family whose children were taken into custody by the agency, and history of a subordinate relationship with the agency, which often reflects the hierarchical nature of families' interactions with formal supports. Often, these three barriers to effective family–agency relations exist in the same case, as the following example illustrates.

A family reunification case, seeking to reunite a child with her family after a 6-month removal, was referred to the MST program by Child Protective Services. The goal of the agency, family, and MST program was reunification, yet the mother, Ms. Jones, was extremely guarded and refused to communicate with representatives of the agency. This refusal to communicate created a major obstacle in achieving treatment goals, as the mother needed to comply with the agency rules to regain custody of her daughter. The therapist's evaluation of the family–agency linkage revealed that although the agency was on board and attempting to cooperate with therapeutic recommendations, the mother was highly suspicious of the agency's motives (e.g., mother retained custody of three other children and feared that they might be removed as well) based on past experiences concerning her daughter's removal. In addition Ms. Jones clearly lacked the skills needed to advocate for herself with the agency (e.g., she frequently became angry and left meetings), and this difficulty was exacerbated by depressive symptoms (e.g., sad affect, irritability, sleep difficulties, hopelessness, and feeling that things will never get better).

Thus, the therapist targeted these three concerns for treatment (i.e., hostile relationship, unempowered relationship, and lack of knowledge and skill). Given that the mother's suspiciousness of and poor skills in interfacing with the agency posed an immediate threat to reunification, the therapist worked with Ms. Jones to identify one person in the organization whom she trusted more than others. The therapist then encouraged the agency to have this person interface primarily with the family until further therapeutic progress could be made. As Ms. Jones seemed to be experiencing a major depression that was affecting her capacity to interface with Child Protective Services as well as with her family and friends, the therapist worked simultaneously to facilitate the treatment of depression. Ms. Jones agreed to obtain a psychiatric evaluation during which an antidepressant was prescribed. To further facilitate the reduction of depressive symptoms, the MST therapist provided cognitive-behavioral therapy that targeted the negative cognitions affecting Ms. Jones's ability to interface with the agency. Based on the therapist's assessment of the fit of the depression, another component of treatment included helping Ms. Jones increase her social support network. After 4–5 weeks of treatment, the depressive symptoms began to improve.

As Ms. Jones felt less irritable and hopeless and had more energy, the therapist moved to target her lack of education and skills in interacting with agency personnel. First, the therapist developed an understanding of exactly what transpires each time Ms. Jones disrupts an agency meeting. Then, the therapist worked with Ms. Jones to interrupt this sequence of events (Principle 5) by providing education, role-play and practice. When Ms. Jones seemed to have mastered these skills, the therapist and mother practiced by meeting with the "trusted" agency worker, then gradually reentered into negotiations with other agency members. By the end of the MST treatment (14 weeks), although still somewhat suspicious of agency workers, Ms. Jones was able to work with them well enough (without the MST therapist's assistance) to accomplish the goal of obtaining custody of her daughter.

As demonstrated by the previous example, one of the goals of MST is to empower families that are linked with agencies to advocate for themselves within that organization. Ideally, when MST treatment is completed, the family will be involved only with agencies that are absolutely necessary for attainment or maintenance of therapeutic goals. Within the context of this relationship, the family should be empowered—family members should be able to interface with the agency with enough savvy to obtain needed services, but overinvolvement or dependence on the organization should not be promoted.

Barriers Pertaining to MST–Agency Linkages

Because many families receiving MST services are embedded in a complex web of community organizations and agencies, a member of the treatment team, usually a clinical supervisor or —depending upon the number of clinical teams comprising the MST program—the MST program administrator is often designated to assist team members with agency interfaces. It should be noted, however, that the community-liaison functions required to ensure ongoing collaboration with agencies that influence family outcomes is part and parcel of each MST therapist's job. In addition, however, because removal of barriers to achieving positive outcomes sometimes requires that agencies, and the MST program, accommodate one another with procedural or policy changes, it is important to establish a vehicle whereby agency and MST staff with the authority to make such changes can have ready access to each other. To this end, having the clinical team supervisor or program administrator (also trained in MST) maintain an extensive working knowledge of the community agencies and ongoing dialogue with pertinent personnel in each agency is useful. Ongoing relations, therefore, are established with police; social service, mental health, and juvenile justice agencies; schools; and any other organizations that have an impact on the lives of youth and families in treatment. The clinical supervisor or program administrator works with the therapists, who should possess similar (though sometimes less extensive) knowledge, to develop strategies that facilitate MST–agency cooperation, thereby increasing the chances of achieving the family's treatment goals.

Commonly encountered barriers between MST programs and other agencies often pertain to a lack of understanding or education on both parts about the informal and formal missions of the respective organizations. Similar to the evaluation of family–agency barriers, the assessment of MST–agency barriers requires an understanding of the agency's culture, formal mission, rules and structure and the key individuals comprising the agency. When such an understanding is developed, interventions to improve MST–agency linkages are often structured in much the same way as for a family-based intervention. That is, the therapist first works to align with the agency and identify common goals. When common goals are established, mutually agreeable interventions can be developed and implemented to reach the goals, as in the following example.

A preliminary evaluation of placement outcomes of one MST program revealed that although youth receiving MST were spending considerably less time in residential treatment facilities, this favorable outcome was being partially offset by an increase in days spent in juvenile justice facilities. To address this difficulty, the MST program administrator and team clinical supervisor met with the director of juvenile justice to develop a plan to divert program youth from correctional placements when therapeutically indicated. During this meeting, it became apparent that barriers to such diversion needed to be addressed within the respective organizations. The first barrier was a lack of knowledge within the juvenile justice system about the MST program and the unusually comprehensive services provided by the MST treatment team. The second barrier was a lack of understanding on the part of the MST treatment team about the rules governing the juvenile justice system and the ways in which these rules could be used to the program's advantage. To address these barriers, the juvenile justice director facilitated the following:

(1) a meeting between the family court judges and the program directors to educate the judges about the program and affirm that the common goals of rehabilitating youth and preserving families were shared by both organizations, (2) a similar meeting with the family court prosecutors and public defenders, and (3) interagency procedures so that the MST treatment team and juvenile justice staff communicated about the appropriateness of placement in detention and possible alternatives to such for those youths in the MST program who were truly at imminent risk of incarceration. Thus, by determining the common goals of the MST program and a key agency, the program was able to develop lines of communication and collaboration that promoted the attainment of family and program goals.

Building Collaborations with Agency Colleagues

As in any other intervention, the success or failure of a given treatment ultimately rests on the shoulders of individual people—family members, the therapist, and professionals from other agencies. Every agency we have collaborated with included incredibly bright, hard-working, and committed professionals, but occasionally there is an individual in an organization who repeatedly seems to impede therapeutic progress, despite the best efforts of agency and MST staff to design strategies to enlist cooperation. An important goal of every MST therapist and program, therefore, is to identify and build strong relationships with the former agency professionals and avoid the latter as much as possible. Such advice may be difficult to heed, however, if the troublesome agency professional is integral to the operation of the organization.

When the "problematic professional" is both impeding treatment and unavoidable, we suggest that this obstacle be addressed first within a meeting of the therapist team and clinical supervisor. The team should be encouraged to approach difficulty in engaging professionals in other agencies in much the same way as they would conceptualize and problem solve difficulty engaging a family in treatment. Thus, the team should make a strength and barrier list about the problematic professional and an assessment of the possible fit of behaviors that impede treatment. Interventions can then be developed that are strength based and emphasize common goals. If the MST program is composed of multiple teams and a program administrator serves as a primary community liaison, he or she should sit in on this initial problem-solving meeting to become aware of strategies the team is designing to address the problem. The team's community liaison may need to invest time in developing a good working relationship with this individual's supervisor as well. In general, however, the supervisor should not be contacted until other interventions are tried, although specific situations may warrant "going over the professional's head."

In the same vein, to accomplish the task of building strong relations with staff from key agencies, MST team members are encouraged to utilize engagement skills similar to those used with families (e.g., emphasizing strengths and common goals). The clinical supervisor and/or program manager taking the lead with community-liaison functions should develop "interventions" to build and maintain affiliations based on an understanding of the strengths and needs of each agency. For example, if increased social contact between an organization and the MST team may improve treatment outcomes for a project, a joint gathering or party may be planned. Our MST organization has attended pot luck luncheons hosted by the Department of Juvenile Justice (DJJ), participated in picnics and games jointly hosted with DJJ and the Mental Health Center, and invited key agency personnel to various parties and educational functions. At times we give doughnuts or fruit baskets to various agency personnel to show appreciation for going beyond the call of duty or to express contrition when we have erred. Great care is taken to keep lines of communication open through phone contacts, formal and informal meetings, letters, and electronic mail. Moreover, the affiliation of MST programs with community agencies is similar to the connections families in treatment have with their social supports in that maintaining a quid pro quo is necessary. Thus, in our relationships with agencies, we try to act with integrity, follow through with promises, and give at least as much as we receive. To the extent that the families and youth in treatment are embedded in these organizations, therapeutic outcome can be impacted by how adept the MST program is with these interfaces.

Conclusion

The MST therapist should acquire an understanding of how families in treatment access and utilize community-based resources. When obstacles or deficiencies in this interface that impact treatment are apparent, an understanding of the fit of this problem within the broader systemic context should be developed. Developing an understanding of the fit will often involve an assessment of the informal and formal resources available to families. When generating interventions, the MST therapist should attempt to empower the family to access more proximal or informal supports, paying careful attention to the promotion of treatment generalization. By understanding the importance of informal and formal resources, how to assess them, common barriers encountered, and steps for overcoming these obstacles, the MST therapist will be better equipped to develop ecologically valid interventions that attain desired outcomes.

III

OUTCOMES AND POLICY

9

Outcomes of MST: Findings from Controlled Evaluations

In this chapter
- The short-term and long-term effects of MST on adolescent behavior, adolescent criminal activity, parental psychopathology, family relations, and out-of-home placements.
- Current studies that are examining the generalizability of MST to other clinical populations and the adaptability of MST to models of service delivery other than home based.
- The cost-effectiveness of MST.

Careful documentation of clinical outcomes produced by MST for children and families has been a high priority since the initial development of this treatment model in the late 1970s. During the 1990s, for example, significant resources have been spent examining the effectiveness of MST in rigorous research studies. In light of our ongoing commitment to examining outcomes, a substantial research base has been developed regarding the effects of MST on adolescent behavior, family functioning, and out-of-home placements. In addition, several major MST-based projects are currently in progress, and these should provide substantive new information during the next few years about the effectiveness of MST with other clinical populations; associations between supervisory support, therapist adherence to MST, and youth outcome; and cost-effectiveness.

Completed and Near-Completed Outcome Studies

Memphis, Tennessee

In 1976 one of us (S. W. H.) took his first academic position in the Department of Psychology at Memphis State University (now the University of Memphis). There, he was principle investigator of the first two evaluations of MST.

INNER-CITY DELINQUENTS

The first MST outcome study (Henggeler et al., 1986) was conducted from 1978 to 1983 on a small budget that made use of graduate students as therapists and data managers and undergraduate students as research assistants. The study used a quasi-experimental design in which a federally funded community delinquency diversion program referred youths and families to the MST condition. The comparison participants were selected from the case files of the diversion program to match the demographic characteristics of the families in the MST condition. An assessment battery, including self-reports, other reports, and observational measures, was administered before treatment and soon after treatment was completed. Findings showed that MST was more effective than usual community services in decreasing adolescent behavioral problems and improving family relations, especially family communication and affect.

Although modest in scope by today's standards (e.g., no follow-up or cost analysis), the study made several contributions to the development and refinement of MST. First, the delivery of MST was originally intended to take place in the well-equipped clinic located in the psychology building at the University. Shortly after beginning the study, however, it became clear that participant attrition was going to be extremely high if the project continued to adhere primarily to a site-based model of service delivery, even if appointment times were made flexible for the families. Because the families of juvenile offenders would often not come to the clinic, the therapists went to the families. Out of this necessity was born the home-based model of service delivery that has characterized subsequent evaluations of MST. As discussed in Henggeler and Borduin (1995), the home-based model has many advantages in addition to improving treatment completion rates (e.g., more valid assessment, improved treatment generalization, and facilitating the therapeutic alliance). The second contribution to the refinement of MST pertained to the observed outcomes at posttreatment. Improved family relations and adolescent behavior supported the social ecological treatment theory of MST, a theoretical model that was consistent with emerging findings from the field of criminology regarding the determinants of delinquency (see Chapter 1). Third, the favorable effects of MST supported the viability of conducting further studies of the effects of MST in treating serious clinical problems.

CHILD ABUSE AND NEGLECT

The first randomized trial of MST and the first evaluation to use a well-specified treatment for the comparison group was conducted by Brunk et al. (1987) with maltreating families referred by the Department of Social Services. Families were randomly assigned to home-based MST versus clinic-based behavioral parent training conditions in a pretest–posttest design. MST was provided by doctoral students in clinical psychology, whereas behavioral parent training was provided by mental health professionals employed at a community mental health center. Several results at posttreatment showed similar improvements across the treatment conditions: Parents reported decreased psychiatric symptomatology, reduced overall stress, and a reduction in the severity of identified problems. Observational measures of parent–child interaction, however, favored the MST condition. Parent–child dyads in the MST condition showed the types of changes in interaction that suggest decreased risk for maltreatment: Maltreating parents controlled their child's behavior more effectively, maltreated children displayed less passive noncompliance, and neglecting parents became more responsive to their child's behavior. Though lacking a follow-up, this study remains one of the few randomized trials of a family-based treatment for child abuse and neglect (Becker et al., 1995). Moreover, as discussed later in this chapter, the Brunk et al. (1987) study served as the forerunner of an important randomized trial of a family-based alternative to out-of-home placement of children taken into custody for abuse or neglect.

Columbia, Missouri

In 1982, another of us (C. M. B.) took his first academic position in the Department of Psychology at the University of Missouri–Columbia. From 1983 to 1986 he conducted a relatively large-scale randomized trial of MST in collaboration with the Missouri Department of Juvenile Justice. Several outcome studies of MST are based on this trial.

JUVENILE SEXUAL OFFENDERS

Though modest in scope and size ($n = 16$), to date, this study (Borduin, Henggeler, Blaske, & Stein, 1990) is the first and only published randomized trial with juvenile sexual offenders. Youths and their families were randomly assigned to treatment conditions: home-based MST delivered by doctoral students in clinical psychology versus outpatient counseling delivered by community-based mental health professionals. Recidivism results at a 3-year follow-up are revealing. Significantly fewer participants in the MST condition were rearrested for sexual crimes (one of eight vs. six of eight), and the mean frequency of sexual rearrests was considerably lower in the MST condition (0.12 vs. 1.62). Moreover, the mean frequency of rearrest for nonsexual crimes was lower for the offenders who received MST (0.62) than for counterparts who received outpatient counseling (2.25). This study represents one of the few challenges to prevailing (and unvalidated) clinical practices for juvenile sexual offenders.

CHRONIC JUVENILE OFFENDERS

In what is arguably one of the most important randomized trials conducted in the field of delinquency, Borduin et al. (1995) compared the effects of home-based MST versus office-based, individual, outpatient counseling in the treatment of almost 200 chronic juvenile offenders. MST therapists were doctoral students in clinical psychology and outpatient counselors were master's-level mental health professionals. Self-report, other-report, and family observational measures were collected at pretreatment and posttreatment assessment sessions, and recidivism was examined at an approximately 4-year follow-up. Remarkably, this complex study was conducted on a small budget by taking advantage of student resources at the university. A downside for conducting complex randomized trials with limited resources, however, is the often considerable lag between the beginning of the study and the publication of manuscripts describing outcomes (see also Henggeler et al., 1986 [which began in 1977]).

Analyses of the pretreatment to posttreatment outcomes indicated that MST, in comparison with individual counseling, effected the types of changes in family functioning that were assumed to lead to reductions in the criminal activity of the chronic juvenile offenders. Family members who received MST reported increased family cohesion and adaptability. Moreover, family members' reports of improved family relations were supported by findings from the observational measures: Family members showed increased supportiveness and decreased conflict–hostility during family discussions. Of note, parents in the MST condition showed greater reductions in psychiatric symptomatology than did parents of offenders in the individual therapy condition.

In light of the improved functioning evidenced by families in the MST condition, one would predict improvement in behavioral problems in the youths, and such was the case. Results from a 4-year follow-up of recidivism showed that youths who received MST were significantly less likely to be rearrested than youths who received individual counseling. As shown in Figure 9.1, offenders who completed MST had lower recidivism rates (22%) than youths in families that dropped out of MST (47%), youths who completed individual counseling (71%), youths who dropped out of individual counseling (71%), and youths in families that refused to participate in either treatment (88%). Moreover, the MST dropouts were at lower risk of rearrest than the individual counseling completers, individual counseling dropouts, and treatment refusers. These differential arrest rates suggest the possibility of a dosage effect, where a partial dose of MST (MST dropouts) is better than no dose (individual counseling groups) but not as beneficial as a full dose (MST completers). In addition, the lack of difference in recidivism rates between individual counseling completers versus dropouts might be anticipated based on the lack of established effectiveness for individually based treatments for delinquency.

A more fine-grained examination of the rearrest data revealed several other favorable effects of MST. First, examination of the recidivists from each group showed that MST youths arrested during follow-up were arrested less often (mean number of arrests for recidivists = 1.71 vs. 5.43) and for less serious offenses than counterparts in the individual counseling condition. Second, youths in the MST condition were less likely to be arrested for violent crimes (rape, attempted rape, sexual assault, aggravated assault, assault/battery) following treatment than were youths in the individual counseling condition. Third, as noted subsequently, youths who received MST had a lower rate of drug-related arrests than individual counseling counterparts (4% vs. 16%).

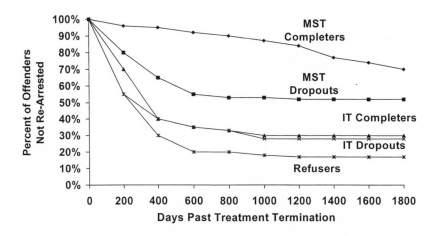

FIGURE 9.1. Missouri delinquency project survival analysis.

Importantly, the effectiveness of MST was not moderated by adolescent age, race (white vs. African American), social class, gender, or pretreatment arrest history. These findings are significant because they show that MST was equally effective with youths and families from diverse cultural backgrounds and with participants presenting a range of serious antisocial behaviors. Such findings conflict with those from much of the child psychotherapy literature in which favorable outcomes are linked with high family resources (e.g., middle class status) and less severe presenting problems at pretreatment. The ability of MST to be equally effective with families of differing sociocultural backgrounds most likely reflects its capacity to be individualized to address the unique strengths and weaknesses of families (see Brondino et al., 1997, for a discussion of this issue).

DRUG USE AMONG SERIOUS JUVENILE OFFENDERS

Prior to the completion of two of the MST trials with serious juvenile offenders (Borduin et al., 1995; Henggeler et al., 1992), analyses were conducted to examine the effects of MST on the drug use of the offenders participating in these studies (Henggeler et al., 1991). Results showed that MST significantly decreased self-reported drug use in the Henggeler et al. (1992) study and significantly reduced drug-related arrests in the Borduin et al. (1995) study. In light of the fact that few treatments of adolescent substance use demonstrate favorable effects in randomized trials (Henggeler, 1997), the aforementioned findings were highly encouraging and, as presented shortly, served as the foundation for a clinical trial focusing specifically on substance abusing and dependent delinquents.

South Carolina

In 1989, at the request of Dr. Gary Melton (formerly at the University of Nebraska, now at the University of South Carolina) and Dr. Jerome Hanley (director of the Child, Adolescent, and Family Services Division of the South Carolina Department of Mental Health), one of us (S. W. H.) collaborated in the design and implementation of a family preservation project, funded by the National Institute of Mental Health (NIMH), that used MST as the treatment model. This project was the first study of MST to be located in a community mental health center and, as such, represented our entry into the field of children's mental health services research. Services research differs from psychotherapy research in its emphasis on issues such as external validity, behavior in real-world settings (e.g., community clinics and managed care organizations), and cost-effectiveness (Hoagwood, Hibbs, Brent, & Jensen, 1995). As a result of the success of this project and the support of policymakers such as Dr. Joseph Bevilacqua, then commissioner of the Department of Mental Health in South Carolina (now with the Bazelon Center in Washington, D.C.), and academics such as Dr. Alberto Santos and Dr. James Ballenger, who were highly supportive of public/academic liaisons to conduct services research, Henggeler took a position in the Department of Psychiatry and Behavioral Sciences at the Medical University of South Carolina in Charleston in 1992. There, he founded the Family Services Research Center (FSRC), whose mission is "to develop and validate clinically effective and cost-effective family-based interventions for youth presenting serious clinical problems." As described next, the FSRC has been relatively successful in fulfilling this mission.

VIOLENT AND CHRONIC JUVENILE OFFENDERS— SIMPSONVILLE, SOUTH CAROLINA

The purpose of this collaboration between the Department of Mental Health and the Department of Juvenile Justice (DJJ) was to investigate whether MST could serve as a clinically effective and cost-effective alternative to incarceration for violent and chronic juvenile offenders and their families (Henggeler et al., 1992). As noted earlier in this volume, incarceration is a costly intervention that most likely does more harm than good, assuming that one goal of incarceration is to decrease rates of future offending. In light of the study's purpose, inclusion criteria for participation were (1) record of violent or chronic (three or more criminal arrests) offending, (2) prediction by probation staff that the youth was at imminent risk of incarceration, and (3) the presence of a parental figure in the youth's life (i.e., youths already in out-of-home placement were excluded). Almost all families of youths who met these criteria agreed to participate in the study.

Families were randomly assigned to treatment conditions: MST versus usual DJJ services. MST was provided using a family preservation model of service delivery (low caseloads, time-limited duration of treatment, 24-hour, 7-day availability of therapists) by master's-level therapists employed by the South Carolina Department of Mental Health (DMH). Usual DJJ services often included incarceration, as predicted by probation staff, and referral to community-based services. Assessment batteries composed of self-report and other-report instruments were administered pretreatment and posttreatment, and a 59-week postreferral follow-up was conducted to examine rates of rearrest and incarceration.

Results showed that MST was effective at reducing rates of criminal activity and institutionalization. At follow-up, youths who received MST had significantly fewer rearrests (means 0.87 vs. 1.52) and weeks incarcerated (means = 5.8 vs. 16.2) than did youths who received usual services. Thus, even though youths in the MST condition spent an average of 73 more days in the community than usual services counterparts, they perpetrated fewer crimes. Incarceration, therefore, did not protect the community, as the youths in the usual services condition reoffended at higher rates based on both arrest data (above) and self-reports on the Self-Report Delinquency Scale (Elliott, Ageton, Huizinga, Knowles, & Canter, 1983). In addition, families that received MST reported increased family cohesion and decreased adolescent aggression with peers in comparison with usual services counterparts. Together, these findings show that MST preserved families while reducing criminal activity and did so at less cost (discussed later in this chapter) than usual DJJ services.

Results from a 2.4-year follow-up supported the longer-term capacity of MST to reduce reoffending (Henggeler, Melton, Smith, Schoenwald, & Hanley, 1993). As shown in Figure 9.2, between-groups differences in recidivism rates were maintained through the follow-up period. By the end of that period, MST had essentially doubled the survival rate (i.e., the percentage of juveniles who had not reoffended) in comparison with usual services. Moreover, consistent with the findings of Borduin et al. (1995), the effectiveness of MST was not moderated by demographic characteristics (i.e., race [white vs. African American], age, social class, gender, arrest and incarceration histories) or mediated by psychosocial variables (i.e., family relations, peer relations, social competence, behavioral problems, and parental symptomatology). Thus, MST was equally effective with youths and families of divergent backgrounds and with varying strengths and weaknesses.

Together, Borduin et al. (1995) and Henggeler et al. (1992) are the first randomized trials in the field of delinquency to demonstrate reductions in

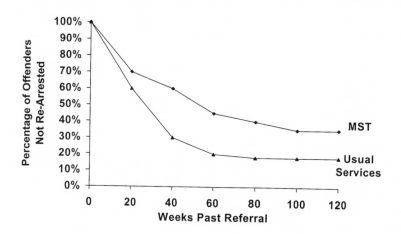

FIGURE 9.2. Simpsonville, South Carolina, project survival analysis.

reoffending among serious juvenile offenders at follow-up. The success of these studies greatly facilitated the development of several other studies and projects that are further examining the viability of MST as a clinically effective and cost-effective family-based treatment for youths presenting serious clinical problems and their families.

SUBSTANCE-ABUSING AND -DEPENDENT
JUVENILE OFFENDERS—CHARLESTON, SOUTH CAROLINA

This randomized trial, funded by the National Institute on Drug Abuse (NIDA), examined the effectiveness of MST with juvenile offenders who met criteria for substance abuse or dependence according to the revised third edition of the *Diagnostic and Statistical Manual of Mental Disorders* (DSM-III-R; American Psychiatric Association, 1987) (Henggeler, Pickrel, & Brondino, 1998). In collaboration with DJJ, eligible youths in the juvenile justice system and their families were recruited for the study and, if agreeable, assigned randomly to either MST or usual community services conditions. MST was delivered by master's-level therapists, and usual community services typically involved referral for office-based group counseling at a local public provider organization. Comprehensive assessment batteries measuring individual, family, peer, and school functioning from multiple perspectives were administered at pretreatment, posttreatment, 6-month follow-up, and 12-month follow-up.

Although the findings have not yet been submitted to peer review and published and many analyses remain to be conducted, several outcomes are noteworthy. First, youths in the MST condition reported significantly decreased drug use at posttreatment. Second, MST reduced rearrests by 26% in comparison with usual services, though this reduction was not statistically significant. Third, at approximately 1 year postreferral, MST had reduced days incarcerated by 46% (569 vs. 1,051) and total days in out-of-home placement by 50% (674 vs. 1,342). This substantive reduction occurred in spite of the fact that youths were not defined *a priori* as at imminent risk of out-of-home placement. Currently, we are examining changes in individual, family, peer, and school functioning through the follow-up periods and evaluating the variables linked with favorable outcome.

Even though the findings regarding clinical outcomes have not yet been published, service and cost-related manuscripts from this project have recently appeared in professional journals. The cost manuscript (Schoenwald et al., 1996) is discussed later in this chapter. The service manuscript pertains to the capacity of MST to address a long-standing problem in the field of substance abuse treatment: high dropout rates (Stark, 1992). In the present study, 98% of the families in the MST condition completed a full course of treatment, which lasted an average of 130 days (Henggeler, Pickrel, et al., 1996). The success of MST in minimizing dropout was most likely due to several aspects of its clinical and service delivery model that are discussed throughout this volume: (1) Therapists are available 24 hours a day, 7 days a week, (2) the MST treatment team and project administrators assume responsibility for achieving treatment engagement and clinical outcome, (3) treatment is strength focused, with goals set primarily by family members, and (4) services are individualized to meet the multiple and changing needs of youths and their families. Thus, by providing services that were highly accessible, fully collaborative, and emphasized family strengths, treatment was provided in full to almost all families.

DISSEMINATION OF MST FOR VIOLENT AND CHRONIC JUVENILE
OFFENDERS IN RURAL SETTINGS—ORANGEBURG AND
SPARTANBURG, SOUTH CAROLINA

Following the success of the Simpsonville project in reducing the criminal activity and out-of-home placements of serious juvenile offenders, NIMH funded a DMH and DJJ collaborative project to study several aspects of the diffusion of MST to community mental health settings (Henggeler, Melton, et al., 1997). Within the context of a randomized design (MST vs. usual services), one aspect of this study was to determine whether the effectiveness of MST could be maintained in the absence of ongoing weekly consultation with an MST expert. Such consultation had taken place in all previous trials of MST and added a significant expense in terms of agency costs for consultation and reduced reimbursement for services because therapists were devoting 5% of their week to the consultation (which was not reimbursable). Other components of the MST training protocol remained in place (i.e., initial 5-day training to orient therapists, periodic booster training, and on-site clinical supervision). Ten master's-level therapists from the community mental health centers participated in the project, and therapist adherence to the MST treatment protocol was assessed from the perspectives of parents, youths, and the therapists at two times during the course of treatment using an instrument developed by Henggeler and Borduin (1992).

Results of the randomized trial indicated that MST improved adolescent symptomatology at posttreatment and decreased incarceration at a 1.7-year follow-up by 47% (average of 30 days per year per youth in the MST condition vs. 70 days per year per youth in the comparison condition). On the other hand, MST had relatively little impact on the criminal activity of the serious juvenile offenders. However, when the associations between treatment outcome and the fidelity of MST implementation were examined, the findings were enlightening. Adherence to the MST treatment principles was an important predictor of key outcomes pertaining to adolescents' criminal activity (arrests and self-reported index offenses), incarceration, and psychiatric symptomatology. Thus, this study clearly showed that clinical outcomes for serious juvenile offenders are directly related to the integrity of MST implementation.

Such findings have extremely important implications for the design of MST dissemination projects. Essentially, it becomes critical to evaluate the therapist, supervisory, consultative, and agency/community factors that are linked with therapist adherence to treatment. Then, strategies must be developed to enhance the salience of factors that are linked positively with adherence and to attenuate the adverse impact of factors that are linked negatively with adherence.

Outcome Studies That Are in Progress

Several studies are being conducted by the FSRC in South Carolina and other studies are being conducted by entities in other states, with ongoing technical assistance and consultation regarding MST from Multisystemic Therapy Services, Inc. Whereas the FSRC has primarily research and development missions, the focus of MST Services, Inc. is on technical assistance and support in the effective dissemination of MST to provider organizations outside the state of South Carolina.

Family Services Research Center
ALTERNATIVE TO PSYCHIATRIC HOSPITALIZATION
OF YOUTHS—CHARLESTON, SOUTH CAROLINA

Currently, 70% of the nation's mental health dollars for children are spent on out-of-home placements such as inpatient psychiatric hospitalization and residential treatment centers that have no established effectiveness (Sondheimer, Schoenwald, & Rowland, 1994) and may do more harm than good (Weithorn, 1988). Thus, a clear need exists for the development of family- and community-based alternatives to these restrictive and expensive mental health services. In collaboration with the DMH and the Institute of Psychiatry at Medical University of South Carolina, we are conducting an NIMH-funded trial of MST as an alternative to the hospitalization of youths presenting psychiatric emergencies such as suicidal and homicidal ideation and psychosis (Henggeler, Rowland, et al., 1997). With random assignment to treatment conditions (MST vs. hospitalization), this is one of the few studies in the field of children's mental health to examine psychiatric hospitalization as one of the treatment conditions and will eventually include a sample of 200 children and adolescents when the project is completed in the year 2000.

As described by Henggeler, Rowland et al. (1997), this project has required revision of the MST clinical protocol to ensure the safety and address the intensive clinical needs (i.e., high rates of internalizing disorders and suicidal ideation) of youths in the MST condition. In comparison with previous trials of MST with youths presenting serious antisocial behavior, considerable increases in and reorganization of clinical resources (i.e., reduced therapist caseload, addition of a crisis caseworker, increased psychiatric consultation and increased clinical supervisory time) are required to meet family clinical needs. In addition, a great deal of administrative time has been devoted to building active collaborations with key stakeholders in the community (e.g., social welfare, juvenile justice, and schools) and in promoting the community's capacity to meet the short-term respite needs of youths and families (e.g., shelters and respite foster homes).

SUBSTANCE-ABUSING PARENTS OF YOUNG CHILDREN—CHARLESTON, SOUTH CAROLINA

In collaboration with state substance abuse and mental health authorities, funded by the Center for Mental Health Services, Substance Abuse and Mental Health Services Administration (SAMHSA), and under the direction of Dr. Susan Pickrel, a quasi-experimental study is evaluating the effectiveness of MST blended with the CRA (Higgins & Budney, 1993) in the treatment of substance-abusing parents or guardians of young children. The CRA has shown considerable promise in treating drug abuse in adults and shares many philosophical, conceptual, and practical similarities with MST. Thus, this study is integrating MST, family-based therapeutic child care, and the CRA to provide comprehensive mental health and substance abuse services to parents and their children. The aims of the project are to increase service accessibility for this difficult-to-reach population, an aim for which MST has a demonstrated track record, and to develop and test an adult-oriented MST model that can achieve clinical aims such as decreased parental drug use and improved parent–child relations.

PREGNANT ADOLESCENTS AND ADOLESCENT PARENTS— SUMTER, SOUTH CAROLINA

In collaboration with Sumter School District 17 and funded by the Head Start Bureau of the Department of Health and Human Services Administration for Children, Youth, and Families, Dr. Pickrel is directing a qualitative and quantitative evaluation of a program of integrated substance abuse, mental health, primary care, and educational/vocational services for pregnant adolescents and adolescent parents. Drawing heavily on MST treatment principles and clinical conceptualizations, this project targets the subpopulation of parents and guardians who have mental health or substance abuse problems and whose children are in Head Start. This project is embedded in a national evaluation of Head Start.

ABUSED AND NEGLECTED CHILDREN TAKEN INTO CUSTODY BY DEPARTMENT OF SOCIAL SERVICES

Funded by the South Carolina Department of Health and Human Services and under the direction of one of us (S. W. H.) and Dr. Cynthia Cupit Swenson, a randomized clinical trial is examining the effectiveness of a family-based system of care and clinical program for maltreated children who enter foster care in comparison with current services in the community. The implementation of this program, the "Charleston Collaborative Project," is the product of cooperative efforts by multiple private (i.e., a child advocacy center) and public (i.e., child protective services, mental health) agencies. The focus of the family-based condition, developed by Dr. Libby Ralston of the Lowcountry Children's Center, is child safety and family reunification, with home- and community-based clinical interventions based on an individualized and comprehensive assessment of trauma, medical needs, family needs and strengths, and risk of maltreatment. Outcome measures pertain to child psychosocial functioning, caregiver functioning (e.g., drug use), reincidence of maltreatment, time in out-of-home placement, and cost of services.

AN MST-BASED CONTINUUM OF CARE

To date, outcome research has focused on the effectiveness of MST using a home-based or family preservation model of service delivery. Yet, MST is a treatment model, not a model of service delivery, and, as such, MST is defined by its nine treatment principles. In other words, MST can be delivered via other models of service delivery, such as outpatient care. In fact, one of us (S. W. H.), among others, delivered MST within the 50-minute hour to families who could attend clinic-based sessions when he was a director at the Family and Health Institute of Memphis in the 1980s.

The goal of this project, which has been funded by the Annie E. Casey Foundation, is to develop and evaluate an MST-based continuum of care for a population of youths returning from residential placement and their families. The project can be conceptualized as a managed care study in which a provider organization has responsibility for providing the mental health and substance abuse services for a high-use population of youths in state custody. To meet the needs of the youths and their families efficiently, the provider organization will develop and specify a range of MST-based services. This range, for example, may include MST-based outpatient treatment in a neighborhood location for situations when less intensive services are sufficient to meet youth and family needs, MST delivered via a home-based model when clinical needs are high; MST-friendly therapeutic foster care (i.e., foster care that involves the youth's family and aims at expeditious reunification of the youth with the family) when the family and kinship network cannot guarantee the safety of the youth, and a short-term restrictive MST-friendly setting when the youth is a serious danger to self or others and the family and kinship network are not yet equipped to meet his or her clinical needs. In collaboration with the Annie E. Casey Foundation and the neighborhood governing board, and under the guidance of one of us (S. K. S.), treatment manuals and training protocols have been developed for the various service components, and the research protocol has been designed. This protocol emphasizes the measurement of treatment implementation, clinical outcomes, and cost-related issues.

Unique aspects of this study are that all services in the provider organization will be based on MST principles, and, consequently, all clinicians will be on the same philosophical, conceptual, and clinical wavelength. Thus, values such as provider accountability for outcomes, commitment to continued quality improvement, emphases on strength-based treatment and family collaboration, and focusing change on the natural ecologies of youths will be shared by outpatient therapists, home-based therapists, foster parents, and clinicians working in a restrictive setting. Moreover, if possible, individuals within the organization will share in the benefits accrued from providing clinically effective and cost-effective services for a population that would otherwise be burdensome and costly for the entity that previously had responsibility for the population.

TARGETING SERVICES AT LOCATIONS WITH A HIGH DENSITY OF MENTAL HEALTH PROBLEMS

Funded by the South Carolina Department of Health and Human Services, the FSRC is developing organizational partnerships in two settings that have a high prevalence of mental health problems. The first setting is a neighborhood that has high rates of crime, children taken into custody, and adolescent drug abuse. In collaboration with neighborhood residents, the FSRC is developing and implementing a range of ecologically based interventions aimed at addressing key problems identified by these residents. The second setting is an inner-city middle school in an economically disadvantaged neighborhood that has high rates of violence, drug use, and dropout. In collaboration with school personnel, neighborhood residents, and staff from state agencies, the FSRC, under the direction of one of us (P. B. C.), is developing, implementing, and evaluating the effectiveness of a set of ecologically based prevention and intervention strategies (including MST). Across both projects, goals will be to promote family and community protective factors while attenuating serious difficulties such as violence and drug abuse.

Controlled Evaluations of MST Conducted by Organizations Distal to the FSRC

One potential criticism of the aforementioned clinical trials is that each was directed by one of the developers of MST. This criticism raises the question of whether MST is effective when examined by investigators who are distal to the developers of MST and to the FSRC. Several studies are currently under way that address this issue. In each, technical assistance and MST consultation are being provided either by the FSRC or MST Services, Inc. When completed, these studies will provide invaluable lessons regarding the conditions needed to support the effective dissemination of MST.

GALVESTON, TEXAS

Under the direction of Dr. Christopher R. Thomas, University of Texas Medical Branch—Galveston, the treatment portion of a randomized clinical trial with juvenile offenders, including a substantive percentage of Hispanic American gang members, was recently completed. Although interpretation of findings is limited by the small sample size in this study (i.e., small samples have low statistical power), this is the first study of MST that included a substantive percentage of gang members or an ethnic group other than African American or Caucasian. Analysis of outcomes should be completed in 1998.

WILMINGTON, DELAWARE

The Department of Services for Children, Youth, and Their Families is conducting a randomized trial of MST as an alternative to placement of serious juvenile offenders in costly out-of-state residential treatment facilities. The impetus for this study was the skyrocketing utilization and costs of such placements and the impression among state officials that such placements were not cost-effective. To the credit of state officials, stakeholders have been convinced of the importance and have consented to support the implementation of a rigorous evaluation of community-based versus institution-based services for serious juvenile offenders. Although recidivism-related findings cannot yet be interpreted because the study has been under way for only 15 months, a preliminary report (Miller, 1997) indicated that substantial cost savings have already been realized.

ONTARIO, CANADA

Under the direction of Dr. Alan W. Leschied, London Family Court Clinic, a study of MST as an alternative to incarceration of moderate- to high-risk juvenile offenders is being conducted across four sites in the Province of Ontario. In Canada, 80% of the funding for juvenile services is devoted to restrictive placements. Thus, the central aims of this study are to reduce crime and protect community safety at a cost savings in comparison with usual services.

Cost Savings and Cost-Effectiveness

Tremendous resources are being spent on mental health, juvenile justice, and substance abuse services that have no demonstrated effectiveness and may do more harm than good (Sondheimer et al., 1994). For example, as noted previously, Burns (1991) concluded that 70% of the nation's mental health dollars for children are spent on restrictive out-of-home placements, which have little documented effectiveness. The development and dissemination of effective community-based services for children, adolescents, and families will most likely not be achieved through the allocation of "new" dollars from fiscally conservative legislators. Rather, the greatest potential for increasing the funding of innovative mental health services will come from the redeployment of existing dollars from institution-based services to community-based programs (Meyers, 1994). To optimize the probability of continued funding for community-based programs, however, consumer satisfaction, clinical effectiveness, and cost savings must be demonstrated.

The first MST trial to attend to issues of cost was the Simpsonville project in which MST was provided as an alternative to incarceration of chronic and violent juvenile offenders (Henggeler et al., 1992). A key finding from this trial was that MST reduced incarceration by an average of 73 days per offender over a 59-week follow-up. Converting this difference to 1998 dollars and assuming that the costs of incarceration are $100 per day, the added costs in the usual services condition was $7,300 per youth (i.e., the cost above and beyond the average incarceration costs of youths in the MST condition). Using 1998 dollar figures, MST program costs average between $4,000 and $5,000 per family, depending on the regional variation in professional salary structures. Thus, in the Simpsonville study, MST program costs were recouped via reduced incarceration approximately 8 months postreferral, at least in theory. Future MST-related reductions in incarceration would represent cost savings.

Several caveats to the above analysis of cost issues should be made. First, the discussion pertains solely to the costs of MST services and incarceration.

Costs associated with possible between-groups differences in the utilization of primary care, social services, and other mental health, juvenile justice, and substance abuse services are not considered. Second, the analysis does not take into consideration the benefits and cost savings associated with decreased criminal activity among MST participants. Criminal behavior, for example, incurs costs in victim medical care, property damage and loss, and time missed from work, for example (Cohen, Miller, & Rossman, 1994). Third, decreasing incarceration in a state facility that has fixed costs will not necessary result in substantive cost savings, especially as compared with decreasing out-of-state residential services that are paid on a per diem basis for each youth placed. These caveats are addressed, in part, by cost-related findings in a recent study of MST described next.

Schoenwald et al. (1996) examined costs of mental health treatment, substance abuse treatment, and out-of-home placement data through approximately 12 months postreferral for 118 youths who participated in the randomized trial of MST with substance-abusing and dependent juvenile offenders that was discussed earlier (Henggeler et al., 1998). Results showed that the incremental costs of MST (i.e., the costs of MST that were above and beyond the usual cost of services for these youths) were nearly offset by the savings incurred as a result of reductions in days of out-of-home placement (i.e., incarceration and residential and inpatient treatment) during the year. The authors concluded that if between-groups differences in service utilization continue over time, the incremental costs of MST will convert to cost savings in a short period. Noteworthy regarding the cost analysis for this study is that the participants were not at imminent risk of out-of-home placement, *a priori*.

When youths are truly at imminent risk for out-of-home placement, as in the Simpsonville study (Henggeler et al., 1992), cost savings have the potential to be substantive. As further examples, our current trial examining MST as an alternative to the hospitalization of youths presenting psychiatric emergencies (Henggeler, Rowland, et al., 1997) includes an extensive cost-effectiveness analysis. Because youths in the comparison condition are averaging almost 2 weeks of extremely expensive inpatient psychiatric hospitalization during the first 4 months postreferral, while such restrictive placements have been largely averted in the MST condition, the cost savings for the MST condition should be substantial. More important, we project that MST will be more effective at ameliorating the psychosocial difficulties that contributed to the decision to hospitalize the youth. If this projection is correct, MST will be both less expensive and more effective than standard treatment of the serious clinical problems addressed in this study. Similarly, preliminary findings from the Delaware project (Miller, 1997) suggest the significant potential of MST to achieve cost savings.

Finally, a recent report from the Washington State Institute for Public Policy (1998) showed that MST was the most cost-effective of a wide variety of treatments to reduce serious criminal activity by adolescents. Indeed, the average net gain for MST in comparison with boot camps was $29,000 per case in decreased program and victim costs.

In conclusion, evidence is emerging that MST is a cost-effective treatment model when used with youths presenting serious clinical problems and their families. MST has been effective at reducing rates of costly out-of-home placements while improving the psychosocial functioning and decreasing the criminal activity of treated youths. The combination of clinical effectiveness and cost savings can provide a potent rationale for the redeployment of funds from institution-based services to effective community-based programs.

Future Directions for MST Outcome Research

We view the refinement of MST as a continuous, ongoing, and dynamic process. The development and validation of treatment conceptualizations and processes that enhance the effectiveness of MST is a continuing goal of the FSRC (see, e.g., the study that blends the CRA for treating adult substance abusers with MST). Critical to this refinement, however, is the rigorous evaluation of enhancements. Enhancements will not be included in the MST treatment model because they "sound" good or "feel" good. Rather, as with all other aspects of MST, enhancements will be incorporated after testing to determine whether they contribute to clinical outcome, cost-effectiveness, or some other important aspect of clinical services (e.g., consumer satisfaction).

MST outcome research is currently proceeding in four related directions.

Generalization to Different Populations of Youths and Families Presenting Serious Clinical Problems

MST has been best validated in the treatment of violent and chronic juvenile offenders and their families, with several studies documenting favorable effects on family relations, adolescent behavioral problems and criminal activity, and rates of out-of-home placement. In addition, rigorous examinations of the effectiveness of MST in treating substance abuse and dependence and serious emotional disturbance in youths are well under way or near completion. Also, as noted previously, studies are examining the effectiveness of MST with gang members, with ethnic groups other than Caucasian and African American, and with substance-abusing parents of young children. Several other projects are in the early stages of implementation or in late stages of planning. These include the following:

• In the field of child welfare, considerable resources are devoted to out-of-home placements for abused children, while little attention is devoted to ameliorating the factors that contributed to the abuse. Directed by Dr. Cynthia Swenson, FSRC, and building on the findings of Brunk et al. (1987), a grant proposing a randomized trail of MST in the treatment of physically abused children and their families has been submitted for consideration.

- The development and validation of services for young children (infants, toddlers, and preschoolers) and their families are the primary research and clinical interests of Dr. Pickrel, who is directing the two studies noted earlier that relate to the parents of young children Pending the results of these studies, we anticipate that the further development of MST services for young children and their families will be an increasing priority for the FSRC.
- Services research and effectiveness studies (in comparison with efficacy studies, see Hoagwood et al., 1995) tend to focus on youths presenting problems of aggression and externalization. For some children and adolescents identified as seriously emotionally disturbed, however, internalizing problems such as anxiety and depression present significant burdens on their capacity to function effectively across home, school, and community contexts. Yet, the vast majority of treatment research with internalizing disorders of childhood has been conducted in university settings, with highly circumscribed samples and minimal family involvement. We plan for MST to be more fully specified for treating internalizing disorders and hope to conduct a randomized trial in comparison with an individually oriented state-of-the-art treatment model.

Cost-Saving and Cost-Effectiveness Studies

During the past few years an increasing percentage of our research resources has been devoted to examining the cost savings and cost-effectiveness of MST. Conducting such studies requires frequent and accurate assessment of service utilization across the major service sectors (mental health, juvenile justice, social welfare, education) by all youths and families participating in a project as well as the accurate delineation of the costs associated with those services. This is an extremely complex task for which we have found expert consultants in health economics to be most helpful. Building on the MST cost-related research noted earlier (e.g., Schoenwald et al., 1996), several cost analysis studies are in progress or planned.

- Drs. Schoenwald and David Ward are directing the cost-effectiveness analyses for our study of MST as an alternative to the hospitalization of youths presenting psychiatric emergencies.
- Dr. Ward is taking the lead in cost-related aspects in the Charleston Collaborative Project, which examines a family-based service for children taken into custody by the Department of Social Services.

- We have recently been funded by NIDA to conduct an extended follow-up of the outcomes in the randomized trial with substance abusing and dependent juvenile offenders (Henggeler et al., 1998). A major aspect of this follow-up is on service utilization and costs of such during the follow-up period. These data will enable a relatively rigorous evaluation of cost-effectiveness.
- Violent and chronic juvenile offenders who participated in the Henggeler et al. (1992) and Borduin et al. (1995) trials are now in their 20s and early 30s. Two of us (S. W. H. and C. M. B.) have a grant application under review that proposes to conduct a 10-year follow-up on these participants, and a major aspect of the follow-up pertains to earnings and service utilization.

Managed Care

We believe that the long-term success of managed care organizations will be predicated on the provision of clinically effective and cost-effective services that receive high ratings for consumer satisfaction. MST, if provided with high treatment fidelity, clearly has the capability of fulfilling these needs. It will be necessary, however, to develop MST service delivery protocols other than home based. The high intensity (and corresponding cost) of home-based services is not needed for many cases, and in other instances, children require short-term placement in out-of-home settings until their safety (or the safety of others) can be secured.

As discussed earlier, the collaboration of the FSRC with the Annie E. Casey Foundation is providing a major step toward the development and validation of an MST-based continuum of care. The journey from a university-based clinical trial that began in 1978 to developing and examining the effects of a managed care entity sometime before the year 2000 has been extraordinary. We believe, however, that this research is the most likely of all our projects to have a substantive impact on the field of children's mental health. In a sense, the Casey collaboration integrates and extends our research during the past 20 years with diverse populations and many key stakeholders. If clinical effectiveness and cost savings can be demonstrated in this project, the stage may be set for the redistribution of funding from institution-based services to family-friendly and community-based services that meet the needs of children and their families.

Dissemination Research

Through the FSRC and MST Services, Inc., MST has been disseminated to 12 states and Canada, and numerous treatment teams have been trained and are receiving ongoing consultation. The critical issue in this work is whether teams that are distal to Charleston are delivering MST with the integrity needed to obtain clinical outcomes. As Henggeler, Melton, et al. (1997) and our extensive anecdotal experience in training suggest, wide variability exists in the implementation of MST across therapists and sites. A major task in the upcoming years is to evaluate those factors that are linked with treatment adherence. As suggested by Schoenwald and Henggeler (in press), these factors most likely relate to characteristics of therapists, supervisory behaviors, agency policies, and system-level variables such as funding regulations. To facilitate an evaluation of the multiple determinants of therapist adherence (and concomitant child outcomes), several projects must be completed first.

- The MST supervisory and consultation protocols must be specified. Measures must be developed to assess adherence to these protocols, and a study must be conducted to examine the associations between MST consultant behaviors, supervisors' behaviors, and therapist adherence.
- Written guidelines for the development and implementation of MST programs in a community should be refined by MST investigators in collaboration with individuals who have expertise in the areas of interagency relations, financing, and community organization.
- When treatment, supervisory, consultation, and organizational protocols are delineated along with corresponding measurement instruments, the conduct of a large-scale dissemination study will be viable.

To facilitate the viability of a large scale dissemination, the Office of Juvenile Justice and Delinquency Prevention (OJJDP), U.S. Department of Justice, has recently funded the development of the MST supervisory protocol and organizational manual. Moreover, several entities (e.g., FSRC, OJJDP, MST Services, Inc., Consortium on Children, Families, and the Law, and several consultants) are in the process of planning the design of the dissemination project and procuring the necessary funding. An important intent of the project will be to gradually transfer the technology of MST to the provider organization—so that the organization will eventually be capable of meeting its own training and consultation needs—while ensuring high, ongoing, and continuous quality assurance.

Epilogue: Policy Implications of the Effectiveness of MST

In this chapter

- The primary implications for policy change posed by the effectiveness of MST—redistribution of funding from institution-based services to community-based services, increased accountability of service providers, and improved training of mental health professionals.
- The major barriers to achieving policy changes.
- A solution for overcoming barriers to policy change.

In a context in which the vast majority of fiscal resources is devoted to removing antisocial youths from their families, schools, neighborhoods, and communities, the capacity of MST to reduce long-term rates of criminal activity at a cost savings has extremely important implications for policymakers, provider organizations, and the fields of mental health and juvenile justice. These implications bear directly on several major concerns of leading policymakers and researchers about the state of mental health and juvenile justice services for children and adolescents. These concerns include the following:

- Some 70% of the nation's mental health dollars for children and adolescents are spent on out-of-home placements (Burns & Friedman, 1990).
- No scientific evidence indicates that the most restrictive and expensive out-of-home placements (psychiatric hospitalization, residential treatment centers, incarceration) are clinically effective (Sondheimer et al., 1994).

- Substantial research indicates that restrictive out-of-home placements may do more harm than good (Weithorn, 1988).
- For adult populations, community-based care is more effective and less expensive than care in the hospital (Kiesler, 1982), which sets the clear precedent for child and adolescent counterparts.
- Traditional office-based, outpatient mental health services for children and adolescents show little evidence of effectiveness (Weisz, Weiss, & Donenberg, 1992).
- No evidence suggests that any treatment for adolescent substance abuse is more effective than any other treatment or no treatment (Henggeler, 1997).
- Emerging community-based services (e.g., wraparound services, intensive case management and home-based services) are being disseminated widely in the absence of adequate evidence regarding their effectiveness.
- With the exception of MST, no treatment of serious antisocial behavior in youth has established long term effectiveness.

Thus, within a context in which tremendous fiscal and personal resources are being used to achieve scant success, the dual promise of MST—clinical outcomes at cost savings—is noteworthy. As such, this epilogue examines the policy implications of the success of MST.

Increase Family- and Community-Based Services, Decrease Residential and Institutional Services

The outcome studies cited in Chapter 9 support the effectiveness of MST in treating youths presenting serious antisocial and their families. Findings demonstrated favorable clinical outcomes (e.g., improved family relations) long-term reductions in criminal activity and incarceration, and cost savings. Logic, reason, and research, therefore, do not support the continued lopsided flow of fiscal resources into expensive, restrictive, and ineffective placements that remove children from their natural social networks to live with individuals who have no emotional attachment to the children or long-term commitment to their care. Similarly, logic, reason, and research do not support the devotion of clinical resources to activities and settings (e.g., group therapy in residential facilities) that have little to do with the children's functioning in their environment, while the factors that promoted the decision to place the child are all but ignored (e.g., parental substance abuse, academic failure, and deviant peers).

Shifting resources from beds in facilities to families and communities will not be easy, however. Substantive barriers include the following:

- Funding mechanisms are often stacked against cost-effective community-based services and favor the use of restrictive services (Meyers,
1994). Why, for example, should a provider organization decide to
provide family preservation reimbursed at $50 per day when residen-
tial treatment is reimbursed at $150 per day? Similarly, we have
encountered cases in which a state agency decided to save money by
having an adolescent incarcerated (which was funded entirely by a
different state agency) rather than treated in the community (where the
agency had to pay for 50% of the treatment dollars).

- Clinicians, supervisors, and administrators often tire of struggling with
the tough clinical cases—those involving parental substance abuse,
youth violence, serious emotional disturbance—in the absence of
evidence or experience indicating their efforts are at all effective.
Placing the youth in a distant facility avoids a major work-related
headache.

- Within all segments of the mental health community, tremendous
vested interests argue and lobby for the expansion of out-of-home
placements, often using invalid data (e.g., from descriptive program
evaluations) with legislators to make their points. For example, we
have heard directors of numerous institutional entities cite wonderful
statistics regarding recidivism rates for offenders who completed their
programs. These statistics have never held up to informed questioning.

- In a similar vein, intervention programs for children are often based
on political expediency (e.g., bootcamps to look tough on crime) or
the charisma and salesmanship of the program developer rather than
on any logical model of why or how the program should work.

- The public often believes that juvenile offenders should be removed
from the community, that all offenders need is discipline, and that the
families of offenders are beyond help. Similarly, slick television
commercials are used to convince viewers that private psychiatric
hospitalization (until insurance coverage expires) is an appropriate
treatment for problems such as childhood depression. Family- and
community-based mental health services do not have the advertising
budgets to compete.

Accountability of Service Providers

Critical to the success of MST, MST-based programs strongly emphasize the
accountability of therapists, supervisors, and administrators for engaging
families in treatment and for attaining desired clinical outcomes. With accountability, however, must come the resources needed to accomplish pro-
grammatic goals as well as rewards for accomplishing such goals. As such,

we strongly advocate that effective therapists, supervisors, and administrators share in the success and cost savings of the program (e.g., profit sharing for managed care organizations, increased salary, and quarterly bonuses). Linking positive contingencies to performance is certainly not a new concept in this nation, though such linkages are rare in the fields of mental health and juvenile justice. Therapists should not be held accountable, however, when they have not received the requisite training and support for working with multiproblem families or when their caseloads are so high that the possibility of designing and implementing well-conceived interventions is negated.

Unfortunately, current mental health and juvenile justice services have almost no accountability to consumers, the public, or funders. For example, no licensing standards in social work, psychology, or psychiatry address the competence of professionals to achieve clinical outcomes with clients. Licensing is based on passing exams and not engaging in unethical contact, with virtually no consideration given to therapeutic effectiveness. Reimbursement is based on the provision of services, not on the outcomes of the services. This lack of accountability can breed a clinical culture that is extremely self-serving. For example, programs may "cream" the client pool, engaging and retaining families that are highly cooperative and "deserving," while terminating (for reasons of family "resistance") families that pose significant clinical challenges. Similarly, therapists remain behind their desks and follow the 50-minute hour rather than exerting the effort needed to truly understand the social ecology of a child. Human nature dictates that if the rewards are equal, individuals usually prefer the easy path to the difficult path.

The development of mechanisms that promote provider accountability is an extremely difficult task for several reasons.

- Accountability requires that performance and outcomes be measured, and under current practice standards, few mental health professionals volunteer for such measurement. Rather, some professionals have argued that "therapy" is art, not science and, therefore, cannot be measured. Similarly, professionals may contend that the benefits of their therapy to clients cannot be quantified.
- The professional guilds may use their influence to resist efforts to promote clinical accountability. In some states, mental health professionals are unionized, and unions generally oppose efforts to develop performance-based criteria for merit salary increases or to terminate members for not meeting minimal performance criteria (see, e.g., attempts to develop merit-pay systems for teachers).
- State budgetary and salary systems rarely have mechanisms for incorporating the types of reimbursement procedures needed to reward successful therapists, supervisors, and administrators. Often, all state employees get the same 2% raise—irrespective of their efforts and

performance. Such a system serves as a disincentive to "go the extra mile" that may be needed to achieve treatment goals in a difficult case.

The Training of Mental Health Professionals

Research findings (e.g., Henggeler, Melton, et al., 1997) demonstrate a clear link between MST treatment fidelity and clinical outcomes, and dissemination experiences continue to strengthen our perception that MST treatment integrity is difficult to achieve. Consequently, the MST training protocol is intensive and ongoing. With a graduate degree taken as a proxy for intelligence, commitment, and some understanding of ethical and clinical (ideally behavioral and pragmatic family therapies) procedures, MST training assumes that treatment integrity will be maintained only through an organizational commitment to continuous quality improvement. Thus, after an initial 5-day orientation to MST (which follows an evaluation of the organization's capacity to provide the supervisory and administrative supported needed for MST), MST consultants provide weekly and continuing quality assurance to therapists, treatment teams, and clinical supervisors. The overriding purpose of this consultation is to facilitate therapist adherence to the MST treatment principles and to help therapists and supervisors develop strategies to overcome barriers to achieving treatment goals with the families. Thus, because outcomes are produced through treatment fidelity, a crucial purpose of training and consultation is to ensure MST treatment adherence.

The vast majority of the clinical world, however, devotes almost no attention to issues of treatment integrity, irrespective of the particular treatment model that is being used. Clinicians are usually free to use whatever treatment model they desire, and whether that model has any empirical support for its effectiveness is rarely considered. Similarly, graduate programs usually teach a variety of treatment approaches, at least some of which have no empirical support, and students are left to choose whichever approach "feels" right. The use of "gut" feelings to make clinical decisions in lieu of evidence from parents, teachers, and so on, is considered perfectly acceptable clinical behavior. After obtaining an advanced degree, clinical supervision is minimal and often consists of an exchange of clinical anecdote or encouragement to catch up on paper work. Moreover, a central premise of graduate (master's- and doctoral-level) training programs is that successful completion of the program earns individuals the right to practice autonomously. Indeed, the very concept of a profession, be it social work, psychology, education, law, or medicine, is that individuals trained and socialized into the profession have earned this right. Thus, it should not be surprising that postgraduate clinical supervision is minimal, or that postgraduate training experiences usually consist of 1- or 2-day workshops in which a therapeutic approach is reviewed but includes no opportunity for follow-up (i.e., was the clinical strategy adopted, and, if so, was it implemented with integrity?). In light of such training, the failure of the field to obtain outcomes with complex cases is not surprising.

Several significant obstacles hinder the development of more effective training protocols.

- Graduate training is primarily conducted by faculty in graduate schools. Graduate faculty are notoriously independent-minded, which is good for academic freedom but bad for efforts to change graduate training practices. Moreover, although these faculty are typically bright and well read, they are often out of touch with the realities of clinical practice in real-world settings.
- Obtaining guild support and consensus on the features of training for empirically based and community-oriented training practices would be near impossible. The guilds are run by individuals who benefited tremendously from the present system and who have long-standing allegiance to clinical models with little clinical support.
- Experienced therapists are usually comfortable with the range of interventions that they use and have little desire to be "required" to adhere to a particular treatment protocol, particularly in light of the professional practice and identity issues raised earlier.
- Knowledge about the individual and organization factors effecting treatment adherence is scant, and, correspondingly, we know little about the parameters of training that are linked with treatment adherence.

A Proposed Solution to the Funding-, Accountability-, and Training-Related Barriers

Across the nation, many efforts are being made to address one or more of the aforementioned barriers. For example, Drs. Jane Knitzer, Columbia University, and Judith Meyers organized a "Work Group on Training in the Public Sector" through Division 37 of the American Psychological Association with the aim of enhancing the training of mental health professionals who work in the public sector; Drs. Barbara Burns, Duke University, and Kimberly Hoagwood, NIMH, are spearheading an effort to develop a national agenda for the development of "effective" mental health services for children, adolescents, and their families. These efforts and those of many other individuals and organizations are well conceived and will certainly bear fruit.

As MST has integrated the best of the empirically based treatment approaches into a comprehensive, yet individualized, treatment model, we believe that dilemmas pertaining to funding, accountability, and training can be addressed simultaneously in a project that integrates several of the important innovations that are being examined across the nation. As such, we propose to develop and evaluate a private MST-based managed care entity with the following characteristics:

- Responsibility for meeting the mental health and substance abuse treatment needs of a predefined high-risk and high-cost population of youths (e.g., violent juvenile offenders, antisocial youths currently in out-of-home placements, and juvenile offenders at imminent risk of incarceration).
- A capitated payment system whereby, for example, the entity receives 75% of the funds that would otherwise have been allocated to serving the youths.
- A small and well-specified continuum of MST-based service components, including, for example, MST outpatient treatment, MST home-based treatment, a family-friendly foster care network that follows MST principles, and a small and short-term MST-friendly setting for securing the safety of youths presenting a danger to themselves or others.
- A rigorous quality assurance system to provide continuous monitoring of treatment integrity and client outcome, with triggers to enhance either or both as needed.
- Competitive salaries for clinicians, supervisors, and other staff, with individual bonuses when performance criteria are met.
- A continuous training protocol provided across service components to ensure that *all* entity staff are on the same conceptual wavelength and to maintain a high commitment to quality assurance and treatment integrity.
- A "no reject" philosophy, so that the managed care organization could not transfer youth to the public sector without cost.

The development and successful evaluation of such an entity would bypass major barriers to obtaining outcomes with children presenting serious antisocial behavior and their families. By definition ("no reject" philosophy, predefined population, fiscal responsibility), the organization would assume accountability for meeting the clinical needs of youths and their families. Along with fiscal incentives, a rigorous quality assurance system implemented within the organization and dedicated to obtaining favorable outcomes would greatly facilitate treatment integrity. Evaluation of the entity would focus on clinical outcomes and cost savings, and the inclusion of a comparison sample (e.g., youth counterparts in out-of-home placement who were not randomly assigned to the managed care entity) would be essential.

References

Achenbach, T. M. (1991). *Manual for the Child Behavior Checklist/4–18 and 1991 profile.* Burlington: University of Vermont, Department of Psychiatry.

Alexander, J. F., Holtzworth-Munroe, A., & Jameson, P. (1994). The process and outcome of marital and family therapy: Research review and evaluation. In A. E. Bergin & S. L. Garfield (Eds.), *Handbook of psychotherapy and behavior change* (4th ed., pp. 595–630). New York: Wiley.

Amato, P. R., & Keith, B. (1991). Parental divorce and the well-being of children: A meta-analysis. *Psychological Bulletin, 110,* 26–46.

American Psychiatric Association. (1987). *Diagnostic and statistical manual of mental disorders* (3rd ed., rev.). Washington, DC: Author.

American Psychiatric Association. (1994). *Diagnostic and statistical manual of mental disorders* (4th ed.). Washington, DC: Author.

American Psychological Association. (1995). Psychological issues related to child maltreatment: Working group reports of the American Psychological Association Coordinating Committee on Child Abuse and Neglect. *Journal of Clinical Child Psychology, 24*(Suppl.), 1–88.

Ammerman, R. T. (1990). Etiological models of child maltreatment: A behavioral perspective. *Behavior Modification, 14,* 230–254.

Asher, S. E., & Coie, J. D. (Eds.). (1990). *Peer rejection in childhood.* New York: Cambridge University Press.

Barkley, R. (1990). *Attention-deficit hyperactivity disorder: A handbook for diagnosis and treatment.* New York: Guilford Press.

Barkley, R. (1991). *Attention-deficit hyperactivity disorder: A clinical workbook.* New York: Guilford Press.

Barkley, R. A., & Associates. *The ADHD report.* New York: Guilford Press.

Barlow, D. H. (1988). *Anxiety and its disorders: The nature and treatment of anxiety and panic.* New York: Guilford Press.

Bateson, G. (1972). *Steps to an ecology of the mind.* New York: Ballantine.

Bateson, G., Jackson, D. D., Haley, J., & Weakland, J. (1956). Toward a theory of schizophrenia. *Behavioral Science, 1,* 251–264.

Baumrind, D. (1967). Child care practices anteceding three patterns of preschool behavior. *Genetic Psychology Monographs, 75,* 43–88.

Baumrind, D. (1971). Current patterns of parental authority. *Developmental Psychology Monographs, 4,* (1, pt.2).

Baumrind, D. (1978). Parental disciplinary strategies and social competence in youth. *Youth in Society, 9,* 239–276.

Baumrind, D. (1983). Rejoinder to Lewis' reinterpretation of parental firm control effects: Are authoritative families really harmonious? *Psychological Bulletin, 94,* 132–142.

Baumrind, D. (1989). Rearing competent children. In W. Damon (Ed.), *Child development today and tomorrow: The Jossey-Bass social and behavioral science series* (pp. 349–378). San Francisco: Jossey-Bass.

Baumrind, D. (1991). The influence of parenting style on adolescent competence and substance use. Special issue: The work of John P. Hill: I. Theoretical, instructional, and policy contributions. *Journal of Early Adolescence, 11,* 56–95.

Baumrind, D. (1993). The average expectable environment is not good enough: A response to Scarr. *Child Development, 64,* 1299–1317.

Beck, A. T. (1993). Cognitive therapy: Past, present, and future. *Journal of Consulting and Clinical Psychology, 61,* 194–198.

Beck, J. S. (1995). *Cognitive therapy: Basics and beyond.* New York: Guilford Press.

Becker, J. V., Alpert, J. L., Bigfoot, D. S., Bonner, B. L., Geddie, L. F., Henggeler, S. W., Kaufman, K. L., & Walker, C. E. (1995). Empirical research on child abuse treatment: Report by the Child Abuse and Neglect Treatment Working Group, American Psychological Association. *Journal of Clinical Child Psychology, 24*(Suppl.), 23–46.

Beitchman, J. H., Zucker, K. J., Hood, J. E., daCosta, G. A., Akman, D. & Cassavia, E. (1992). A review of the long-term effects of child sexual abuse. *Child Abuse and Neglect, 15,* 537–556.

Bergin, A. E., & Garfield, S. L. (Eds.). (1994). *Handbook of psychotherapy and behavior change* (4th ed.). New York: Wiley.

Beutler, L. E., & Hill, C. E. (1992). Process and outcomes research in the treatment of adult victims of childhood sexual abuse: Methodological issues. *Journal of Consulting and Clinical Psychology, 60,* 204–212.

Bierman, K. L., & Montminy, H. P. (1993). Developmental issues in social skills assessment and intervention with children and adolescents. Special issue: Social skills assessment and intervention. *Behavior Modification, 17,* 229–254.

Block, J. H., Block, J., & Gjerde, P. F. (1986). The personality of children prior to divorce: A prospective study. *Child Development, 57,* 827–840.

Borduin, C. M., Henggeler, S. W., Blaske, D. M. & Stein, R. (1990). Multisystemic treatment of adolescent sexual offenders. *International Journal of Offender Therapy and Comparative Criminology, 35,* 105–114.

Borduin, C. M., Mann, B. J., Cone, L. T., Henggeler, S. W., Fucci, B. R., Blaske, D. M., & Williams, R. A. (1995). Multisystemic treatment of serious juvenile offenders: Long-term prevention of criminality and violence. *Journal of Consulting and Clinical Psychology, 63,* 569–578.

Brondino, M. J., Henggeler, S. W., Rowland, M. D., Pickrel, S. G., Cunningham, P. B., & Schoenwald, S. K. (1997). Multisystemic therapy and the minority client: Culturally responsive and clinically effective. In D. K. Wilson, J. R. Rodrigue, & W. C. Taylor (Eds.), *Health and behavior in minority adolescent populations* (pp. 229–250). Washington, DC: APA Books.

Bronfenbrenner, U. (1979). *The ecology of human development.* Cambridge, MA: Harvard University Press.

Brown, B. S. (1995). Reducing impediments to technology transfer in drug abuse programming. In T. E. Backer, S. L. David, & G. Soucy (Eds.), *Reviewing the behavioral science knowledge base on technology transfer* (National Institute on Drug Abuse Research Monograph No. 155; NIH Publication No. 95-4035, pp. 169–185). Rockville, MD: National Institute on Drug Abuse.

Brunk, M., Henggeler, S. W., & Whelan, J. P. (1987). A comparison of multisystemic therapy and parent training in the brief treatment of child abuse and neglect. *Journal of Consulting and Clinical Psychology, 55,* 311–318.

Bukowski, W. M., Newcomb, A. F., & Hartup, W. W. (1996). *The company they keep: Friendship in childhood and adolescence.* New York: Cambridge University Press.

Burns, B. J. (1991). Mental health service use by adolescents in the 1970s and 1980s. *Journal of the American Academy of Child and Adolescent Psychiatry, 30,* 144–150.

Burns, B. J., & Friedman, R. M. (1990). Examining the research base for child mental health services and policy. *Journal of Mental Health Administration, 17,* 87–97.

Chambless, D. L., & Gillis, M. M. (1993). Cognitive therapy of anxiety disorders. *Journal of Consulting and Clinical Psychology, 61,* 248–260.

Cherlin, A. J. (1992). *Marriage, divorce, remarriage* (2nd ed.). Cambridge, MA: Harvard University Press.

Cicchetti, D., & Bukowski, W. M. (1995). Developmental processes in peer relations and psychopathology. *Development and Psychopathology, 7,* 587–589.

Cochran, M. (1993). Parenting and personal social networks. In T. Luster & L. Okagaki (Eds.), *Parenting: An ecological perspective* (pp. 149–178). Hillsdale, NJ: Erlbaum.

Cohen, M. A., Miller, T. R., & Rossman, S. B. (1994). The costs and consequences of violent behavior in the United States. In A. J. Reiss, Jr., & J. A. Roth (Eds.), *Understanding and preventing violence* (pp. 67–166). Washington, DC: National Research Council, National Academy Press.

Cohen, R., & Siegel, A. W. (Eds.). (1991). *Context and development.* Hillsdale, NJ: Erlbaum.

Cohn, A. H., & Daro, D. D. (1987). Is treatment too late: What ten years of evaluative research tells us. *Child Abuse and Neglect, 11,* 433–442.

Craske, M. G., & Barlow, D. H. (1990). *Therapist's guide for the Mastery of Your Anxiety and Panic (MAP) program.* Albany, NY: Graywind.

Crouter, A. C., & McHale, S. M. (1993). The long arm of the job: Influences of parental work on childrearing. In T. Luster & L. Okagaki (Eds.), *Parenting: An ecological perspective* (pp. 179–202). Hillsdale, NJ: Erlbaum.

Cummings, E. M., & Davies, P. T. (1994). *Children and marital conflict.* New York: Guilford Press.

Day, C., & Roberts, M. C. (1991). Activities of the Child and Adolescent Service System Program for improving mental health services for children and families. *Journal of Clinical Child Psychology, 20,* 340–350.

Deblinger, E. (1995, January). *Cognitive behavioral interventions for treating school age sexually abused children.* Paper presented at the San Diego Conference on Responding to Child Maltreatment, San Diego, CA.

Dishion, T. J., Patterson, G. R., Stoolmiller, M., & Skinner, M. L. (1991). Family, school, and behavioral antecedents to early adolescent involvement with antisocial peers. *Developmental Psychology, 27,* 172–180.

Doherty, W. J., & Needle, R. H. (1991). Psychological adjustment and substance use among adolescents before and after parental divorce. *Child Development, 62,* 328–337.

Duchnowski, A. J. (1994). Innovative service models: Education. *Journal of Clinical Child Psychology, 23*(Suppl.), 13–18.

Dumas, J. E., & Wahler, R. G. (1985). Indiscriminate mothering as a contextual factor in aggressive-oppositional child behavior: "Damned if you do and damned if you don't." *Journal of Abnormal Child Psychology, 13,* 1–17.

Dunn, J. (1994). Stepfamilies and children's adjustment. *Archives of Disease in Childhood, 73,* 487–489.

Dunn, L. M., & Markwardt, F. C., Jr. (1970). *Peabody Individual Achievement Test.* Circle Pines, MN: American Guidance Service.

Elliott, D. S. (1994). *Youth violence: An overview.* Boulder: University of Colorado, Center for the Study and Prevention of Violence, Institute for Behavioral Sciences.

Elliott, D. S., Ageton, S. S., Huizinga, D., Knowles, B. A., & Canter, R. J. (1983). *The prevalence and incidence of delinquent behavior: 1976–1980.* Boulder, CO: Behavioral Research Institute.

Elliott, D. S., Huizinga, D., & Ageton, S. S. (1985). *Explaining delinquency and drug use.* Beverly Hills, CA: Sage.

Elliott, D. S., Huizinga, D., & Morse, B. J. (1985). *The dynamics of deviant behavior: A national survey progress report.* Boulder, CO: Behavioral Research Institute.

Emery, R. E. (1988). *Marriage, divorce, and children's adjustment.* Beverly Hills, CA: Sage.

Emery, R. E. (1992). Family conflict and its developmental implications: A conceptual analysis of deep meanings and systemic processes. In I. V. Shantz & W. W. Hartup (Eds.), *Conflict in child and adolescent development* (pp. 270–298). London: Cambridge University Press.

Emery, R. E. (1994). *Renegotiating family relationships: Divorce, child custody, and mediation.* New York: Guilford Press.

Fantuzzo, J. W., DePaloa, L. M., Lambert, L., Martino, T., Anderson, G., & Sutton, S. (1991). Effects of interparental violence on the psychological adjustment and competencies of young children. *Journal of Consulting and Clinical Psychology, 59,* 258–265.

Farrington, D. P. (1987). Epidemiology. In H. C. Quay (Ed.), *Handbook of juvenile delinquency* (pp. 33–61). New York: Wiley.

Farrington, D. P. (1991). Childhood aggression and adult violence: Early precursors and later-life outcomes. In D. J. Pepler & K. H. Rubin (Eds.), *The development and treatment of childhood aggression* (pp. 5–29). Hillsdale, NJ: Erlbaum.

Farrington, D. P., Loeber, R., & Van Kammen, W. B. (1990). Long-term criminal outcomes of hyperactivity–impulsivity–attention deficit and conduct problems in childhood. In L. Robins & M. Rutter (Eds.), *Straight and devious pathways from childhood to adulthood* (pp. 62–81). New York: Cambridge University Press.

Federal Bureau of Investigation. (1996). *Uniform crime reports.* Washington, DC: U.S. Government Printing Office.

Federal Register. (1977, December 29). p. 65083, §121a.5.

Federation of Families for Children's Mental Health. (1995, July). *Principles of family involvement in the development and operation of managed health and mental health care systems for children and youth.* Alexandria, VA: Author.

Fine, M. J., & Carlson, C. (Eds.). (1992). *The handbook of family–school intervention: A systems perspective.* Boston: Allyn & Bacon.

Foa, E. B., Rothbaum, B. O., Riggs, D. S., & Murdock, T. B. (1991). Treatment of posttraumatic stress disorder in rape victims: A comparison between cognitive-behavioral procedures and counseling. *Journal of Consulting and Clinical Psychology, 59,* 715–723.

Foa, E. B., Rothbaum, B. O., & Steketee, G. S. (1993). Treatment of rape victims. *Journal of Interpersonal Violence, 8,* 256–276.

Forehand, R., & Long, N. (1988). Outpatient treatment of the acting out child: Procedures, long term follow-up data, and clinical problems. *Advances in Behavior Research and Therapy, 10,* 129–177.

Forman, S. G. (1993). *Coping skills interventions for children and adolescents.* San Francisco: Jossey-Bass.

Frauenglass, S., Routh, D. K., Pantin, H. M., & Mason, C. A. (1997). Family support decreases influence of deviant peers on Hispanic adolescents' substance use. *Journal of Clinical Child Psychology, 26,* 15–23.

Frick, P. J., Lahey, B. B., Loeber, R., Stouthamer-Loeber, M., Christ, M. A. G., & Hanson, K. (1992). Familial risk factors to oppositional defiant disorder and conduct disorder: Parental psychopathology and maternal parenting. *Journal of Consulting and Clinical Psychology, 60,* 49–55.

Gambrill, E. D. (1977). *Behavior modification: Handbook of assessment, intervention, and evaluation.* San Francisco: Jossey-Bass.

Greenberg, L. S., & Johnson, S. M. (1988). *Emotionally focused therapy for couples.* New York: Guilford Press.

Greenberg, L. S., & Pinsof, W. M. (1986). Process research: Current trends and future perspectives. In L. S. Greenberg & W. M. Pinsof (Eds.), *The psychotherapeutic process: A research handbook* (pp. 3–20). New York: Guilford Press.

Grych, J. H., & Fincham, F. D. (1992). Marital conflict and children's adjustment: A cognitive-contextual framework. *Psychological Bulletin, 111,* 434–454.

Haley, J. (1976). *Problem solving therapy.* San Francisco: Jossey-Bass.

Harrison, A. O., Wilson, M. N., Pine, C. J., Chan, S. Q., & Buriel, R. (1990). Family ecologies of ethnic minority children. *Child Development, 61,* 347–362.

Hawkins, J. D., Catalano, R. F., & Miller, J. Y. (1992). Risk and protective factors for alcohol and other drug problems in adolescence and early adulthood: Implications for substance abuse prevention. *Psychological Bulletin, 112,* 64–105.

Hawkins, J. D., & Lam, T. (1987). Teacher practices, social development, and delinquency. In J. D. Burchard & S. N. Burchard (Eds.), *Prevention of delinquent behavior* (pp. 241–274). Newbury Park, CA: Sage.

Henggeler, S. W. (1989). *Delinquency in adolescence.* Newbury Park, CA: Sage.

Henggeler, S. W. (1991). Multidimensional causal models of delinquent behavior and their implications for treatment. In R. Cohen & A. W. Siegel (Eds.), *Context and development* (pp. 211–231). Hillsdale, NJ: Erlbaum.

Henggeler, S. W. (1994). A consensus: Conclusions of the APA Task Force Report on innovative models of mental health services for children, adolescents, and their families. *Journal of Clinical Child Psychology, 23*(Suppl.), 3–6.

Henggeler, S. W. (1996). Treatment of violent juvenile offenders—We have the knowledge: Comment on Gorman-Smith et al. (1996). *Journal of Family Psychology, 10,* 137–141.

Henggeler, S. W. (1997). The development of effective drug abuse services for youth. In J. A. Egertson, D. M. Fox, & A. I. Leshner (Eds.), *Treating drug abusers effectively* (pp. 253–279). New York: Blackwell.

Henggeler, S. W., & Borduin, C. M. (1990). *Family therapy and beyond: A multisystemic approach to treating the behavior problems of children and adolescents.* Pacific Grove, CA: Brooks/Cole.

Henggeler, S. W., & Borduin, C. M. (1992). *Multisystemic Therapy Adherence Scales.* Unpublished instrument, Department of Psychiatry and Behavioral Sciences, Medical University of South Carolina.

Henggeler, S. W., & Borduin, C. M. (1995). Multisystemic treatment of serious juvenile offenders and their families. In I. M. Schwartz & P. AuClaire (Eds.), *Home-based services for troubled children* (pp. 113–130). Lincoln: University of Nebraska Press.

Henggeler, S. W., Borduin, C. M., & Mann, B. J. (1993). Advances in family therapy: Empirical foundations. In T. H. Ollendick & R. J. Prinz (Eds.), *Advances in Clinical Child Psychology* (Vol. 15, pp. 207–241). New York: Plenum.

Henggeler, S. W., Borduin, C. M., Melton, G. B., Mann, B. J., Smith, L., & Hall, J. A., Cone, L., & Fucci, B. R. (1991). Effects of multisystemic therapy on drug use and abuse in serious juvenile offenders: A progress report from two outcome studies. *Family Dynamics of Addiction Quarterly, 1,* 40–51.

Henggeler, S. W., Cunningham, P. B., Pickrel, S. G., Schoenwald, S. K., & Brondino, M. J. (1996). Multisystemic therapy: An effective violence prevention approach for serious juvenile offenders. *Journal of Adolescence, 19,* 47–61.

Henggeler, S. W., Melton, G. B., Brondino, M. J., Scherer, D. G., & Hanley, J. H. (1997). Multisystemic therapy with violent and chronic juvenile offenders and their families: The role of treatment fidelity in successful dissemination. *Journal of Consulting and Clinical Psychology, 65,* 821–833.

Henggeler, S. W., Melton, G. B., & Smith, L. A. (1992). Family preservation using multisystemic therapy: An effective alternative to incarcerating serious juvenile offenders. *Journal of Consulting and Clinical Psychology, 60,* 953–961.

Henggeler, S. W., Melton, G. B., Smith, L. A., Schoenwald, S. K., & Hanley, J. H. (1993). Family preservation using multisystemic treatment: Long-term follow-up to a clinical trial with serious juvenile offenders. *Journal of Child and Family Studies, 2,* 283–293.

Henggeler, S. W., Pickrel, S. G., & Brondino, M. J. (1998). *Multisystemic treatment of substance abusing and dependent delinquents: Outcomes, treatment fidelity, and transportability.* Manuscript submitted for publication.

Henggeler, S. W., Pickrel, S. G., Brondino, M. J., & Crouch, J. L. (1996). Eliminating (almost) treatment dropout of substance abusing or dependent delinquents through home-based multisystemic therapy. *American Journal of Psychiatry, 153,* 427–428.

Henggeler, S. W., Rodick, J. D., Borduin, C. M., Hanson, C. L., Watson, S. M., & Urey, J. R. (1986). Multisystemic treatment of juvenile offenders: Effects on adolescent behavior and family interactions. *Developmental Psychology, 22,* 132–141.

Henggeler, S. W., Rowland, M. D., Pickrel, S. G., Miller, S. L., Cunningham, P. B., Santos, A. B., Schoenwald, S. K., Randall, J., & Edwards, J. E. (1997). Investigating family-based alternatives to institution-based mental health services for youth: Lessons learned from the pilot study of a randomized field trial. *Journal of Clinical Child Psychology, 26,* 226–233.

Henggeler, S. W., Schoenwald, S. K., & Pickrel, S. G. (1995). Multisystemic therapy: Bridging the gap between university- and community-based treatment. *Journal of Consulting and Clinical Psychology, 63,* 709–717.

Henggeler, S. W., Schoenwald, S. K., Pickrel, S. G., Brondino, M. J., Borduin, C. M., & Hall, J. A. (1994). *Treatment manual for family preservation using multisystemic therapy.* Columbia, SC: Department of Health and Human Services.

Hetherington, E. M. (1993). An overview of the Virginia longitudinal study of divorce and remarriage. *Journal of Family Psychology, 7,* 39–56.

Hetherington, E. M., & Clingempeel, W. G. (1992). Coping with marital transitions. *Monographs of the Society for Research in Child Development, 57,* 1–229.

Higgins, S. T., & Budney, A. J. (1993). Treatment of cocaine dependence through the principles of behavior analysis and behavioral pharmacology. In L. S. Onken, J. D. Blaine, & J. J. Boren (Eds.), *Behavioral treatments for drug abuse and dependence* (National Institute on Drug Abuse Research Monograph No. 137; NIH Publication No. 93-3684, pp. 97–122). Rockville, MD: National Institute on Drug Abuse.

Higgins, S. T., Budney, A. J., & Bickel, W. K. (1994). Applying behavioral concepts and principles to the treatment of cocaine dependence. *Drug and Alcohol Dependence, 30,* 87–97.

Hinshaw, S. P., Lahey, B. B., & Hart, E. L. (1993). Issues of taxonomy and comorbidity in the development of conduct disorder. *Development and Psychopathology, 5,* 31–49.

Hoagwood, K., Hibbs, E., Brent, D., & Jensen, P. (1995). Introduction to the special section: Efficacy and effectiveness in studies of child and adolescent psychotherapy. *Journal of Consulting and Clinical Psychology, 63,* 683–687.

Hobfoll, S. E. (1991). Traumatic stress: A theory based on rapid loss of resources. *Anxiety Research, 4,* 187–197.

Hollon, S. D., Shelton, R. C., & Davis, D. D. (1993). Cognitive therapy for depression: Conceptual issues and clinical efficacy. *Journal of Consulting and Clinical Psychology, 61,* 270–275.

Hooper-Briar, K., Broussard, C. A., Ronnau, J., Sallee, A. L. (1995, Summer). Family preservation and support: Past, present, and future. *Family Preservation Journal,* pp. 5–24.

House, J. S., Landis, K. R., & Umberson, D. (1988). Social relationships and health. *Science, 241,* 540–545.

Howell, J. C. (1995). Gangs and youth violence: Recent research. In J. C. Howell, B. Krisberg, J. D. Hawkins, & J. J. Wilson (Eds.), *A sourcebook: Serious, violent, and chronic juvenile offenders* (pp. 261–274). Thousand Oaks, CA: Sage.

Hoza, B., Molina, B. S. G., Bukowski, W. M., & Sippola, L. K. (1995). Peer variables as predictors of later childhood adjustment. Special Issue: Developmental processes in peer relations and psychopathology. *Development and Psychopathology, 7,* 787–802.

Huesmann, L. R., Lefkowitz, M. M., Eron, L. D., & Walder, L. O. (1984). Stability of aggression over time and generations. *Developmental Psychology, 20,* 1120–1134.

Jastak, S., & Wilkinson, G. S. (1984). *Wide Range Achievement Test—Revised.* Wilmington, DE: Jastak.

Kazdin, A. E. (1988). *Child psychotherapy: Developing and identifying effective treatments.* New York: Pergamon Press.

Kazdin, A. E. (1994). Psychotherapy for children and adolescents. In A. E. Bergin & S. L. Garfield (Eds.), *Handbook of psychotherapy and behavior change* (pp. 543–594). New York: Wiley.

Kazdin, A. E. (1995). *Conduct disorders in childhood and adolescence* (2nd ed.). Thousand Oaks, CA: Sage.

Kendall, P. C. (1993). Cognitive-behavioral therapies with youth: Guiding theory, current status, and emerging developments. *Journal of Consulting and Clinical Psychology, 61,* 235–247.

Kendall, P. C., & Braswell, L. (1985). *Cognitive-behavioral therapy for impulsive children* (1st ed.). New York: Guilford Press.

Kendall, P. C., & Braswell, L. (1993). *Cognitive-behavioral therapy for impulsive children* (2nd ed.). New York: Guilford Press.

Kendall-Tackett, K, Williams, L., & Finkelhor, D. (1993). Impact of sexual abuse on children: A review and synthesis of recent empirical studies. *Psychological Bulletin, 113,* 164–180.

Kiesler, C. A. (1982). Mental hospitals and alternative care: Non-institutionalization as potential policy for mental patients. *American Psychologist, 37,* 349–360.

Knitzer, J., Steinberg, Z., & Fleisch, B. (1990). *At the schoolhouse door: An examination of programs and policies for children with behavioral and emotional problems.* New York: Bank Street College of Education.

Kratzer, L., & Hodgins, S. (1997). Adult outcomes of child conduct problems: A cohort study. *Journal of Abnormal Child Psychology, 25,* 65–81.

Kumpfer, K. L. (1989). Prevention of alcohol and drug abuse: A critical review of risk factors and prevention strategies. In D. Shaffer, I. Philips, & N. B. Enzer (Eds.), *OSAP Prevention Monograph—2: Prevention of mental disorders, alcohol and other drug use in children and adolescents* (pp. 309–373). Rockville, MD: Office for Substance Abuse Prevention, U.S. Department of Health and Human Services.

Lamborn, S., Mounts, N., Steinberg, L., & Dornbusch, S. (1991). Patterns of competence and adjustment among adolescents from authoritative, authoritarian, indulgent, and neglectful homes. *Child Development, 62,* 1049–1065.

Laub, J. H., & Sampson, R. J. (1994). Unemployment, marital discord, and deviant behavior: The long-term correlates of child misbehavior. In T. Hirschi & M. R. Gottfredson (Eds.), *The generality of deviance* (pp. 235–252). New Brunswick, NJ: Transaction.

LeCroy, C. W. (Ed.). (1994). *Handbook of child and adolescent treatment manuals.* New York: Lexington Books.

Lefley, H. P. (1996). Impact of consumer and family movements on mental health services. In B. L. Levin & J. Petrila (Eds.), *Mental health services: A public health perspective* (pp. 81–96). New York: Oxford University Press.

Leitenberg, H. (1976). *Handbook of behavior modification and behavior therapy.* Englewood Cliffs, NJ: Prentice Hall.

Lenhart, L., & March, J. S. (1996). Treatment of psychiatric disorders in children and adolescents. In B. L. Levin & J. Petrila (Eds.), *Mental health services: A public health perspective* (pp. 210–233). New York: Oxford University Press.

Linehan, M. M. (1993). *Cognitive-behavioral treatment of borderline personality disorder.* New York: Guilford Press.

Loeber, R. (1990). Development and risk factors of juvenile antisocial behavior and delinquency. *Clinical Psychology Review, 10,* 1–41.

Maccoby, E. E., & Martin, J. A. (1983). Socialization in the context of the family: Parent–child interactions. In E. M. Hetherington (Ed.), *Handbook of child psychology: Vol. 4. Socialization, personality, and social development* (pp. 1–101). New York: Wiley.

Mann, B. J., Borduin, C. M., Henggeler, S. W., & Blaske, D. M. (1990). An investigation of systemic conceptualizations of parent–child coalitions and symptom change. *Journal of Consulting and Clinical Psychology, 58,* 336–344.

Marcenko, M. O., & Meyers, J. C. (1991). Mothers of children with developmental disabilities: Who shares the burden? *Family Relations, 40,* 186–190.

Mason, A., Cauce, A. M., Gonzales, N., & Hiraga, Y. (1996). Neither too sweet nor too sour: Problem peers, maternal control, and problem behavior in African American adolescents. *Child Development, 67,* 2115–2130.

McMahon, R. J., & Wells, K. C. (1989). Conduct disorders. In E. J. Mash & R. A. Barkley (Eds.), *Treatment of childhood disorders* (pp. 73–132). New York: Guilford Press.

Meichenbaum, D. (1977). *Cognitive-behavior modification: An integrative approach.* New York: Plenum.

Meichenbaum, D. (1993). Changing conceptions of cognitive behavior modification: Retrospect and prospect. *Journal of Consulting and Clinical Psychology, 61,* 202–204.

Meichenbaum, D. (1994). *A clinical handbook/practical therapist manual for assessing and treating adults with Post-Traumatic Stress Disorder (PTSD),* Waterloo, Canada: Institute Press.

Melton, G. B., & Pagliocca, P. M. (1992). Treatment in the juvenile justice system: Directions for policy and practice. In J. J. Cocozza (Ed.), *Responding to the mental health needs of youth in the juvenile justice system* (pp. 107–139). Seattle, WA: National Coalition for the Mentally Ill in the Criminal Justice System.

Mendel, R. A. (1995). *Prevention or pork?: A hard-headed look at youth-oriented anti-crime programs.* Washington, DC: American Youth Policy Forum.

Meyers, J. C. (1994). Financing strategies to support innovations in service delivery to children. *Journal of Clinical Child Psychology, 23*(Suppl.), 7–12.

Miller, M. L. (1997). *The multisystemic therapy pilot program: Fifth quarter status report.* Wilmington, DE: Delaware Department of Services to Children, Youth, and Their Families.

Miller, T. R., Cohen, M. A., & Rossman, S. B. (1993). Victim costs of violent crime and resulting injuries. *Health Affairs, 12,* 186–197.

Minuchin, P. P. (1985). Families and individual development: Provocations from the field of family therapy. *Child Development, 56,* 289–302.

Minuchin, S. (1974). *Families and family therapy.* Cambridge, MA: Harvard University Press.

Moffitt, T. E. (1993). Adolescence-limited and life-course-persistent antisocial behavior: A developmental taxonomy. *Psychological Review, 100,* 674–701.

Mulvey, E. P., Arthur, M. A., & Reppucci, N. D. (1993). The prevention and treatment of juvenile delinquency: A review of the research. *Clinical Psychology Review, 13,* 133–167.

Munger, R. L. (1993). *Changing children's behavior quickly.* Lanham, MD: Madison.

Najavitz, L. M., Weiss, R. D., & Liese, B. S. (1996). Group cognitive-behavioral therapy for women with PTSD and substance use disorder. *Journal of Substance Abuse Treatment, 13,* 13–22.

Nelson, K. E., & Landsman, M. J. (1992). *Alternative models of family preservation: Family-based services in context.* Springfield, IL: Charles C. Thomas.

Newcomb, A. F., & Bagwell, C. L. (1995). Children's friendship relations: A meta-analytic review. *Psychological Bulletin, 117,* 306–347.

Office of Juvenile Justice and Delinquency Prevention. (1997, May). *Juvenile Justice Bulletin—Treating serious antisocial behavior in youth: The MST approach.* Washington, DC: U.S. Department of Justice.

Office of Technology Assessment. (1991). *Adolescent health: Vol. II. Background and the effectiveness of selected prevention and treatment services* (pp. 499–578). Washington, DC: U.S. Government Printing Office.

Oliver, J. E. (1993). Intergenerational transmission of child abuse: Rates, research, and clinical implications. *American Journal of Psychiatry, 250,* 1315–1324.

Ollendick, T. H., & Cerny, J. A. (1981). *Clinical behavior therapy with children.* New York: Plenum.

Olweus, D. (1980). Familial and temperamental determinants of aggressive behavior in adolescent boys: A causal analysis. *Developmental Psychology, 16,* 664–660.

Oswald, D. P., & Singh, N. N. (1996). Emerging trends in child and adolescent mental health services. In T. H. Ollendick & R. J. Prinz (Eds.), *Advances in clinical child psychology* (pp. 331–365). New York: Plenum Press.

Parke, R. D., Burks, V. M., Carson, J. L., Neville, B., & Boyum, L. A. (1994). Family–peer relationships: A tripartite model. In R. D. Parke & S. G. Kellum (Eds.), *Exploring family relationships with other social contexts. Family research consortium: Advances in family research* (pp. 115–145), Hillsdale, NJ: Erlbaum.

Parke, R. D., & Kellum, S. G. (Eds.). (1994). *Exploring family relationships with other social contexts. Family research consortium: Advances in family research.* Hillsdale, NJ: Erlbaum.

Patterson, G. R. (1979). *Living with children.* Champaign, IL: Research Press.

Patterson, G. R. (1982). *Coercive family process*. Eugene, OR: Castalia Press.

Patterson, G. R., Capaldi, D., & Bank, L. (1991). An early starter model for predicting delinquency. In D. J. Peppler & K. H. Rubin (Eds.), *The development and treatment of childhood aggression* (pp. 139–168). Hillsdale, NJ: Erlbaum.

Patterson, G. R., & Reid, J. B. (1984). Social interactional processes in the family: The study of the moment by moment family transactions in which human social development is embedded. *Journal of Applied Developmental Psychology, 5,* 237–262.

Patterson, G. R., & Stouthamer-Loeber, M. (1984). The correction of family management practices and delinquency. *Child Development, 55,* 1299–1307.

Pecora, P. J., Fraser, M. W., Nelson, K. E., McCroskey, J., & Meezan, W. (1995). *Evaluating family-based services.* New York: Aldine DeGruyter

Pepper, S. C. (1942). *World hypotheses.* Berkeley: University of California Press.

Pierce, G. R., Sarason, B. R., & Sarason, I. (1995). *Handbook of social support and the family.* New York: Plenum.

Piercy, F. P. (1986). *Training manual: Purdue brief family therapy.* West Lafayette, IN: Center for Instructional Services.

Plas, J. M. (1992). The development of systems thinking: A historical perspective. In M. J. Fine & C. Carlson (Eds.), *The handbook of family–school intervention: A systems perspective* (pp. 45–56). Needham Heights, MA: Allyn & Bacon.

Polk, K. (1984). The new marginal youth. *Crime and Delinquency, 30,* 462–480.

Poole, E. D., & Rigoli, R. M. (1979). Parental support, delinquent friends, and delinquency: A test of interaction effects. *Journal of Criminal Law and Criminology, 70,* 188–193.

Pulkkinen, L., & Pitkanen, T. (1993). Continuities in aggressive behavior from childhood to adulthood. *Aggressive Behavior, 19,* 249–263.

Quick, J. D., Nelson, D. L., Matuszek, P. A. C., Whittington, J. L., & Quick, J. C. (1996). Social support, secure attachments, and health. In C. L. Cooper (Ed.), *Handbook of stress, medicine, and health* (pp. 269–287). Boca Raton, FL: CRC Press.

Reiss, D., & Price, R. H. (1996). National research agenda for prevention research: The National Institute of Mental Health Report. *American Psychologist, 51,* 1109–1115.

Resick, P. A., & Schnicke, M. K. (1992). Cognitive processing therapy for sexual assault victims. *Journal of Consulting and Clinical Psychology, 60,* 748–756.

Resick, P. A., & Schnicke, M. K. (1993). *Cognitive processing therapy for rape victims.* Thousand Oaks, CA: Sage.

Rife, J., & Belcher, J. (1994). Assisting unemployed older workers become re-employed: An experimental evaluation. *Research on Social Work Practice, 4,* 3–13.

Robin, A. L., Bedway, M., & Gilroy, M. (1994). Problem-solving communication training. In C. W. LeCroy (Ed.), *Handbook of child and adolescent treatment manuals* (pp. 92–125). New York: Lexington Books.

Robin, A. L., & Foster, S. L. (1989). *Negotiating parent–adolescent conflict: A behavioral–family systems approach.* New York: Guilford Press.

Robins, L. N. (1966). *Deviant children grown up.* Baltimore: Williams & Wilkins.

Rodick, J. D., & Henggeler, S. W. (1980). The short-term and long-term amelioration of academic and motivational deficiencies among low-achieving inner-city adolescents. *Child Development, 51,* 1126–1132.

Sampson, R. J., & Laub, J. H. (1990). Crime and deviance over the life course: The salience of adult social bonds. *American Sociological Review, 55,* 609–627.

Sampson, R. J., & Laub, J. H. (1993). *Crime in the making: Pathways and turning points through life.* Cambridge, MA: Harvard University Press.

Sanders, M. R. (1996). New directions in behavioral family intervention with children. In T. H. & R. J. Prinz (Eds.), *Advances in clinical child psychology* (Vol. 18, pp. 283–330). New York: Plenum.

Santos, A. B., Henggeler, S. W., Burns, B. J., Arana, G. W., & Meisler, N. (1995). Research on field-based services: Models for reform in the delivery of mental health care to populations with complex clinical problems. *American Journal of Psychiatry, 152,* 1111–1123.

Sattler, J. M. (1992). *Assessment of children.* (3rd ed., rev.). San Diego: Sattler.

Schachar, R., & Wachsmuth, R. (1990). Oppositional disorder in children: A validation study comparing conduct disorder, oppositional disorder, and normal control children. *Journal of Child Psychology and Psychiatry, 31,* 1089–1102.

Scherer, D. G., Brondino, M. J., Henggeler, S. W., Melton, G. B., & Hanley, J. H. (1994). Multisystemic family preservation with rural and minority families of serious adolescent offenders: Preliminary findings from a controlled clinical trial. *Journal of Emotional and Behavioral Disorders, 2,* 198–206.

Schoenwald, S. K., & Henggeler, S. W. (in press). Services research and family based treatment. In H. Liddle, G. Diamond, R. Levant, & J. Bray (Eds.), *Family psychology intervention science.* Washington, DC: American Psychological Association.

Schoenwald, S. K., Henggeler, S. W., Brondino, M. J., & Donkervoet, J. C. (1997). Reconnecting schools with families of juvenile offenders. In J. L. Swartz & W. E. Martin, Jr. (Eds.), *Applied ecological psychology for schools within communities: Assessment and intervention* (pp. 187–205). Mahwah, NJ: Erlbaum.

Schoenwald, S. K., Ward, D. M., Henggeler, S. W., Pickrel, S. G., & Patel, H. (1996). MST treatment of substance abusing or dependent adolescent offenders: Costs of reducing incarceration, inpatient, and residential placement. *Journal of Child and Family Studies, 5,* 431–444.

Schwartz, G. E. (1982). Testing the biopsychosocial model: The ultimate challenge facing behavioral medicine? *Journal of Consulting and Clinical Psychology, 50,* 1040–1053.

Seaburn, D., Landau-Stanton, J., & Horwitz, S. (1996). Core techniques in family therapy. In R. H. Mikesell, D. Lusterman, & S. H. McDaniel (Eds.), *Integrating family therapy: Handbook of family psychology and systems theory.* Washington, DC: American Psychological Association.

Serbin, L. A., Schwartzman, A. E., Moskowitz, D. S., & Ledingham, J. E. (1991). Aggressive, withdrawn, and aggressive/withdrawn children in adolescence: Into the next generation. In D. J. Peppler & K. H. Rubin (Eds.), *The development and treatment of childhood aggression* (pp. 55–70). Hillsdale, NJ: Erlbaum.

Sisson, R. W., & Azrin, N. H. (1989). The community reinforcement approach. In R. K. Hester & W. R. Willer (Eds.), *Handbook of alcoholism treatment approaches: Effective alternatives* (pp. 242–258). New York: Pergamon Press.

Small, S. A. (1990). Preventive programs that support families with adolescents.

Carnegie Council on Adolescent Development: Working papers. Washington, DC: Carnegie Corporation of New York.

Sondheimer, D. L., Schoenwald, S. K., & Rowland, M. D. (1994). Alternatives to the hospitalization of youth with a serious emotional disturbance. *Journal of Clinical Child Psychology, 23* (Suppl.), 7–12.

Stark, M. J. (1992). Dropping out of substance abuse treatment: A clinically oriented review. *Clinical Psychology Review, 12,* 93–116.

Stattin, H., & Magnusson, D. (1989). The role of early aggressive behavior in the frequency, seriousness, and types of later crime. *Journal of Consulting and Clinical Psychology, 57,* 710–718.

Steinberg, L., Lamborn, S. D., Darling, N., Mounts, N. S., & Dornbusch, S. M. (1994). Over-time changes in adjustment and competence among adolescents from authoritative, authoritarian, indulgent, and neglectful families. *Child Development, 65,* 754–770.

Stevenson, D. L., & Baker, D. P. (1987). The family–school relation and the children's school performance. *Child Development, 58,* 1348–1357.

Stokes, T. F., & Baer, D. M. (1977). An implicit technology of generalization. *Journal of Applied Behavior Analysis, 10,* 349–367.

Stroul, B. A., & Friedman, R. M. (1986). *A system of care for severely emotionally disturbed children and youth.* Washington DC: Georgetown University Development Center.

Stroul, B. A., & Friedman, R. M. (1994). *A system of care for children and youth with severe emotional disturbances* (rev. ed.). Washington DC: Georgetown University Child Development Center, National Technical Center for Children's Mental Health, Center for Child Health and Mental Health Policy.

Swartz, J. L., & Martin, W. E., Jr. (Eds.). (1997). *Applied ecological psychology for schools within communities: Assessment and intervention.* Mahwah, NJ: Erlbaum.

Swenson, C. C., & Kolko, D. J. (1997, January). *Psychosocial evaluation and treatment of physically abused children.* Workshop presented at the San Diego Conference on Responding to Child Maltreatment, San Diego, CA.

Taylor, H. G. (1988). Learning disabilities. In E. J. Mash & L. G. Terdal (Eds.), *Behavioral assessment of childhood disorders* (2nd ed., pp. 402–450). New York: Guilford Press.

Thomas, C. R., Holzer, C. E., & Wall, J. A. (1996, October). *Delinquency and violence in current, past, and never gang members.* Poster presented at the annual meeting of the American Academy of Child and Adolescent Psychiatry, Pittsburgh, PA.

Thornberry, T. P., Huizinga, D., & Loeber, R. (1995). The prevention of serious delinquency and violence: Implications from the program of research on the causes and correlates of delinquency. In J. C. Howell, B. Krisberg, J. D. Hawkins, & J. J. Wilson (Eds.), *A sourcebook: Serious, violent, and chronic juvenile offenders* (pp. 213–237). Newbury Park, CA: Sage.

Tolan, P., & Guerra, N. (1994). *What works in reducing adolescent violence: An empirical review of the field.* Boulder: University of Colorado, Center for the Study and Prevention of Violence, Institute for Behavioral Sciences.

Tully, J. (1995, Fall). SAMSHA assists grass-root effort. *Substance Abuse and Mental Health Services Administration News, 3,* 2–3.

Uehara, E. (1990). Dual exchange theory, social networks, and informal social support. *American Journal of Sociology, 96,* 521–557.

Unger, D. G., & Wandersman, A. (1985). The importance of neighbors: The social, cognitive, and affective components of neighboring. *American Journal of Community Psychology, 13,* 139–169.

U.S. Department of Health and Human Services, Administration for Children and Families, U.S. Advisory Board on Child Abuse and Neglect. (1993). *Neighbors helping neighbors: A new national strategy for the protection of children.* Washington, DC: Author.

U.S. General Accounting Office. (1992). *Federal jail bedspace: Cost savings and greater accuracy possible in the capacity extension plan* (Publication No. GAO/GGD-92-141). Washington, DC: Author.

Vissing, Y. V., Strauss, M. A., Gelles, R. J., & Harrop, J. W. (1991). Verbal aggression by parents and psychosocial problems of children. *Child Abuse and Neglect, 15,* 223–238.

von Bertalanffy, L. (1968). *General systems theory.* New York: Braziller.

Vondra, J., & Belsky, J. (1993). Developmental origins of parenting: Personality and relationship factors. In T. Luster & L. Okagaki (Eds.), *Parenting: An ecological perspective* (pp. 1–35). Hillsdale, NJ: Erlbaum.

Wahler, R. G. (1980). The insular mother: Her problems in parent–child treatment. *Journal of Applied Behavioral Analysis, 13,* 207–219.

Wahler, R. G., & Dumas, J. E. (1989). Attentional problems in dysfunctional mother–child interactions: An interbehavioral model. *Psychological Bulletin, 105,* 116–130.

Wahler, R. G., & Graves, M. G. (1983). Setting events in social networks: Ally or enemy in child behavior therapy? *Behavior Therapy, 15,* 19–36.

Wahler, R. G., & Hann, D. M. (1987). An interbehavioral approach to clinical child psychology: Toward an understanding of troubled families. In D. H. Ruben & D. J. Delprato (Eds.), *New ideas in therapy: Introduction to an interdisciplinary approach* (pp. 53–78). New York: Greenwood Press.

Walker, C. E., Bonner, B. L., & Kaufman, K. L. (1988). *The physically and sexually abused child: Evaluation and treatment.* New York: Pergamon Press.

Washington State Institute for Public Policy. (1998). *Watching the bottom line: Cost-effective interventions for reducing crime in Washington.* Olympia, WA: Evergreen State College.

Wechsler, D. (1991). *Manual for the Wechsler Intelligence Scale for Children* (3rd ed.). San Antonio, TX: The Psychological Corporation.

Weisz, J. B., Donenberg, G. B., Han, S. S., & Kauneckis, D. (1995). Child and adolescent psychotherapy outcomes in experiments versus clinics: Why the disparity? *Journal of Abnormal Child Psychology, 23,* 83–106.

Weisz, J. B., Donenberg, G. B., Han, S. S., & Weiss, B. (1995). Bridging the gap between laboratory and clinic in child and adolescent psychotherapy. *Journal of Consulting and Clinical Psychology, 63,* 688–701.

Weisz, J. B., Weiss, B., & Donenberg, G. R. (1992). The lab versus the clinic: Effects of child and adolescent psychotherapy. *American Psychologist, 47,* 1578–1585.

Weisz, V., & Tomkins, A. J. (1996). The right to a family environment for children with disabilities. *American Psychologist, 51,* 1239–1245.

Weithorn, L. A. (1988). Mental hospitalization of troublesome youth: An analysis of skyrocketing admission rates. *Stanford Law Review, 40,* 773–837.

Wellman, B., & Wortley, S. (1990). Different strokes from different folks: Community ties and social support. *American Journal of Sociology, 96,* 558–588.

Wierson, M., & Forehand, R. (1994). Parent behavioral training for child noncompliance: Rationale, concepts, and effectiveness. *Current Directions in Psychological Science, 3,* 146–150.

Wolpe, J. (1961). The systematic desensitization treatment of neuroses. *Journal of Nervous and Mental Disease, 132,* 189–203.

Wolpe, J., & Lazarus, A. A. (1966). *Behavior therapy techniques: A guide to the treatment of neuroses.* London: Pergamon Press.

Index